NO BED of ROSES

My Sideline View of the Wisconsin Badgers' Return to Greatness

CHRIS KENNEDY

TRAILS BOOKS
Madison, Wisconsin

Library of Congress Control Number: 2007934903
ISBN 13: 978-1-931599-99-3

Editor: Mark Knickelbine
Designer: Colin Harrington
Cover Photo: David Sandell

Printed in the United States of America by Sheridan Books.

12 11 10 09 08 07   6 5 4 3 2 1

Trails Books, a division of Big Earth Publishing
923 Williamson Street • Madison, WI 53703
(800) 258-5830 • www.trailsbooks.com

TABLE OF CONTENTS

ACKNOWLEDGEMENTS

My dad. *For being the first guy to throw a football to me. For fanning the fire in me. The first guy to tell me to write a book about all this.*

My mom. *Never a day has gone by where you haven't shown your unconditional love and support of everything I do. And for my speed.*

My sister Katie. *You keep raising the bar and showing me how possible everything in the world is with your achievements.*

Vern and Cyndi. *I couldn't have asked for more caring and supportive stepparents.*

Adam Mertz—*Your stellar input, information gathering, and editing help were second only to your friendship.*

Phil Chavez—*You and I sharing our memories is one of my favorite things to do and I look forward to your friendship the rest of our lives. Sorry, there's no chapter in here called "Chev" like you requested. Maybe in the sequel.*

Laura Mills—*You're invaluable as a friend and confidante and a much better writer than I. The time you took to read my rough, and I mean rough, manuscript puts me in your debt.*

Terry Frei—*Always kind and free and honest with your advice on an industry I knew nothing about.*

Vince Sweeney—*Your generosity and advice was so helpful.*

Sara Algoe—*Your simple and supportive nudging that I needed to write more if I was to ever finish this book was taken to heart. Here it is.*

Mark Knicklebine—Your belief and editing and advice made this dream of mine a reality. You're a pro and a gem in the industry. I feel lucky to have you as my editor.

Eva Šolcová—Your care and attention to the book is very much appreciated.

The Capital Times—Madison's afternoon newspaper and its first-rate sports photographers provided all the great action photos.

Coach Quinn—Your belief in me at an early age fostered much of the success I went on to have in my life. I couldn't have asked for a better role model or coach. I owe you too much to ever thank you enough.

Coach Rice—Your encouragement and support ever since I was in high school has helped sustain me. Your success as a coach is due to your commitment and kindness as a human being.

Coach Alvarez and his staff—You guided and taught me on the path of my dreams and I'm ever grateful for the opportunity.

My teammates—When I first came to play football for the Badgers, it because of my personal goals. I stayed because of you and our goals as a team. It is with honor that I can call myself your teammate for eternity.

And finally, I'd be remiss if I didn't thank friends, family, and fans, too many to name individually, who along the way supported me as I've been rumblin', bumblin' and stumblin' through the years.

INTRODUCTION:
WAITING AT THE DOOR

It was early December of 1993; I sat outside the office awaiting a meeting with arguably the most powerful man in the state of Wisconsin at the time, Barry Alvarez, head coach of the Rose Bowl-bound University of Wisconsin Badgers.

I was a reserve wide receiver on the team and a member of Alvarez's first class at the university just three years earlier. During my time on the team, we went from 1-10 to 10-1. From worst to first, one of the fastest turnarounds achieved by any program in college football history. Coach Alvarez was the general, and I was one of the soldiers of this crusade.

In a couple of weeks, the team would leave for Pasadena to play in our school's first Rose Bowl game in 31 years. Before that season, college football experts and even Badgers fans would have considered our feat nearly impossible. But I didn't, my teammates didn't, and our coaches didn't. So while others doubted, we worked hard enough and played well enough to make it happen. The state, the university, and the team were brimming with unprecedented pride and excitement.

Two days before this meeting, I checked the roster posted in our locker room, which listed the players who would be suiting up for the Rose Bowl game. Qualifying for the Rose Bowl was beyond my wildest dreams, and I looked for ways to let that fact sink in. I thought seeing my name in print on the roster would be one of those ways; however, my name wasn't listed. I was instantly plunged into my worst nightmare. At the doorstep of the biggest game of my life, I was locked outside.

My experience on the team had led me to believe that nothing was impossible. I set the meeting with Coach Alvarez because, well, a senior player like me being left off the roster, it seemed...impossible.

As I sat and waited on the lobby's bright red couch, my position coach, Jay Norvell, came to me to issue a warning. Alvarez was by no means pleased to have to deal with my situation amid the mayhem of preparing for the biggest game of his coaching career. This coaching staff ran things with an iron fist and pounded flat anything they saw as a distraction from their mission, their total focus on winning the Rose Bowl game. Norvell said I was on the cusp of not even being flown out to Los Angeles to watch the game, much less suit up for it. He said I could be deprived of my Rose Bowl ring.

Norvell suggested I be grateful and positive in my meeting with Alvarez or I could smear the four years I'd spent in the program. I thought that my experience as a Badger had already been sufficiently defiled by the fact that I wasn't being allowed to join my teammates on the sidelines. But I said nothing in response. Maybe in a way he was looking out for me, but I wanted nothing to do with him at that moment.

I noticed Norvell and some other coaches entering Alvarez's office; this was not a good sign. It meant they were taking time away from game preparation to discuss my situation, and I doubt they appreciated that. But I was no longer concerned about what these guys thought of me, even though all I'd wanted during my whole career was to earn their respect. This newfound emotion was both liberating and frightening.

I had arranged this meeting with Alvarez to set the record straight. I felt I'd been left off the travel squad as punishment for something I didn't do, and I wanted to tell my side of the story. I wasn't sure how it would go. I felt I'd been a team player and wanted to finish out the last few weeks of my career that way.

Part of me questioned why I should continue practicing for a team that seemed ungrateful for my efforts. Why show up for work if the boss doesn't consider you an employee? I considered quitting. Had I known I was this unappreciated and seemingly expendable, I'd have quit a long time ago. But I'd come this far and would get a trip to Pasadena with my teammates and a Rose Bowl ring out of the deal, so why quit now? It was a matter of principle. But was the principle worth giving up even the bare minimum of perks I'd earned?

I also considered that it didn't matter what I wanted to do; there was no mistaking who was in charge of anything to do with the football program—Coach Alvarez. The only power a player has in big-time college football is that given him by the coaching staff. It occurred to me that Coach Alvarez may have already decided to kick me off the team. Why deal with the mess of my situation when he had the biggest game of his life and all the national attention on him?

I felt a little guilty about taking time away from the head coach to press a personal issue. But this really was about more than that to me. If I was on the team and contributed to its current status as Big Ten champions, shouldn't I be rewarded as such? I needed to find out what it really meant to be a member of this team.

The coaches exited Alvarez's office a few moments later and I was called in. Coach Alvarez was sitting behind his big, uncluttered desk. It struck me that he and I had never sat one on one like this before.

We shook hands and then sat down to decide my fate.

To understand how we got to that meeting, you need to understand where we started. The 1994 Rose Bowl wasn't just the product of a singular 10-1-1 season; rather, it was the culmination of an epic four-year journey.

As a member of that caravan for its duration, I'll do my best to share my experiences in the hope that you can see what it means to be a college football player. If I'm not completely accurate, I apologize. I did take some pretty big hits.

A college football player is most visible when he is in front of the crowds and the television cameras, but the majority of his time is spent outside of the spotlight, balancing his schedule, enduring practices and injuries, and handling his student-athlete life. Though college football boasts many fans, very few of them have any idea what it's like to be on the inside. Like church, "Many attend, few understand."

Mine was an incredible and rewarding journey, but certainly no bed of roses. Here's how it started.

CHAPTER ONE:

STATE OF FOOTBALL

Wisconsin may not get much credit for being a football-crazy state, like, say, Texas, but it is. I know because I was born and bred in Waunakee, Wisconsin, 10 minutes outside of Madison. In Wisconsin, weddings and funerals are scheduled around Badgers football on Saturdays and Packers football on Sundays. Badgers and Packers logo shirts are worn until they fall apart. I was at a wedding where the groomsmen wore bow ties and cummerbunds featuring Packers helmets. And I've heard of a funeral where a man was buried in a Green Bay Packers casket. Wisconsin football fans truly live and die with their teams. My father was a 21-year-old junior at the University of Wisconsin when I was born. So when I say I was born to play football for the Wisconsin Badgers, I mean it literally.

On Friday nights, high school football rules, certainly in my small town. Waunakee High has had just three head coaches since it first started playing football back in the 1950s: Dick Trotta, Gayle Quinn, and Pat Rice. Quinn and Trotta are in the Wisconsin High School Coaches Hall of Fame, and Rice is on his way. I'm proud that my dad, four of his brothers, my cousins, and I all played for the Waunakee program. We're part of the rich tradition that has put Warriors football among the 50 winningest programs in the entire nation and the second winningest team in the state, behind only Schofield DC Everest.

I was fortunate to grow up in a working-class neighborhood filled with many boys my age. We played every sport under the sun, but football was a favorite. My friends and I would often play in the Smiths' backyard because their father volunteered to be the all-time quarterback for our games. "Make a hard right at the tree and I'll get you the ball before you get to the bushes," he would whisper, as he drew up patterns on the palm of his big hand. Our imaginations were as active as our bodies.

Other times, my dad, Bill Kennedy, and I would play catch until it was too dark to see the ball. If Dad wasn't available, I'd improvise by throwing the ball up onto the roof and attempting to catch it in its unpredictable descent off the rain gutter.

If we weren't playing football, we were watching it. The fall weekends of my youth were booked. Dad and I watched Waunakee High School games on Friday night, UW games on Saturday, and Packers games on Sunday. My mom, Linda Endres, watched a lot of the games as well and became a football expert by proxy. While she may not know the intricacies of a play, she has no problem screaming, "Get him!" at a Badgers lineman chasing the opponent's quarterback.

I recall my dad taking a couple of my friends and me to a football game when we were in elementary school. My young eyes had never seen such an electrifying event. It seemed the whole town was there, and their stirring created a magnetic buzz in the dark, crisp air. Four light towers shed a hard, clear illumination on the freshly painted field and the area just outside of it. The marching band offered a heart-thumping soundtrack. The public-address announcer's voice reverberated through my head and extended out past the cornfields into the night sky. I knew something important was happening. The carnival was in town.

I stood as close as I could to the field, which was laid out as reverently and pristinely as an altar. I got as close as the ropes would allow me to worship accordingly. The players ran by to take the field, only inches from where I stood. They looked like gladiator giants, heroic warriors going off to battle. It almost didn't seem right that I could stand so close to these guys who were like superheroes to me. It felt like I was standing inside the bat cave while Batman and Robin were readying for a mission. I didn't fully understand the game nor comprehend what it took to play it, but I knew, without a doubt, that I wanted to be on that field.

I felt I would just be killing time until I was old enough to play high school football. It seemed like an eternity, the six or so years I'd have to wait to wear the purple, silver, and white jersey of a Waunakee Warrior. I yearned to be out under those lights and buried in a huddle. In the fabric of those Friday night games, my destiny as a football player was woven.

POP WILLIAM

I played tackle football as soon as I could, in fifth grade. Since my father was one of my first coaches, he had a watchful eye over my practice habits. My dad was raised on a dairy farm—one of 11 children. He believed in working hard, doing your job, and being quiet about it. I remember his disappointment one particular practice, when the coaches asked for a volunteer and I didn't jump in on a drill. My dad yelled my name, but it was too late; someone else went in. I was in the middle of a fun conversation with a teammate and didn't want to be interrupted. I didn't think it was that big of a deal, but he didn't look at me the rest of practice or speak to me in the car on the way home.

That night, my parents called me into the living room and told me that they were removing me from the team. They reasoned that if I didn't want to try, then they weren't going to waste their time driving me to any more practices and games. To make matters worse, my father said that he would continue to coach the other players because they wanted to be there and he didn't want to let them down. I hated that my parents were disappointed in me, and I was mortified to think of the humiliation of having to turn in my pads in front of my friends and teammates. I begged my parents to let me continue playing and promised I would give full effort from then on. They acquiesced, and I was allowed to stay on the team.

In the game played the following Saturday, I was a terror. I became fully aware that I could be constantly moving around, making plays all over the field. I started playing with a passion and realized how much more success I could have when I gave full effort. Working harder than the other players allowed me to have more impact and hence, more fun.

My father evaluated my play, mostly focusing on areas of improvement, but noting some of the good things as well. He never let me get too high or too low on myself. I remember scoring on a touchdown run at the end of a game in which we were getting beat handily. That night before I went to sleep, he told me he was proud that I'd scored at the end because it showed that I hadn't quit just because the team had no chance of winning.

Immediately following many of my Saturday morning youth football games, my father and I would rush to Camp Randall Stadium and arrive just in time for the kickoff of the Badgers game. The energy surrounding the stadium and in the stands was overwhelming. The upper deck reached as high as any building I'd ever seen. It was a Midwestern Disneyland.

Sometimes we'd get Badgers tickets through my uncle and his friends. If we didn't already have tickets for a game, my father and I would circle the stadium looking for the best deals from scalpers. Often, I'd still be wearing my dirtied youth football jersey, which my father likely leveraged: "Hey buddy, my son is over there and he just wants to watch the game." Across the street from the stadium, I remember standing on the lawns of multi-kegger fraternity parties while my dad would haggle over tickets with a drunken student.

My favorite part of the games was when Wisconsin scored a touchdown or made a big play. I remember how happy all these adults, including my father, looked after UW won. My father and his friends, normally reserved men, looked like little kids, laughing, high-fiving, jumping up and down. I wished I could do that for them, make them feel that way. I would one day, I told myself.

GREAT EXPECTATIONS

My transition from neighborhood pick-up games to organized sports went well. I played on an all-star youth basketball team, qualified for a national track meet, and was voted MVP of my eighth-grade football team.

As a freshman at Waunakee High School, I broke the unofficial rushing-yardage record with 1,069 yards in six games. In one game, I ran for 296 yards on 10 carries and made five touchdowns. I was pulled out of the game in the third quarter so as to not run up the score. Upon being told by a student manager that I was just shy of 1,000 yards for the season, I begged the coach to put me in for one carry in the fourth quarter. He reluctantly said yes to one play. We were on our own 5-yard line, and I ran into the huddle and asked the linemen to give me a big hole to run through because I was only getting one carry. They gave me that hole, and I ran through it for a 95-yard touchdown.

Word spreads fast in small towns like Waunakee (population 6,000 at the time), and I was tabbed as a contender for the varsity tailback position the next year as a sophomore. Strangers seemed to know who I was. I'd bump into them at a gas station or at the grocery store, and they'd wish me luck or embarrass me by saying something like, "This is Chris Kennedy, he's going to be the starting tailback next year and break all the rushing records." No pressure, though.

Here I am as a Waunakee Warrior, charging into a future I was sure would be full of football glory.

THE MIGHTY QUINN

While my dad's influence remained strong, the circle of men I needed to please with my efforts expanded to include my high school football coaches, especially the head coach, Gayle Quinn.

He had been coaching high school football for so long that my father and three of my uncles had played under him. Quinn was a strict disciplinarian. He taught his players to carry themselves with class and had us address all adults as "Sir" and "Ma'am." I recall one game in high school where I had a bloody snot in my nose that I dispelled quickly over my right shoulder. The gob just missed hitting a referee. I responded, "I'm sorry, SIR." I hoped the classy remark might redeem me from my grotesque gesture. It did. In fact, our team's decorum often impressed the referees enough to write letters to our school lauding the character of its football players. Quinn used to say he was more proud of that than our wins, and I sort of believed him.

Coach Quinn didn't allow players to have long hair. He thought short hair made one look more respectable and argued pragmatically that the closer the helmet is to your head, the better it works. If a player didn't have his hair cut by the time fall practice started, Quinn became his barber. He definitely was a better coach than a barber, but then Vidal Sassoon didn't use a tape cutter to style hair.

Coach Quinn was old-fashioned, but I respected and worked hard for him. He was a man's man, a man of his word, and a man who believed that a handshake meant more than any legal document ever could. He was John Wayne, Clint Eastwood, and Knute Rockne all wrapped up in a mesh baseball cap and cardigan sweater with a football helmet insignia on it. He didn't say much, so when he spoke you listened. He expected toughness, both mental and physical, from his players. He preached the importance of character. Coach Quinn emphasized discipline, pride, and hard work. His authority trumped all. I never questioned it, not even the time he berated me at practice in front of the whole team: "Kennedy! That's not good enough! Run it again, boys."

I was playing fullback, and my assignment on the play was to block the middle linebacker. I blocked him but didn't move him very far, and the tailback, following my lead, tripped over my legs. Coach Quinn blew the whistle and made us run the play again. He demanded that I move the linebacker out of the way, so there'd be no chance of the tailback tripping over me. The linebacker was tough and didn't want to let me do that to him. We ran the play again, and again I failed to move him far enough for Quinn. The linebacker grew tired so Quinn substituted another linebacker to replace him. I was pissed off. I didn't move the replacement far enough, but managed to hurt him in the process. Quinn then lined up four other linebackers to take me on one by one, and I had to block and move each of them. By the time I got to the last guy I was like a rabid pit bull. I was embarrassed and angry and frustrated and exhausted, but I summoned myself and drove the final guy almost off the practice field, continuing even after the whistle blew as my own form of protest. Biting down hard on my mouth guard, I turned and glared at Quinn through my face mask. Quinn just nodded with a slight smile and said, "That's how you should do it every time, now grab some water." He set the standards high, and I couldn't handle disappointing him.

Most importantly, Coach Quinn truly cared about his players as people more than players. We innately knew this, which is why so many of us abided by his strict doctrine.

Coach Quinn took a liking to me and essentially saved my life in some ways. I was a pretty cocky freshman football player. I'd unofficially set a school record for most yardage gained in a season. I believed that my performance as a freshman made me one of the best running backs to ever come through this school. I already assumed I'd be offered a scholarship to a top Division I-A school. I felt my grades only needed to be the minimum required to get into college, which at the time was somewhere around a 2.2 grade point average. Sure, I could try harder at schoolwork, but I had bigger concerns. My sports, my football would take precedence over all else. The fact that I was undermining myself academically didn't register any significance with me.

My mom (great parenting here) shared with a guidance counselor her concerns that her son was headed in the wrong direction. More to the point, her son was simply being an ignorant punk who wouldn't listen to his mother. The guidance counselor, at my mom's prompting, spoke with Coach Quinn, who went to work on me.

At the beginning of my sophomore year in 1987, Quinn nominated me for a leadership conference. I would be one of two representatives from the sophomore class to attend. I'd never thought of myself as a leader of anything other than my own whims and desires. I'm sure some teachers and administrators had their doubts, as I did, but Quinn was not to be questioned on matters of character.

Being selected for this leadership conference changed my life. It dawned on me that I was capable of being a leader, and I wanted to be one. I felt comfortable and similar to the other kids from schools around the state. Many were achievers in both sports and academics, and were good people to boot. It became painfully obvious to me where I was lacking—schoolwork—and I knew I had to get my act together. I managed to end up with better than a B average when I graduated from high school, despite my rocky first couple of years. As it turned out, it was academics, not sports, that gave me the opportunity to play football at UW.

SOPHOMORE JINX

My sophomore year, Waunakee switched from the Capitol Conference, where we were one of the biggest schools, to the Badger Conference, where we were the smallest. We had less than half the student enrollment of some of our competitors. This discrepancy did not bode well for our football team, and we ended up with a .500 record.

Personally, I had become the second-team tailback at the start of my sophomore season. Unfortunately, the week of our opening game, I came down with mononucleosis. Some folks joked that this was the "kissing disease." While it was unlikely, I felt guilty because I was dating a senior girl (rare for an underclassman, but my varsity status wasn't just limited to the field) and figured I contracted the disease during one of our kissing sessions. Now, I questioned why I was jeopardizing my career over a girl. But I was a young man and a football player, and I figured I would make it all work somehow.

I was in no laughing mood when the doctors told me I'd have to sit out four to six weeks, over half the season, because my spleen was enlarged and therefore vulnerable. "One good hit and that'll burst," the doctor warned my mother and me, "and your life will be in an ambulance driver's hands." Mothers love hearing that stuff.

I'd never had to sit out a football game since I first started playing in the fifth grade. Never in all the times I'd imagined being on my high school football field had I envisioned myself on the sidelines as a street-clothed exile. With no visible injury, like a casted leg or arm, the fans and former players I looked forward to playing in front of had no clear indicator of why I wasn't playing. I was going out of my mind.

After four weeks, I insisted on a check-up and demanded the doctor give me a green light. He refused, so I found another doctor who did. I couldn't take it any longer; I'd risk a burst spleen over ruptured pride.

In my first game back against Portage, future UW teammate Mike Thompson's team, I was a maniac. Coach sat me out the first half of the game, and I was pacing on the sidelines growling that I was ready to play. I bothered the coaches enough to put me in the game. I was screaming in the huddle, trying to get everyone pumped up, and I remember the upperclassmen just laughing at me through their mouth guards. I got to carry the ball several times for big gains and stayed on the field long enough to help secure the win. I knew I was back on track.

We lost the next game against state runner-up Monroe High, but I got significant playing time. I lined up against Badgers recruit Eric Benswchal, all 6' 4", 250 pounds of him, and for the first time in my career I got knocked on my back. The highlight of the game for me was my open-field tackle on all-state running back Rick Gordon. I remember thinking I'd had him around the waist but it turns out I was grabbing onto his huge leg.

I had managed to salvage my season somewhat and earned a varsity letter, but it was still a disappointing year.

COME ON, JUNIOR

As my junior year began, I knew how important it was for me to have a good season if I was to gain interest for potential scholarship offers. But instead of breaking records, I broke bones.

In the first quarter of the season opener, I was reaching my left arm out for a first down, my legs wrapped by a couple of defenders, when another player landed on my outstretched arm. I felt a sharp rush of pain up my shoulder and neck. Something just sounded and felt wrong in my shoulder. I couldn't lift my arm away from my hip. Due to the adrenaline, I was able to keep playing but my ineptitude at taking or delivering a hit with only one good shoulder overshadowed whatever courage I displayed by remaining on the field. I had sprained my left shoulder.

Later, as I exited the tomb-like silence of our locker room, I was distraught over the loss of a game I had no doubts we'd win. I eschewed any words of consolation from my girlfriend and friends. I insisted on walking to my car alone.

On the windshield wiper was a handwritten note from my father. He told me to keep my head up. I was a leader of the team and I had to act like one. He encouraged me to use my disappointment as the fuel to come back strong for the next game. It was what I needed to hear to snap me out of my funk. I think it was even nicer to know I had someone who understood me so well and cared about me so much.

Still, the team struggled on the field as I struggled with my shoulder injury. And then things took a turn for the worse.

In the second-to-last game of the year, against rival Middleton High School, I suffered a concussion and a broken nose on the same play. I was diving over a pile for extra yards when my legs got swept out from underneath me. I was holding onto the ball with my right hand and couldn't get my left down in time to break my fall. So my head did that for me. My helmet slid down and smashed my nose, and I went head over heels. I got up and took part in a few more plays but realized I didn't know what I was doing. I was seeing way too many stars in the sky.

The trainers saw that my nose was broken and that I didn't know it was Friday night. They took me into the locker room, helped me off with my shoulder pads, and opened my locker for me since I couldn't remember my combination.

My teammate and fellow running back, Trent Schwenn, and I had developed an especially close rapport with one of the younger custodians, who would open the gym for us at night so we could go in and shoot hoops after hours. As I was brought into the locker room, my head reeling, I remember that custodian saying, "Chris, you might wanna look in the mirror." I went to the mirror and saw my nose hanging toward the left side of my face. After he and the other custodian led me out to meet my mom, they joked, "There goes your modeling career." (How wrong they were. More on that later.)

The emergency room that night was full of high school football players, strapped to gurneys, some still in their pads. There were so many of us, we had to share a large makeshift room. I recognized another player who I'd competed against earlier in the year. He'd broken his leg. He was a tough guy so to hear him scream as they manipulated it made me queasy. The doctor told me I should have surgery as soon as possible, and I did a few days later.

I watched my team win our final game of the year through my blackened eyes and a protective beak worn over my nose. My college football aspirations looked as bleak as my face.

LAST HURRAH

I spent the off-season of my junior year pursuing interests outside of sports like never before. I ran for student council and won. I acted in the school play. I was on the mock trial team. I sang and danced in the swing choir. I studied hard and became an A student. I got my driver's license and went out a lot on weekends.

Perhaps I dove into these outside pursuits to escape the pressures I'd placed on myself to succeed in football. I wanted to distract myself from the possibility that I might not succeed on the gridiron like I'd always imagined. I needed to realize I was good at many things and didn't require football success to define me.

While most seniors enter their final year confident and feeling like they own the world, my mind was full of desperation and panic. Time was short—eight games—to gain the interest of college recruiters. The team was in rough shape with only 11 seniors. When our rival school, Middleton, showed up to play us and saw our sideline, a player asked me, "Where's the rest of your team?"

On game tapes, Coach Quinn pointed out that I wasn't waiting for the holes to open up, I was just ramming into the backs of the linemen, trying to create something. I was forcing things. But the noise of anxiety in my head was too loud to hear what he was saying, and I continued to spin my wheels, or rather, my cleats.

The team went 2-6 for the 1989 season. I gained more than 100 yards only three times. Worse yet, I never really even allowed myself to relax, play the game, and enjoy my teammates and the experience. I had burdened myself too heavily with my individual goals to do that. To compound this, I felt I let everyone down: my teammates, my father, Coach Quinn, and myself.

After the season, Coach Quinn kept telling me we needed to talk. Some Division II and III schools were interested. I avoided him; I just didn't want to face the facts. I had fallen painfully short of my expectations of high school grandeur. My dream of being a Badgers football player was going to stay a dream. Finally, I told Coach Quinn I was through with football.

AFTER THE FALL

A month or so after the season, over the Christmas break, it sort of sank in that I would never play football again. While my high school career had not gone as I thought it would, I still loved the sport and knew I could play it well. I was feeling lost without the identity being a football star had given me.

What would my relatives talk to me about at family gatherings? Homework? Ever since I could remember, my family members spoke to me about their hopes for the upcoming football season. I loved it and got excited by it. I was the football player.

If my football days were over, I figured I would be a less interesting person. What would I have to set myself apart from the crowd? I would be average. I'd tried so hard to be impressive and above average for most of my life; now I needed to figure out some other way to make people proud of me.

I started seriously considering the possibility of playing for the Wisconsin Badgers. I'd already been accepted at the school in November and was planning on attending for the 1990 school year anyway. A wave of life washed through me at the thought of playing again. I could create a whole new football path. I met with Coach Quinn the first day back from break and told him of my plans.

Coach Quinn contacted the new UW coaching staff headed by a guy named Barry Alvarez. They requested game tape on me.

The protocol was for a player to send a tape of his best game or two. For me, it was probably the Middleton game in which I played every down—offense, defense, and special teams. I'd amassed more than 100 yards of offense, recorded many solo tackles, and almost blocked a punt on defense against a team that made it to the state semifinals. I played with a tireless passion and was voted the player of the game by my coaches and teammates. Despite my efforts, we'd still lost that game, 28-0.

I failed to see how sending them a game where my team had been shut out was going to make the kind of grand impression I was looking to make, especially given the many outstanding players the UW coaching staff was recruiting.

I collected all the game tapes from my junior and senior seasons, and put together my own highlight reel. This was 1990, a millennium ago technology-wise.

For a couple of weeks, I spent free periods, study halls, and after school time sitting in the cramped, little audiovisual office viewing play after play, selecting the good ones and recording them onto a master. I edited them as tightly as possible for someone with no more editorial pedigree than knowing how to press the Record and Stop buttons on two big, bulky VCRs.

The tape was rough but ambitious. Most guys on the University of Wisconsin Badgers, and on any Division I-A football team, had played on successful teams, and if they had not, they were at least successful players. I was neither. We sent it off to the UW football office with our fingers crossed.

Three days later, Scott Seeliger, the one coach retained from the previous staff by the new head coach, said that I was invited to be a walk-on candidate that fall. Alvarez wanted to institute a healthy walk-on program, similar to the one at Nebraska, where he'd played and coached. I was ecstatic, especially proud because I felt I created the opportunity and made it happen.

Quinn gave me his thoughts on the situation, "They'll take a look at you. But let me say this, big-time college football is not fun. I think football should be fun. Why don't you consider playing at a smaller state school?" Coach Quinn made good points, and I couldn't argue with his logic but I was on a mission. Playing football for Wisconsin was the only path to the fulfillment of my football dreams.

CHAPTER TWO:
BARRY NEW
ENVIRONMENT

Just before the new year of 1990, my senior year in high school, Notre Dame defensive coordinator Barry Alvarez was hired as head coach at UW. I can't imagine anyone in Madison who wasn't swept into the big news—except perhaps some Williamson Street residents who felt the only legitimate sport on campus was hackey sack.

Alvarez was chosen by the new athletic director, Pat Richter. A legend with the Badgers, he had earned nine letters (three each in football, baseball, and basketball). He was on the last UW Rose Bowl team in 1963 and then went on to play for the Washington Redskins for eight seasons. He had a nice corporate job with Oscar Mayer before he agreed to pull his alma mater's athletic department finances out of the cardinal red. The main cause of this plight was an underwhelming football team, which had won just six games in three years under head coach Don Morton. A successful football team was the only way to right the athletic department ship, and Richter felt Alvarez had the experience and fire to guide it.

The word on Alvarez was that he was a player's coach. As a player that sounds good, though what other kind of coach would he be? An equipment manager's coach? Anyway, I watched the Notre Dame bowl game on New Year's Day, and the commentators mentioned the hiring often. Good publicity for UW. I cheered for Notre Dame—I had just decided I was going to walk on at UW.

I was excited and nervous about having a top-caliber coach. Would he be too hard on me? Would he be the motivator they said he was and help catapult me to great success? Would he have Wisconsin playing for the national title, like Notre Dame? Or would he be another UW coach who didn't fulfill his promise?

Coach Alvarez came in with a definite vision for football success at the University of Wisconsin. In his opening press conference as the new coach, he boldly told fans to buy their season tickets now because they wouldn't be available long. Alvarez put together an experienced, hard-working coaching staff, one of the most important things a head coach can do. Coach Alvarez and his veteran staff brought in a new attitude and a new lexicon.

Coach Alvarez needed coaches and players who would buy into the blue sky he said was behind the dark clouds that had hung over the UW football program for so long. He wanted guys who would commit themselves to an idea, who had faith in the great unknown, and who were willing to do it the hard way without any shortcuts.

Bucky Badger wasn't the only one holding high hopes that Barry Alvarez would save the UW football program.

MEET AND GREET

In the spring of my senior year in high school, I was named the captain of the track team. I'd run varsity track since I was a freshman as a long sprinter and as part of several relays. Our 4 x 400-meter relay team had one of the top times in the state, and I was focused on us winning the state championship. Since I wasn't good enough to make the state meet in my individual events, I put extra emphasis on the relay. I learned the importance of teamwork and being a good leader. It paid off: We qualified for the state track meet at the sectional finals on our home track.

Capitalizing on my impending trip to the state track meet as a great talking point, I visited the UW football offices and met Coach Alvarez.

My first meeting with Alvarez was brief, a quick chat in the hallway. He was tan and neatly dressed: well-pressed slacks and shirt, and polished shoes. He was a broad man with drooped eyelids and piercing blue eyes. He wore a big gold bowl ring on his right hand. He had an air of confidence; I felt intimidated, like a kid trying to impress him.

I then met with the receivers coach, Jay Norvell, a tall, young black man with a pencil-thin moustache and short-cropped hair. I'd heard that he played at Iowa as a defensive back, his dad was a higher-up in the athletic department, and that he was now a "volunteer" coach on the staff.

I honestly can't remember how it was decided I'd be a wide receiver, other than by default because of my size. I stood 5'10" and weighed about 170 pounds. Coach Quinn told me I had the guts and work ethic to be a great lineman, but unless we acquired some sort of time machine to travel back to the turn of the century, I was more than 100 pounds below the necessary weight to play on the line. I knew I wasn't quick enough to be a running back, but felt I had enough speed and the good hands needed to be a receiver. I caught a lot of passes out of the backfield in high school, and my high school coaches told recruiters I had a knack for getting open. Plus, I liked the idea of being on offense.

Ever since I was a kid, the allure of scoring a touchdown was what made football my favorite sport. Essentially, the offense creates, the defense destroys. I wanted to be the one who attacked, the one the opponent had to figure out how to stop. I think most offensive players feel this way.

Coach Norvell was very casual in flip-flops and sweats. He was friendly and confident, and told me he was glad to hear about the state track meet. "That'll put you in good shape heading into summer conditioning." He told me there'd be several other recruits at the state meet and congratulated me for being in their good company. He wished me luck and told me they'd be in touch.

My 4 x 400-meter relay team finished second at the state track meet. I was disappointed we came up short in our quest for a state championship but more sad to be finished with high school sports. I was proud, though, to have finished on the winner's platform with a medal draped around my neck. I hoped this momentum would carry into my summer training and help me become a Badgers football player in the fall.

I must admit, while inspired and excited about the opportunity, I had only a vague notion of what it would take to play for UW. I had some trepidation about my chances. While most players would be riding waves of confidence into their tryouts for the team, I'd be vigorously dog-paddling in a rough sea of hope.

Despite my disappointing high school football career, I was ready to open myself up again, to dream big and to make it happen. To work harder than I ever had before. My football life had been resurrected.

IT'S A CRUEL, COOL SUMMER

I, along with the rest of the team, received letters throughout the spring and summer from different members of the coaching staff, most of whom I hadn't met. The letters were very rah-rah and spoke of the excitement and promise that lay ahead for us. For some reason, virtually every coach on the staff had a wife who was expecting. Many of the coaches included inside jokes in these letters about having babies—stuff like one coach's kid being so big that he was already on the depth chart at linebacker, or kicking so hard that they'd offered him an early punting scholarship. Since most of us players had never met these coaches, the jokes were lost on us.

I saved a few of the letters I found particularly inspiring. I really liked defensive backs coach Paul Jette's letters. Coach Jette ended up being one of my favorite coaches because he didn't seem to feel the need to bully his players to get them to perform. In one of his letters, he wrote, "The precious nugget that lies at the heart of every Badger is that you strive to be something more than you are." God, I really felt that was true with me, and I wanted to be coached by a man who would write something like that.

Another one of the letters talked about the summer conditioning program at the stadium. I called the football office and asked whether I could attend. The response was something like, "Sure, we meet four days a week at 6 a.m. Knock yourself out, kid."

The strength coach was a big guy who was not well-liked by the players. It was a relief to many when he resigned a year later after it was revealed that he had put his girlfriend on the athletic department payroll for work she wasn't doing. Word was he left college football and became an artificial limb salesman in somewhere in the Midwest. Now, at least he could profit from any handouts.

WORKIN' IT OUT

As I had done the previous summer, I worked at my Uncle Dave's store, Kennedy-Hahn TV and Appliance, as a delivery driver and appliance installer. My usual hours were 7 to 4; however, the summer conditioning program consisted of 6 a.m. workouts, four days a week. The workouts usually took an hour or so, and I knew I'd be reporting late for work nearly every day. Uncle Dave was a fair but tough boss, and our family, while disposed toward nepotism (my grandpa and a handful of his siblings worked for Dave at some point), also didn't play favorites.

In fact, my family was often harder on each other than they would be on others. Case in point, my grandfather, Bernard Kennedy, was the Westport town chairman, an elected position. In the winter, when snow needed to be plowed from the streets, he would instruct the drivers to clear his street last.

I was reticent to ask for special treatment on the schedule, but I also knew that Dave was a huge football booster, a season ticket holder, and an athlete himself. I told him of my predicament, that I needed to make money but working out with the team this summer would get me in shape and possibly ingratiate me with the coaching staff. He and the delivery foreman, Rick, worked out an amended schedule for me. I was trying to play for the Badgers, for gosh sakes, and these guys wanted to help. Instead of the others in the warehouse being jealous of my accommodated schedule, I became admired. They'd drill me with questions about the team, the speed and strength of the players, and my own progress.

I couldn't have asked to work for better people. No matter how solitary your goals may be and how much of the work you have to do on your own, you cannot avoid how much you need others' help in pursuit of your dreams.

So my summer schedule consisted of rising at 5:30 a.m. to attend the conditioning workouts, then reporting to work in the warehouse and doing extraneous deliveries the early teams didn't have room for or that came in late. I'd usually punch out around 5:30 p.m. every day.

The summer workouts were held at Camp Randall Stadium. My commute was only about 15 minutes, and I'd park my car in the empty lot beside the stadium. Most of the players had scooters or rode bikes. I couldn't believe those little scooters could support such big guys. Imagine an elephant on a bicycle.

I also couldn't believe how many different kinds of Wisconsin football shorts, shirts, and shoes the current players had. You could easily spot the newbies, soon-to-be freshmen and transfers: We were the ones with no Wisconsin football paraphernalia.

I knew no one at the workouts and stayed mostly to myself. These guys were all veterans and I was not even a rookie yet. A few players introduced themselves to me. They all looked like they were about 40 years old to me at the time. I'd never seen so many big guys in one place before. They all moved so well, too. They were fast. It was scary to see a guy 230 pounds sprinting almost even with me. Dangerous, really.

I recognized most of their names, if not their faces. I'd only attended one game the season prior. I guess I'd just been busy and they'd just been struggling so much, the games just weren't that fun. And at that game, I must admit I hadn't really imagined myself playing at UW.

A lot of the veterans were friendly to me but also seemed to watch me a bit closely, wondering what kind of crop this new coach Alvarez was bringing in. Even though I wasn't a recruit, I sensed some of this understandable curiosity from these guys. I'm sure they didn't feel threatened by me; but the new staff made it known that nothing from the old regime was sacred, and everyone would be re-evaluated. This likely explained the high attendance at these voluntary workouts. This, and the excitement that's intrinsic in new hope.

A few of us newbies soon bonded. A couple of black guys from Los Angeles had been in town for the summer to take some classes and one of them, Donny

Gray, was a fellow receiver. We were instantly connected: we were rookies, overwhelmed, and not morning people.

Donny was a really friendly, laid-back guy from Inglewood, California. I was impressed by how openly emotional and vulnerable Donny was. He would walk up to me during a particularly tough practice, put his arm around me and say, "Kill me, Chris. You love me right? Just do it. Put me out of my misery." I'd laugh. He'd fake crying, and yell, "Why do we do this?" Donny had an infectious laugh, and he started most sentences with a prolonged, "Shooooooooooot."

Donny was one of only a few black walk-ons. His friend, Kareem, had been recruited to play quarterback for Morton, but quit when Alvarez took over. Kareem loved Madison, though, so he decided to stay and talked some of his LA friends, like Donny, into attending the school.

The other member of their crew was Jade Freeman, another really nice, laid-back kid from Inglewood who lasted a year as a defensive lineman. I remember Jade teasing me about my Wisconsin accent and how I said the word "bag." I argued that I didn't have an accent. I pronounced the word properly: "beyyyy-g."

Donny and I, along with the other receivers, would catch balls from the quarterbacks to help them warm up. They threw the ball so hard I honestly felt like they were trying to break my hands. The passes came much, much faster than any I'd ever caught before. The ball hurt so much when I caught it that my face would start to get hot, but I pretended like it was no big deal. If you let the ball hit your body at any point, you had a guaranteed bruise.

It was quite a mix of guys on the team. Black and white guys from the south, the north, small towns, and major cities. Big and strong, short and fast, big and fast, short and strong. Smart and not-so-smart. Humble and cocky. Individuals and team players. Religious and pagan.

Almost all players—starters, walk-ons, backups—had been successful up to this point in their lives. They were the best at their schools, their conferences, and their states. Many hadn't had to deal with much failure until they arrived at the university, and some were more equipped to deal with this than others. As we sat and stretched in our various position lines, I was reminded of an ad, I'm pretty sure it was Nike, showing row upon row of guys stretching before practice, that read, "What's it feel like to be just another high school star?"

I liked the stretching but was always torn. Part of me wanted to really relax, get my body limber and ready, and enjoy the nice, quiet summer morning, while the other part of me wanted to get through the stretching so we could just get the drills over with.

The workouts were tough with several strength coaches assigned to different stations. Each station would present a different challenge. The most dreaded was the stair station, which consisted of running to the top of the stadium and back.

The stadium's upper deck stairs are noticeably steeper and tougher to climb than those in the lower deck. What started as a sprint in the first part of the stairs slowed to a heavy-breathing, slow-walking leg heave to make the final stairs. Many a time I thought I wasn't going to get my leg high enough, and I would just crash face-first into the concrete.

One morning when we were running the stadium steps drill, the strength coaches made a contest out of it. We all split into five lines. On the whistle, the first player in line started sprinting up the steps. As the first player reached about a third of the way up, the coaches would blow the whistle again, and the next player would sprint, and so on. If you were able to catch up to the guy in front of you, the coaches would reward you with a Wisconsin Football conditioning shirt. I really wanted that shirt; it would be proof that I was actually working out with the team. This wasn't the kind of shirt you could buy at a sports store. You had to earn it.

So I situated myself behind a young lineman, who happened to be in my line, and easily "caught" him before we reached the top. The coach blew the whistle and yelled, "There's our first shirt of the day. Come on, guys! Have some pride, don't let anyone catch you!" I felt sort of bad for the lineman. It really wasn't fair, but it wasn't my fault he was in line with me and I happily got my shirt after practice. I made sure to wear it as much as possible around the stadium so people would know I was a football player and so they didn't try to kick me out of any facilities.

There were more agility drills involving jumping, rolling, and change of direction. The guys were intense and attacked each drill with tremendous focus. I was already getting a taste of the work ethic required to play at the Division I-A college football level. I worked very hard to not be a weak link.

At the end of every workout, we'd all come together, arms high, and yell something for the day. Halfway through the summer it switched from "Badgers!" to "Cal!" our first opponent for the fall season. By mid-summer, some of the guys knew my name. I started to feel like I was on my way to being a member of the team.

I thought it was pretty cool to walk freely around the football facility as if I belonged there. I guess I sort of did now. It was very rewarding to be sweated through your clothes standing in the cavernous stadium, exhausted but invigorated. I savored the sight of the glowing sun as I caught my breath. It felt like I had earned the privilege of the view. This was one of those rare moments during my career when I actually felt that I made it, that I was doing something special.

After the workouts, I'd hurry down to the refreshment room, located next to the weight room. The refreshment room had two big percolating sports-drink dispensers. I loved the white drink that tasted like a vanilla shake and was supposedly good for putting on weight, which I needed to do. There were also huge trays of muffins and bagels every morning. I'd eat one, throw a few in my pocket, and eat them on my way to work.

Most of the players went back to bed or lifted weights. Many were taking a class or two in the summer. Very few worked jobs like me. It was an exhausting schedule, but I was a driven man and thought nothing of it. I needed to gain as much confidence as I could possibly get for the fall and this hard work was filling the larder.

SOARING IN

The university summer freshman orientation program is known as Student Orientation Advising and Registration—SOAR. Incoming freshmen spend the day learning about life at the university and what to expect in the coming year through presentations, skits, and short tours of the campus.

John Alby, a guy I'd met at Badger Boy's State that previous summer, was in my SOAR group. Badger Boys State is a weeklong leadership camp attended by two male junior students from every high school in the state, selected by their school administration and faculty. Students are selected on the basis of excellence in school, in sports, and in community service. It's an honor to attend, and I met some really great guys. John was one of them; he was from Appleton, and I learned he was also walking onto the football team. We were both supposed to report to the stadium to meet with recruiting coordinator Rob Ianello after the morning session. We were happy to know we'd be meeting him together, and I was very excited about the caliber of guys I was going to be calling my new friends and teammates.

A couple of the girls at SOAR overheard us talking about being on the team, and the word spread throughout our orientation group that we were football players. We instantly became the most interesting people in the group. Several girls introduced themselves to us. John and I got their dorm room numbers for the fall and they asked us for ours. We both quickly concluded that it was going to be pretty nice being UW football players.

John and I walked to the football offices, which were housed in the stadium. I told John I'd been working out with the team that summer, and he got nervous. "Whoa, man, I gotta get in shape." I told him not to worry about it; I wasn't any less nervous than he was and didn't know if I was ahead of him. He wondered whether it was bad that he hadn't been invited by the team to do the summer workouts. I assured him it wasn't anything special to work out with the team; I just happened to live close by and was able to make the workouts. It struck me that we could be so cool and confident just minutes earlier at the SOAR presentation and yet quickly turn into such worrywarts about football practice.

Once inside the offices, we were greeted by a sweet-looking, longtime receptionist who told us that everyone called her "Ski." I thought about how homey everything was feeling so far. Little did I know I could probably count the number of times I would speak with Ski on my fingers for the rest of my four years on the team.

Nonetheless, John and I waited in the lobby. It was an impressive lobby. A few oversized pictures of home game crowds, portraits of former Badgers star players like Tim Krumrie and Al Toon, and, displayed in a case, Alan Ameche's Heisman Trophy from back in 1954. It was exciting and overwhelming to think that skinny, scared, 18-year-old freshmen like us were going to be playing in front of those crowds, against guys like Krumrie, Toon, and Ameche, guys good enough to win the Heisman Trophy and play in the NFL. We sure weren't in high school anymore.

Coach Rob Ianello, a friendly guy dressed in a red sweat suit, came into the waiting area to greet us and to bring us into his office just down the hall. During our meeting, he vigorously chewed his gum, yawned big, and spoke with a slight southern drawl. We sat across from him, and his first question was, "How many pretty girls were in your orientation group?" We chuckled and said a few.

Coach Ianello informed us we'd be notified when to report and told us to be in the best shape of our lives when we reported to fall camp. He said that Coach Alvarez wanted to give walk-ons a shot, so we should be ready to take advantage of the opportunity. He told us that we were lucky to be in Alvarez's first class, a fact we'd be able to brag about to our grandkids someday. I was 18, and the thought of having grandkids couldn't have been further from my mind, much less what I'd be bragging about to them. I wasn't concerned with any epic ramifications of playing for the team. I was much more concerned with the immediate tasks at hand, getting used to this completely foreign stage of my life, and being away from my parents and out on my own for the first time.

Coach Ianello ended the meeting by wishing us luck and giving us one last word of advice. "Oh, yeah, fellas?" he said. "Both Coach Alvarez and Coach Jacques have daughters in your class, so find out who they are…and stay away from them." We chuckled. He didn't. Message received.

FRESHMAN REPORT

Early August in Wisconsin brings humidity, mosquitoes, and the sound of coaches' whistles echoing through the air. This August of 1990, it was time for Barry Alvarez's first recruiting class to report for duty. Both scholarship and non scholarship players were asked to report four days earlier than the varsity. There were a lot of players—50 or so—about half of whom were not on scholarship. Coach Ianello wasn't kidding about Alvarez wanting to open up the team and have a strong walk-on program like they had at Nebraska.

We all reported to the lakeshore dorms at UW-Madison. My father and sister Katie drove me to the camp. The scene closely resembled a typical college drop-off day, though this group had more minorities, more intensity, and much bigger dudes. It was a veritable Who's Who of high school football stars. Nearby, I recognized prized in-state recruit Dustin Rusch, all 6' 4", 280 pounds of him, hugging his girlfriend goodbye.

My father and I said hello to my position coach, Jay Norvell. "Well, Chris should be a little ahead of the game from coming in all summer," Norvell reassured me and my father. I was happy he knew I'd been doing that. Of course, coaches know everything that happens on their football team.

My father and I are not demonstrative people save for big moments like this. He gave me a quick, firm hug and said, "Well, show 'em what you've got." In these kinds of big moments in life, simple statements are loaded, and his meant a lot. It meant, I'm proud of you, I wish you the best of luck, and I'm behind you all the way. And you're on your own.

My sister hugged me and mentioned something about trying not to get killed. Good advice from both. I said goodbye to the family I'd known and hello to my new family. This camp was full of athletic-looking strangers who were going to be my brothers in a sense that all teams are social families.

At our first team meeting, there was a nervous, intense energy. There was naturally a lot of "sizing up" going on. I wondered whether, in their minds, other players gave me more or less credit than I deserved. These guys looked younger and smaller than the varsity players I'd been working out with over the summer, so I wasn't too intimidated. Of course, they were still bigger than me.

Jon Alby and Matt Morris, of cross-town rival school Middleton, were among the few guys I knew. I was quite jealous of Matt and his successful high school career: all-state, 1,000-yard rusher for the state champion team. He had accomplished all the things I'd imagined I would do in high school. I always wondered how I would've done if I'd had the opportunities he had—a bigger school, a bigger and better team, and nicer facilities. Who was better? It seemed that now would be the time to find out.

Matt didn't harbor any of the animosity toward me that I had toward him. If he had a chip on his shoulder, I never saw it; mine, on the other hand, made me look like the hunchback of Notre Dame. I simply wasn't on his radar. In these new surroundings, though, Matt's laid-back nature quickly disarmed me and we became fast friends. He was a smart guy and a good athlete. Whatever differences I thought we had, we were both in the same boat now. We were both walk-on wide receivers, undersized local boys.

Matt, however, didn't seem to have anything to prove like I did. He was one of the most honest, straightforward guys I'd met in my life. He was a quick learner and helped me to catch on during practices and meetings. He impressed me with his skills. After only a few practices, I had an answer to my question: Matt was a better football player than I was. Strangely enough, that realization eased my tension.

You could tell by our roommate assignments that the coaching staff had made the same assessment. I was assigned a walk-on lineman, and he was assigned Theo Carney, a black scholarship running back from Milwaukee. When Matt, another player, and I walked into Matt and Theo's room, Theo blurted, "Hey! White guys!" Theo was funny. He had an Eddie Murphy delivery to everything he said. He was also quite a piano player, as he proved later on at camp.

The first morning of camp, we were shuttled in small busses the short distance to the stadium where we went through a battery of physicals, measurements, and fittings that resembled a military enlistment.

In line to get weighed, I was behind Mark Montgomery, a scholarship fullback from Minneapolis. Mark stepped on the scale and it read 188 pounds. Mark apparently disagreed, saying, "Ain't no way I'm some 180! I'm 200!" He looked at me incredulously and yelled again, "I'm 200!" The scale responded only with its original answer.

I stepped on the scale and registered at 168 pounds. This meant little to me, but I mocked being pissed to lighten the mood. "No way! I'm 170 at least!" No one laughed. Overwhelmed newbies make for a tough crowd. As I eavesdropped on other players' weights, I became aware I was one of the lightest players there, and it made me a bit self-conscious. Standing in line at the next station, I asked Mark what the big deal was. He shook his head and said, "Man, they see 180's they'll put me at DB [defensive back]. I'm a fullback. A fullback!" I didn't really care where the coaches put me, as long as they put me somewhere.

When it was time to be fitted by Bill Losby, the droll, sarcastic equipment manager, I asked for big shoulder pads. As an undersized linebacker/fullback in high school, I preferred to look bigger than I was in an attempt to improve my intimidation factor. Bill shook his head, explaining that a receiver needs to have the smallest shoulder pads possible for mobility purposes. I stubbornly insisted I'd be fine with the bigger ones. He acquiesced. Turns out Bill was right. I traded them in after one day for a smaller pair as he suggested, realizing it was rather important for a receiver to be able to lift his arms above his head to catch a ball once in awhile.

I had always had quite a bit of difficulty finding a helmet that fit right, through pee wee leagues to high school. My head just didn't seem to be made for a helmet, or vice versa. Every time I removed my helmet, it felt as if I was tearing out all the hair on my head. For the entire season, my forehead was chronically marked with a big red bruise that replicated the size and shape of the pad on the front of my helmet. There were also periodic zits to accent the bruise, thanks to the sweat pinched in by the helmet.

Bill summed up my problem sweetly: "You guys with those high foreheads are a pain in my ass."

One could tell right away this was top-notch in Division I-A college football equipment. In high school, the thigh pads went into the actual pants, and the hip and tail pads were belted into them as well. The pads never really stayed where they were supposed to. I was constantly readjusting them for both comfort and protection during my high school games. Now, at Wisconsin, we were given girdles, spandex shorts that had places for all these pads, and they were very effective at keeping everything firmly in place. Very efficient and self-contained, attributes appreciated by anyone who has ever had a tail pad dangerously close to entering where the exit is.

After completing all our tests and getting all our equipment fitted, we were bussed back to the dorms. I piled into a van with a group of guys and sat next to a young, Tom Cruise-looking guy. He was friendly and introduced himself to me as Jeff Messenger. I was familiar with the name of the Wisconsin state high school player of the year. I'd probably read 20 articles on how happy the staff was to get one of the state's top recruits to come to Wisconsin. At that moment, I was really struck with the caliber of athlete I was sitting shoulder-to-shoulder with, and it affirmed even more how hard I was going to have to work to succeed.

That next morning at breakfast, I sat alongside Mike Verstegen, a Wisconsin native and star high school football and basketball player. At 6' 6" and only about 210 pounds, Mike looked like a basketball player. When he told me the coaches were going to redshirt him and make him an offensive lineman, I was skeptical. No way this tall, skinny guy was going to be a Big Ten lineman. Later, in the off-season, I remember him complaining that he was sick and tired of eating all the time. The coaches had him on something like a five-meal-a-day regimen, along with a devilish workout routine. By that next fall, Mike was up to 260 pounds. With his height and frame, Mike ended up with a playing weight of 315 pounds in his junior and senior years, and into his professional career with the New Orleans Saints.

The linemen go through the most drastic body changes of any position on the team. I remember at a weigh-in, as many of us stood around with our shirts off to be weighed, a big lineman pointed at my puny frame and exclaimed, "These little guys get to be all *ripped* and I gotta be all fat. Nice!"

The next year, I spoke to another gargantuan lineman in the making, Jamie Vanderveldt. Jamie was big but still relatively normal-sized, with handsome, chiseled features. He was quite downtrodden at the prospect of plumping his good looks. As a young veteran, I took it upon myself to try to persuade him that it was just a little challenge he had to face but it could be overcome, "Look, any guy who's good looking and in shape can get women. So what? Big deal. The guy who's all thick and got some gut on him, if he still gets the women…well, he's the real stud." He seemed to like that reasoning. The coaches should've thanked me; Jamie ended up being a real solid lineman in the program, and I don't think it's too presumptuous of me to say it was all because of my little pep talk.

Practice officially started for us freshmen with a 7 a.m. wake-up. We had 45 minutes to eat breakfast, get suited up, and be on the field. I preferred eating a good-sized breakfast as soon as I got up, and by the time I was in uniform and stretched, it was digested sufficiently to let me practice comfortably, without any hunger pains. But some guys didn't like eating right before practice so they stayed in bed a bit longer and skipped breakfast, practicing on an empty stomach. These guys played hungry in more ways than one, I guess.

According to NCAA rules, the first few days of fall practice couldn't be in full gear—probably to allow players a little time to get into shape before slamming into each other—so we suited up in only our helmets with our names written in tape on them. This was so the coaches could get our names right as they derided us. Instead of "Hey, YOU, get your ass in position," it could now be, "Hey, Kennedy, get your ass in position!" The personal touch.

Underneath our practice jerseys, we wore spider pads—soft, small shoulder pads—and thigh pads with shorts. We were protected but still not in full pads. The workouts were full speed and just as intense as if we were in full pads, however, so it probably would've been safer for us to be in full dress.

Each coach ran a different station, and the players were separated into six different groups. We rotated from station to station at breakneck speed to the sound of the bullhorn.

I'd never seen coaches, or anyone for that matter, who worked with so much enthusiasm and intensity. They seemed like generals, preparing an army for an imminent battle, who wished they had more time but didn't, so they were trying to squeeze in an overly heavy workload.

The warm smiles and encouragement they'd been giving us all summer and greeted us with when we reported quickly transformed into scowls and criticism. They seemed to have a seething intolerance for mistakes, especially mental ones: running the wrong route, jumping offsides, falling for a head fake, and getting beat deep.

The coaches had little tolerance for not doing things their way. Run a designated pass route 11 yards instead of 10 and you'd hear a coach yell, "Hey! If you wanna run your own routes, go down to the park and get off my field!"

I felt an extreme cognitive dissonance as the urge to jump in and impress the coaches and my teammates in drills and scrimmages battled with my fear of making a mistake and getting singled out for verbal abuse by the intense coaches. It was strangely exhilarating.

Many of us had never worked out this hard before. It was exhausting to summon up all of my mental and physical energy on a play, still make a mistake and have to do it over again.

At the end of a long practice, just when we thought we were finished and ready to head into the locker room, they'd have us run wind sprints or do up/downs. Up/downs are when you fire your feet up and down in a football stance, then upon a whistle, drop to your stomach, do a designated number of push-ups, and roll from side to side as quickly as possible in whichever direction the coaches were pointing. Sometimes we were forced to hold a push-up position for an extended period of time. While our arms felt like noodles and sweat dripped into our eyes, we had to summon whatever reserves of strength we had left to not collapse, lest we cause the whole team to start over and have to do this again.

Our minds and bodies spent, we limped our way back to the dorms, ate dinner in a quiet daze, and retired to our rooms, where some of us overachievers attempted to navigate through our thick playbooks and make sense of them.

I think most of us were surprised to learn how little we know about a sport that we were stars in back in high school. I think we could get away with not having great technique in high school because most of our competition didn't either, and we were likely able to beat them just on our abilities. Some players quit after the first day.

The physical exhaustion gave way much sooner than the mental exhaustion. This is why some of the finely conditioned guys walked out of a camp—not because they couldn't handle the physical punishment, though some couldn't; mainly, they couldn't control their minds enough to focus and get the hard tasks asked of them finished.

As I lay wide awake in the dark, small, dorm room, shell-shocked by the hurricane pace of things, I shared with my roommate how much more difficult this all was than I had expected. He made me feel like a wimp, a lonely one at that, when he said he actually didn't think camp was that tough. The next night after practice, I came back to an empty room. He'd quit. Chump.

We were given an hour or so before lights out to make calls from the few pay phones in the lobby. I stood in line for a long time, with my quarter in hand, and waited anxiously to call my father. I told him of the intensity, the fast pace, and the cut-throat nature of camp. I admitted to feeling a bit overwhelmed, perhaps looking for a much-needed, sympathetic ear. He replied enthusiastically, "Yeah, but is there any other place you'd rather be?" I could've listed about three million other places but chose to just fake it and say, "Nope, guess not."

When I hung up that phone, I realized that even though my father was only about a distance of 10 miles away, we may as well have been a solar system apart. There was no way anyone in the outside world would understand what I was going through. I was on my own.

Well, that was only partly true. There were teammates experiencing this along with me, and my only hope of survival was that they were feeling as anxious, vulnerable, and lost as I felt. I realized how important it was going to be to make connections. I was going to have to break out of my shyness and insecurities, and get to know these guys if I was going to make it through all this, through the next practice.

The coaches continued to be hard on us. Little did I know at the time, they were being extra hard on us to thin the herd, to get rid of the guys who weren't really committed. They didn't have to cut anyone; guys who couldn't take it cut themselves. Coach Alvarez used the "ham and egg breakfast" analogy to explain the meaning of commitment: "The chicken was involved, but the pig was committed." An old joke, but he wasn't kidding. As hard as it was, I wasn't going to quit; they were going to have to throw me out. I had too much to prove.

After practice one day, perhaps in an attempt to boost our spirits and remind us where we were, we were taken to a special room in the stadium to get our pictures taken for the game programs. I guess this made us officially members of the team. Not as ceremonial as I'd imagined, but I didn't care.

The pictures were taken in an old room filled with memorabilia. The whole scene had a traditional, classic, country club feeling to it. As a lifelong Badgers fan, this felt like something special to me; it reenergized me to think that all this isolated, hard, sometimes lonely work was for a purpose.

There were several sets of red blazers and blue- and red-striped ties that we all shared to get our individual pictures taken. When I put my blazer and tie on, and coiffed my hair for the picture, safety Melvin Tucker stood next to me and pronounced, "Ladies and gentlemen, Richie Rich!" If it was an insult, it was a pretty tame one; if it was a compliment, I'm not sure I got it. I smiled and nudged by him, looked in the mirror and realized I did look a bit like Richie Rich. I was a white kid with brown hair, parted slightly to one side…close enough.

In full embrace of the Richie Rich mindset, I smiled big for the picture. As I later perused through the headshots in game day programs, I noticed I was one of only a handful of players who actually smiled for their photos. The rest of the guys posed as if it was their mug shot for the Madison police. I was fine with smiling, I didn't feel I needed a tough-guy pose to prove my mettle. Did these guys think opposing players would go through the game day program to see who they should avoid? It was funny for me to see some of my teammates, who I knew were total goofballs, looking like such tough guys in their photos. It might have fooled the fans, but not me. I often heard girls comment on how cute it was that I was smiling and if you care to search them out, you'll notice in all four pictures of my career, my piano keys are showing.

A fellow smiler was Henry Searcy, a defensive back from Georgia. Henry was often smiling in real life, so the picture was representative of him. He was always talking, fast and with a heavy southern accent, so that most of the time no one understood what he was saying. But it sounded fun and was certainly lively.

Henry loved to playfully taunt people. One summer workout, we were doing sprints up the stadium steps, and he and wide receiver Lionel Crawford got into a little verbal tussle. Henry told Lionel, whom he often teased by telling him he looked like a monkey, to run fast because there was "a banana up there waiting at the top of the stairs for you." During the ooohs and ahhhs from those around, Lionel quickly responded, "Searce, you better run fast, there's speech lessons up there waitin' for you."

Media Day occurred halfway through fall camp. It was held at the stadium for press and fans to meet and take pictures of the players. Since the team hadn't been all that good, turnout was pretty low. Many guys jokingly took pictures of each other. Terry Glavin, a dry, sarcastic player, asked Henry whether he wanted some pictures of Glavin posing. Henry, without missing a beat, pointed to the upper deck of the stadium and said, "Sure, Glav, go up to OO."

To the kids at Media Day, anyone in a football uniform is a hero.

I told a clueless reporter that I was Nick Polzynksi, our 320-pound senior captain. He took my picture as a bunch of guys laughed, then he thanked me and walked away looking puzzled.

I signed my first autographs as a Badgers player during those Media Days, mostly for little kids who didn't know better and for my wiseacre sister. In fact, most of the attendees were family coming to visit with their sons for the first time since fall camp started. All my parents showed up, along with my sister, so I had a decent crowd around me, especially considering I was a walk-on. Some of the starters had a pretty steady crowd of actual fans around them. It was strange to see guys who'd just been yelled at during practice a few hours earlier now signing autographs in public. I can't think of another situation where you are exposed to humiliation and adulation in such short order.

I made it through the four-day freshman camp intact. Coach Alvarez addressed us after the last practice. He said we got some nice work done, but he thought some of the guys had reported a bit out of shape. He warned us the pace would increase a few notches when we reported tomorrow with the varsity. It was not what I or any of the other exhausted freshmen wanted to hear. Just when I thought I had the pace down, they were going to intensify it! Welcome to college football, where you can't get comfortable.

WHAT'S IN A HOLY NAME?

Our four-day camp over, a leaner and meaner freshman crew now joined the varsity, who reported directly to the Holy Name Seminary, a large, four-story fortress located just outside of Madison. Holy Name was a working seminary where men left society, practiced chastity, and dedicated themselves to God. Replace "God" with "Football," and the place couldn't have been more appropriate for us. Coaches are generally a paranoid bunch; during the school year, black plastic covered the chain-link fences next to the stadium to obscure any views of what was taking place at practice. Holy Name's seclusion was perfect.

Security personnel were stationed at the entrances of the driveway and the building. The players figured the security served the dual purpose of keeping the public out and keeping us in. Part protectors, part wardens.

The spartan Holy Name environment allowed the coaching staff to have the full focus of the players for the two weeks before school and the start of the season. It's an overwhelming football barrage: seven hours of practice per day, five hours of meetings, a couple hours of film, and a couple hours of eating.

At the team meetings, the coaches quickly established themselves as a cocksure bunch. They had the vocal intensity and physical movements of professional wrestlers. It seemed like each coach was competing to top the other when it was his turn to address the team. They spoke with the seriousness of military commanders and made us feel as if bullets were flying and many innocent lives were at stake for the next day's practice.

We sat in the auditorium according to our year, seniors in the front and freshmen in the back. Seats were assigned in alphabetical order. Nikki Kemp, a 215-pound fullback and light-skinned black guy from the East Coast, sat to my left. His parents were diplomats or something to that effect. Nikki was a nice, soft-spoken guy, though he invaded my space often by hogging the armrest. When I complained, he justified it by saying he had to lean into me because to his left was Ben Hoffman, a 300-pounder, who Nikki said, "kicked off too much heat."

Ben Hoffman was barely 6' and a block of a man. He had three things most of us freshmen didn't have: a moustache, a wife, and a kid. He was 18 going on retirement. This made him easy fodder for the hecklers, but he was a sweetheart of a guy from a small farming town and took it all in stride. He quit after a year; the demands of family probably took priority over those of football.

With Nikki leaning into me, I was smashed into the guy to my right, Lee Krueger, a 260-pound nose tackle from Michigan. Lee had one of the biggest hearts and heads on the team. He was a true warrior. Lee was a backup tackle who got in a decent amount of plays per game. During the season he would always be limping around in the locker room or at the training table with an ice pack bandaged to each knee. But when the game came around on Saturday, his play didn't show any signs of weakness. A true tough guy. There were many guys like him on the team, and they gained a lot of my respect; no one watching them would ever know how much pain they sucked up.

Coach Alvarez—a.k.a. Alvy, as many coaches and players came to call him, mostly behind his back, more for brevity than for derogatory purposes— addressed the team at the beginning of each nightly meeting. He'd discuss the practices and the overall progress of the team. He usually mentioned retraining our brains from losing to winning.

Often, Alvy would bring in motivational speakers or professional players to give speeches. A player favorite was Bill Collier, an old high school football coach with big ears, who made funny faces and spoke in a wild manner. He was like a stand-up comedian; one time he brought in doctored-up pictures of the coaching staff, with their heads inserted on bodies in goofy poses or shirtless models and displayed them on a big screen.

Collier quoted Teddy Roosevelt's famous saying about the importance of being the man, "…actually in the arena. Whose face is marred by dust, sweat, and blood. Who strives valiantly…." He had this speech memorized and he said it with his eyes closed and with a reverent tone. It hit home that we were doing it, that all the bruises and pain were worth it because we were in the arena, on the team, and that was the best place to be.

Collier showed us an image of his Seymour High School championship football team. The picture was taken after the team from the little Wisconsin town won the title, and it featured the players, still in uniform, bunched together, celebrating. He said there were two key players missing from the picture, two of his stars. He pointed to a smaller player in the back of the picture. Collier explained that this guy desperately wanted to be in the picture but was too small to be seen. The two key players, who were bigger guys, hoisted him up on their shoulders so he was visible to the camera. They did this at the expense of being seen themselves. "That," Collier said, "is what a championship team looks like."

Alvy also brought in Madison's new chief of police, Richard Williams, who I think was Madison's first black chief of police. He was a nice, jovial guy. He was self-deprecating about his own high school football days and told us he respected us. Officer Williams also said something that stuck with me. He said, "One thing I know about you all, is you got the fire inside. The fire inside. That's a great kind of thing to have. Hold onto it."

This first season with the new coaching staff brought a lot of optimism—maybe too much. One night, the senior captains were fired up and screaming that "anyone who doesn't believe we can win the Big Ten title should just get up and get the hell out now." Coach Alvarez stepped forward and said, "I don't think you can win the Big Ten." Mouths were agape as the room fell silent. We freshmen let out a silent sigh of relief that Alvy said what we were all thinking. He explained that the team won just two games the previous season and to think we were going to win the Big Ten now was a bit ridiculous. Alvy spoke of the importance of keeping our goals realistic and attainable. I think we found out then that this guy Alvy was in control and was going to be direct and honest and spare no feelings in his evaluations.

At our wide receiver position meetings, pages were added to our playbooks after nearly every practice, so that they now resembled Manhattan phone books. An example of one play: Pro right Z-motion, Y flag 56. The Z receiver (flanker) lines up on the left side of the formation and goes in motion on the quarterback's first call, timing it so that by the time the ball is snapped, he ends up on the right side of the formation past the X receiver. Z then runs a rounded 6–10 yard out-pattern toward the sideline. As soon as Z hits the six-yard mark and makes his cut, he must immediately get his head around to locate the ball that will be bulleting to his ultimate destination about two yards from the sideline. The X receiver (split end), already lined up on the right, runs a 6–10 yard slant toward the goal post. He is not mentioned by name in the play call but knows his route simply by the 56 call. The Y, or tight end, would run a flag route, which I believe is a six yard button hook. These routes are all based against a defense in a cover 3 formation. However, should the defense be in cover 1, 2, or 5, the Z would convert the route to a fade pattern down the sideline, and the X and Y receivers would convert their routes accordingly. In fact, every play call had multiple routes depending on the defensive formation. And we had to learn dozens of such plays.

My summer workout buddy, Donny, and I helped each other remember the plays. Let's say Donny was given a play in the huddle that he was unsure of. He couldn't tell anyone he didn't know it lest he be screamed at, so as he exited the huddle, he'd quickly mouth the play to me standing behind the huddle. He'd say something like 63 Y-stick. I'd hold up eight fingers and make an out motion with my right hand to trace an eight-yard out route. And Donny did the same for me. Sometimes we'd do this when coach called on us in our position meetings as well. It was nice to be completely real with somebody like Donny, who didn't put on a front of being any tougher or smarter than he was, though he was tougher and smarter than he let anyone see.

The limited recreation time (about an hour or so) between the team meeting and lights-out was spent hanging out in our rooms commiserating, although some players would play one of the four outdated video games in a small basement room in the seminary. I didn't find playing a game with graphics a shade more sophisticated than Pong to be much of a temptation.

The rooms were small and had two single beds, a desk, and no air conditioning in the August heat. Each player usually brought a fan, and guys would use both: one by the window and the other oscillating between the two beds.

My freshman year, the commiseration room happened to be the room I shared with Ed Primus. Ed was a linebacker from a small town in northern Wisconsin who chewed tobacco constantly and called everyone "Hmongs." Ed's spit cups were like landmines in our cramped room. He had a great sense of humor. His laugh sounded like a belt sander on a fresh piece of lumber. Ed was a straight-shooter who didn't really care much about what anyone thought of him, and he was fun to be around because of it.

Ed once told me of an argument he had with his linebackers coach, Kevin Cosgrove, over his getting removed from one of the special teams. He went into Cos' office and the conversation went like this:

Ed: "Coach, I'm gettin' dicked."
Cosgrove: "Primo, you're not gettin' dicked."
Ed: "I'm gettin' dicked."
Cosgrove: "You're not gettin' dicked."
Primus shrugged. "Gettin' dicked!"
Cosgrove: "Not gettin' dicked!"
Ed: "Dicked."
Cosgrove: "Not dicked!"

And so on. It could be reasonably argued that all football players have a screw or two loose, especially linebackers. Ed had enough to fill a toolbox.

Anyway, everyone liked Ed, and I was nice enough, so our room was the meeting place. Coach Ianello called our gatherings "the fellowship of the miserable." I found that to be a misnomer, because it made us feel less miserable to gather around and share our stories. It was reassuring to know you weren't the only player who was having a tough time. It helped us to bond as teammates.

Many guys calculated the days until Holy Name was over and talked about the fun we would have back on campus. We imagined all the college girls eagerly awaiting our arrival. It was painful to think of all the other students partying during welcome week while we were subjected to mandatory lights-out after being banged up and bruised from practicing all day.

Sometimes we'd question why we played this sport. One scholarship player I roomed with said in all seriousness that he wished he'd get injured so badly he wouldn't have to play, to face the pressure. I think he was having a bad day. I realized that whether you were a walk-on or a scholarship athlete, no one had it easy. We wondered what our friends were doing. We told jokes. We had farting contests.

We talked about women a lot, or the lack thereof at this place. The only females around were a few nuns visiting the premises and the female trainers. We debated about which of these student trainers was the best looking. I don't know whether there was ever a consensus pick but they all got better looking as the days went along.

A number of freshmen, myself included, came to camp with high school sweethearts back home. My girlfriend, Nicole Lubcke, was an athlete herself and supported what I was trying to do. I met her at a track meet my junior year. But she was now a high school senior, and the demands of high school track were so unlike what I was experiencing now; she was left virtually clueless about what I was going through in this new world, a world only a few miles away but one she could never enter. This eventually caused a divide between us.

We wondered what our girls were doing now that we were stuck out at this remote site. We imagined them having fun at pool parties with lecherous guys taking advantage of our absence. Guys would often profess their undying love for their high school sweethearts—something I would later come to expect from each new crop of freshman players.

One of them, Pete Monty, missed his girl and his home so much that he even had his bags packed one night ready to return home to Colorado. My campus roommate and good friend, Phil Chavez, talked him out of it. He even threw in the hard fact that in a few months, the player likely wouldn't even be dating her anymore. And he turned out to be quite the accurate soothsayer. He was the original Dr. Phil.

Maintaining a high school relationship into college is virtually impossible, and mine was no different. One semester into my college career it was over. Nicole would come to visit me on campus sometimes, and other times I would drive out to her house and pick her up. It started to make me feel like I hadn't left high school going on our dates like this; I wanted to establish myself as a college guy now. I wanted to explore all the corners of this big university, and as they say, he travels fastest, who travels alone. Our breakup was inevitable.

You could spend almost your entire nightly free hour standing in line at one of the four pay phones in the seminary. Lines were typically 10 players deep, and if your conversation took too long you'd be bombarded with notebooks, socks, jocks, and so forth. It was interesting to see big, tough athletes whining to their parents, girlfriends, and buddies about how hard camp was and how much their coach yells at them. Telephones made them uncharacteristically vulnerable. Homesickness spread throughout the camp.

To lighten up the mood and break things up a bit in the middle of camp, the coaches announced there'd be a team talent show. Over the next four years, I saw some doozies. One guy, Todd Anthony, played a bass guitar solo every year. Todd was a friendly guy from Minnesota who was easy to make laugh. Theo Carney played piano, and he played it well. I wonder whether Theo missed his calling as a lounge piano player in some hotel bar in the Caribbean. A few guys did a take on the famous *Saturday Night Live* skit, "Da Bears," but substituted Coach Alvarez for Mike Ditka and Da Badgers for Da Bears. Nick Rafko, upon much prodding, got up and did a dead-on impersonation of Bill Murray in *Caddyshack*.

One year my roommate, Alex Illich, and I joked that we would each do a Shakespeare soliloquy while holding a skull. We dared one another to do it. Funny idea, but not going to happen. Though I chose to become an actor later in life, I never had the guts to act in front of that audience, even though the players were supportive and loud—much like a hooting and hollering USO audience. I guess when you're desperate for entertainment, the bar is pretty low.

Our meals at the seminary were catered by a separate catering company and were fit for a king. Full salad bars at every meal. Two or three entrée choices. Fruit bar. Dessert bar. Juice bar. Good hearty food and plenty of it. All you could eat. As Lamark Shackerford, a scholarship nose guard, once noted about the leftovers in the refrigerator, "Man, they be feeding us like whole steaks and shit…for snacks!" I don't think there's anywhere else you'd get steak for a snack, except maybe in the bear cage at the zoo.

My freshman year, Coach Alvarez noticed that some of the players were dragging after a few days into camp and addressed it at one of our nightly team meetings. "Guys, I know. You're hurt. It's hot out. The coaches are yelling at you. The pace is fast. Freshmen, you've never experienced anything like this. You don't know the plays, it's tough." Wow, this guy is so in tune with us, I thought. He really is a player's coach. Then Alvarez continued, "But you know what? NOBODY CARES! We all got problems! Everybody's got their own stuff to deal with, and they don't care what you're dealing with. Get over it! The only person who cares is your mom and that's cuz she has to. So you take care of your own business. Nobody cares!"

This sounded a little harsh to us and we repeated it often to each other jokingly, and not so jokingly, sometimes. But it was the hard truth of our situation, and as my life progressed I found that it became more and more true. No one else feels the importance of your problems like you do. Everyone has problems, so there's no point in feeling sorry for yourself.

Though Alvarez welcomed the veterans, he showed a special affinity toward us, his first freshman class. He put out a rule: no harassment or hazing of the underclassmen. He reasoned that we're a team and some of the freshmen would be playing this year so he didn't want any divisions. The veterans began to resent us a bit for this. We were the golden children who couldn't be touched. The horror stories of a veteran making a newbie sing his high school fight song or the Oscar Mayer wiener song would only be a myth to us. Many of them didn't think it was fair they had been forced to go through it and we weren't.

At the end of the last non-padded practice, Mike Tams, a senior receiver, called over all the receivers into a huddle. He explained, rather heatedly, "The DBs will be coming after us tomorrow, trying to take us out, cheap shots and all to establish themselves as bad-asses. So be ready and don't take any of their shit!" With widened eyes and nervous stomachs, we freshmen nodded and gulped. It's one thing to run next to, work out with, and practice against these upperclassmen without pads, but add the element of full pads and potential cheap shots with the intent to hurt you, well, that was territory we'd have been happy to leave uncharted.

I doubt if many freshmen got a good night's sleep that evening. It's a dreadful feeling knowing you'll have to wake up at the break of dawn, with the birds sweetly chirping in the fountain courtyard, and throw on full pads and a helmet, pull a smelly jersey over your shoulder pads, bite down on a mouth guard, and start slamming into people.

Team managers were assigned the task of walking down the corridors and knocking on every player's door as a "courtesy" wake-up call. The echoing chambers of the seminary made sure you could hear the managers as they began at the end of the hallway and made their way toward your door. I still get chills when I think of being awakened to the sounds of loud door pounding followed by a terse "Wake up!" Sometimes it integrated into a dream of being a death row inmate, hearing the guards' footsteps walking down the corridor coming to lead him to the gas chamber. *Dead man practicing!*

Holy Name had a small chapel on the third floor where a priest would say a mass at 6 a.m., half an hour before the managers would start knocking wake-ups to the team. I decided this would be a good time to reconnect with my Catholic upbringing, and so a few times I set my alarm accordingly so I could attend. This didn't endear me to my Holy Name roommates; I asked God for their forgiveness on top of my other requests, which included not getting seriously injured that particular day. Being raised a Catholic, I turned to God when I was scared or felt out of control, which wasn't often, but training camp certainly qualified. I guess I was trying to work every angle, and angel, I could.

The daily mass attendance was typically limited to me, sophomore walk-on defensive back Bernie Caputo, and senior all-America defensive lineman Don Davey. Since they were both defensive players, I really hoped they meant it when they wished me peace during the short ceremony.

All the players, regardless of religious affiliation, were required to go to mass every Sunday while the team stayed at Holy Name. Father Tom Burke, the team chaplain, led the mass. Burke performed a sort of non-denominational, inclusive sermon at mass and always did his best to tie in Christ's message with playing football for Wisconsin. "Jesus wants you to be peaceful, yes, but not on the football field. That's a time where you're to use the talents he blessed you with by giving a full effort." I guess Jesus appreciated a good form tackle as much as any other fan. Father Burke would usually try to incorporate some humor as well: "God doesn't discriminate. He loves everyone, except for the Michigan Wolverines." I chuckled; I thought the effort was endearing, but it seemed to fall mostly on bored ears.

The first day with pads on, with more bravery than talent, I entered the field of play with the veterans. On my first play, I was sent on a short route and thrown the ball...and to the wolves, so to speak. Of all the options possible on that play, the quarterback chose to throw the ball to me. I snagged the ball from the air, using all my focus, and was hit from behind and driven into the ground. Without thinking about it, I jumped up and ran back for the next play. What didn't hit me was that I'd already taken my first collision and survived. Turns out the worry was all for naught, as I learned I was tough enough to take the hits and focus on playing football. Don't get me wrong, the hits could really hurt—some of them take your breath away and ring your ears—but it was nothing I couldn't handle.

The quarterbacks threw the ball so hard, you'd think they got extra points if they broke a receiver's finger. A good receiver must catch the ball with his hands, not letting the ball hit his body. If you let the ball hit your arm or stomach, you risk having it bounce off you and fall to the ground.

You had to wear gloves to save the skin on the palms of your hands. Lest you still think receivers have it easy, consider that we usually spend a lot of time on the turf leaping up to pull down passes, sliding to catch low throws, and diving for out-of-reach passes. Any exposed skin is a canvas for turf burns, which, if you haven't had one, is like a carpet burn times ten. All season long, arm scabs are opened and re-opened daily. Some players would try to combat this by wearing rubber elbow pads and taping their wrists, but usually not until an ugly scab had already formed.

One day at practice, I got hit so hard on a slant route by 240-pound linebacker Duer Sharp that a bizarre thing happened to my body. As I picked myself off the grass and made my way back to the huddle, I couldn't stop sneezing. I bet I sneezed more than 20 times in a row, no easy task with a mouth guard in! It's difficult to remove a mouth guard during a sneezing fit, at least with all one's fingers intact.

At a later practice, I had a chance to avenge Duer's hit on me; my assignment on one play was to crack block him. Crack blocks are those that receivers make on unsuspecting linebackers who are watching the backfield play. Before a crack block, I'd prepare myself and plan what part of my body was going to take the brunt of the collision. Depending on how I used my body, it could be my ribs, my head, or my back. I really wanted it to be on the torso, in order to avoid my head. A solid knee thrust to your noggin could easily knock you out. On this play, the ball snapped and I ran at Duer but for some reason didn't completely throw my shoulder, laying into him with all I had—I don't know, I didn't want to hurt him I guess. This was a big mistake. Duer chucked me aside like a rag doll and I got screamed at by my coaches for letting him make the tackle. I learned very quickly that if I was to have any impact on the field, much less survive, I would have to bring everything I had on every play. My high school coach, Gayle Quinn, always said the guys who stand around on a football field are much more apt to get hurt than the guys who are flying around and playing hard. This was especially true when players were stronger, faster, and bigger than they are in high school.

MIKE DEVRIES/CAPITAL TIMES

My pal and roommate, Sam Veit.

Football players, regardless of position, all live with a lot of pain. No one leaves a football game feeling 100 percent healthy. The logistics of the physical sport just don't allow it. (Well, maybe not punters; sorry, Sam Veit, my friend and former roommate. I know you were an option quarterback in high school and a good all-around athlete. You still didn't take many licks on that field. Good thing, as it may have prevented you from having all that poise to pick up the errant snaps and still manage to bury our opponents deep in their own territory. It also might have damaged that precious noggin of yours that was always getting you on the Academic all-Big Ten teams.)

During the first week of practice at Holy Name, the word around was that we'd get a free pass to leave the grounds after our Saturday afternoon practice. The coaches were able to use this as blackmail. If we had a mistake-filled practice, the coaches would say, "Oh, there's no way we're letting you leave on Saturday with the kind of unfocused practice we just had. We'd better have practice Saturday night because we need it."

Players knew we were constantly being evaluated and judged. The anxiety sometimes caused teammates to become enemies. There were fights nearly every day during drills and scrimmages. The coaches loved this and even took note of the players who got involved in the frays. I remember Coach Norvell complimenting my fellow receiver, Vince Zullo, for jumping in to defend a few offensive mates in a ruckus with some defensive players from the previous day's practice.

We were practicing twice a day in full pads during the hottest days of the summer. The humidity was high and the temps were above 90 degrees much of the time. Underneath our pads and helmets, the heat was almost unbearable. The trainers set up small medic tents, making the perimeter of the practice field look like a military base camp. The tents were stocked full of medical supplies and cots. As the summer sun forced sweat out of our every pore, the trainers always had water bottles and towels soaked in ice water to squeeze down our necks in between plays. Some players lost 6-7 pounds of sweat per practice, according to the mandatory weigh-in chart before and after practice.

Large garbage cans full of ice water would be nearby after practice for guys to immerse themselves in. They looked so refreshing, but I never got to use one; it was understood that the limited number of these would be occupied by the big starting offensive linemen.

The rest of us would jump in the Seminary pool, which was indoors and unheated so that it felt like the same temperature as the ice water garbage cans. The cold immersion felt therapeutic and refreshing as we wore our shorts or just our girdles. (Not overly hygienic, though—thank God for chlorine.)

The post-practice pool scene resembled the one in *Caddyshack* where the caddies only have 15 minutes to use the country club pool and they all invade it and act crazy. Some guys would have diving contests and several nut bags would belly flop off the diving board. I remember linebacker Aaron Norvell, younger brother of Coach Norvell, being particularly talented at some crazy dives. Most of us preferred to wait out our post-practice exhaustion lounging against the pool walls and bicycle kicking our feet under the water. This was a great tension breaker and seemed to refurbish our tired bodies and minds.

There were moments of levity in practice, too. One of the blocking drills we did as receivers was to sprint about 10 yards to a life-size dummy bag, held by another player, and drive our shoulders into the bag, taking it down to the ground. One practice, fellow receiver Reggie Torian, feeling a bit overwhelmed by the practice, purposely overdid his enthusiasm at taking down the dummy. Reggie sprinted out and executed the take down, but instead of jogging back to his place at the back of the line as routine, he picked up the dummy, jumped up with it squeezed between his legs, and dropped it to the ground. It was a well-executed pile driver of which any WWF wrestler would've been proud. But Reggie didn't stop there; he then put the dummy into a head lock and kept punching it. He was screaming incoherently at it the whole time. After standing up and throwing it back down to the ground again, Reggie kicked it one last time for good measure before returning to the huddle. While our coach got a bit upset, Reggie's antics were a great comic relief and tension breaker for us receivers performing the drill.

Reggie was good for that; he did perfect Beavis and Butthead imitations on the sidelines. He was a world-class hurdler on the track team and preferred track to football, choosing one year later to quit the football team and focus solely on track. He went on to win an NCAA title in the hurdles and to compete in the World Track and Field Championships.

The team somehow redeemed itself by Saturday, and Coach Alvarez announced that we were permitted to leave the Holy Name confines for the night. We were duly warned that we had to be back by 1 a.m. or hell was to be paid.

The players showered fast and furiously, skipping the meal provided in the cafeteria, so we could get out of there. Those who had vehicles sprinted to them and piled in as many guys as possible. The effect was like clowns piling into a circus car. I'd say every vehicle, including mine, was over the legal weight and passenger limits. Those who were unlucky enough to not fit into any cars had the option of taking shuttle vans to a local theater complex to see a movie. I felt sorry for them, but many of them said just getting out of Holy Name and sitting in an air-conditioned movie theater was exhilarating enough.

On campus, there were conjugal visits for the lucky older guys who'd already established some sort of college life. I drove a few fellow teammates, Jon Alby, Chris Hein, and Tim Ott, to my dad's house to relax.

My father and sister Katie arrived just a bit after we did and later admitted to me that when they saw my car parked out front, they were concerned I'd quit the team. My sister wrote me in a note that she was a little crushed to think that I'd given up so easily and was heartened when she realized I hadn't. Katie and I had fought plenty in our youth but now I was really beginning to understand that she was with me, and her note inspired me to keep playing and be a good example for her. Katie was an excellent athlete at Waunakee and led her basketball team to a state championship.

Anyway, the guys and I just sat in some air conditioning and reveled in not being at Holy Name. Returning to the seminary that evening felt like flying back into the cuckoo's nest.

SENIORITY

As difficult as the seminary time was, each year it became a little bit easier. Plus you started to get more perks as you got older. The seniors were housed on the third floor of the seminary and had their own rooms. The other players were on the fourth floor, one more set of stairs to climb at the end of the day, and they also had to share their rooms.

When I was a senior, I was quite familiar with the building and the grounds of Holy Name. One night, I discovered a darkened side wing on the third floor with working phone jacks (I don't know why it took me four years to figure this out). I had a phone in my luggage that I intended to bring to my apartment once camp was over, and I plugged it into the jack one night after practice and it worked! No more standing in line for me. I was able to sneak away down the dark hallway and make calls during our nightly free time. It was a major discovery that I didn't even trust my best friends on the team with. I feared word would spread and the coaches would catch wind of it, disconnect it, and punish me.

One night, I got carried away in a conversation with my girlfriend, Stephanie, and lost track of time. It was 11:01 and we were to be in our rooms, lights out at 11:00 sharp. I abruptly hung up and sprinted down the darkened corridor toward the main hallway where the seniors were housed. I hoped the assistant coach assigned to our floor was a couple of minutes late this evening. I turned the corner and saw a few guys standing in their doorways but the hallways were empty. I jogged with the phone tucked tightly under my arm, hoping no one would figure out what I was holding. I was only about 10 steps from my room when defensive backs coach Tom McMahon was coming out of a neighboring room conversation. We locked eyes and he looked down at his watch. I looked at him naively, expectantly. Since he was one of the friendlier coaches, I hoped he would casually warn me and say good night. Unfortunately, he made an uncharacteristic angry face and said, "You're late, Kennedy." I was a bit taken aback and all I could say was sorry. Coach McMahon shook his head, "Unacceptable." He walked away angry.

I walked into my room and cursed to myself. How could I have been so careless? I wasn't even talking about anything important. Coach McMahon was going to tell Coach Alvarez and the whole staff. I was going to cause our already exhausted team to run extra laps tomorrow because of my mishap. Worse yet, they could use my discrepancy to take away our Saturday night leave privileges. I imagined the coaches using me as an example of not following rules, and the resulting looks of disappointment from coaches and players alike. I feared a lecture about my indiscretion might snowball into a diatribe about how we couldn't win with guys like me not following the rules, and doing their own thing. I sat against my bed, too filled with self-hatred to sleep, dreading the next day's practice. Frustrated and angered to tears.

I prayed the next morning at chapel that nothing would be said about it. I cringed through most of the practice and felt guilty joking around with some of the guys, knowing that I might be personally responsible for the denial of the leave privileges we all so deserved. I held my breath as Coach Alvarez addressed the team after practice. I stood toward the back already looking and feeling disappointed in myself.

Miraculously, despite how upset he seemed the night before, Coach McMahon must've not told anyone because Coach Alvarez said nothing about it. I made it a point to make eye contact with McMahon and there was no disappointment on his face this time. It was almost as if he'd forgotten. I wanted to thank him but felt it was smarter to not even call attention to it in case he had just forgotten. Either way, a bullet dodged.

At the end of camp, after two weeks of two-a-day practices, the team *needed* to start hitting opponents; we were aching to get the season started. The grueling experience was over. We happily bid adieu to Holy Name. We couldn't wait to get to school, have only one practice per day, and see women again! Praise God. The college life: Holy be thy name was over.

CHAPTER THREE:
FIRST AND TENETS

Scholarship players were required to live in the dorms for the first three years of their schooling. As a walk-on, I was thankfully free of that requirement. Most athletes lived in the lakeshore dorms on the UW campus, a group of old brownstone three-story buildings with ivy creeping up them. They were traditional, charming, and quiet buildings located near the stadium, with views of the lake. The lakeshore dorms had refined names like Kronsage, Bradley, and Adams.

I chose to live in the southeast dorms, three bland high-rise complexes that resembled public-housing projects from third-world countries. They had melodious names like Ogg Hall. The southeast dorms were located right off the main streets of the university and near the popular State Street and downtown Madison. They had lovely views of traffic. I was in the Witte B tower. Each Witte tower had 800 students in residence, about the equivalent of my entire high school. I wanted to be in the mix of the regular student body. I felt the need to get out from under the ominous shadow football posed over my life, and getting far away, literally and figuratively, from the stadium was a way of keeping sane.

I wasn't the only player to do this. There were a handful of non-scholarship players in Witte and the other southeast dorms. Tim Ott and Phil Chavez were in Ogg. Vince Zullo and Chad Cascadden were in Witte. Ed Primus was in Sellery.

We southeast dormers walked together to the stadium most often for our 6 a.m. winter conditioning workouts in the freezing cold three days a week. Out of our proximity grew a bond. We called each other in the early morning as backup alarm clocks, out of camaraderie and misery loving company. It's a little discouraging to have to start our day when other dorm mates were just ending theirs.

I would get up at 5:30 a.m. and go to a brutal morning conditioning, shower in time to attend my 8:50, 9:55, and 11 a.m. lectures, and return home to find my roommate and most of my floor still asleep.

I felt like a coal miner most of the time— rising early and returning home exhausted, bruised, and underpaid. A player starts to wonder whether he's really "experiencing" college, since he isn't given much time to meet anyone outside of his football obligations, including his own dorm mates.

Was all this sacrifice really worth it—especially to a non-scholarship player who has a slim chance of getting any playing time? This inner conflict was almost constant for me. I was a young man who wanted to assert his newfound independence, a necessary ingredient in the transition to manhood. Yet I felt I was being told by the football program what to do with nearly every waking hour of my existence. Even more frustrating, I felt I was being controlled by coaches who didn't feel any need to get to know much about me personally.

The new general, sizing up his troops.

UW COACHES

Coach Alvarez had to quickly put together a team composed of players left over from his unsuccessful predecessor's squad, and from his own 11th-hour recruiting efforts. He also needed to turn to the student body, to the non-scholarship athletes better known as walk-ons. He allowed 140 players to attend his first fall camp, more than usual for a college football team. He knew many would probably leave; but Coach Alvarez believes in the old adage, the cream will rise to the top. I'm very thankful for that because if he'd made the cutoff at 130, I probably would have had to buy student tickets to get into the games.

By the time the first two weeks of fall camp were over, there were already 40 fewer players around. Scholarship guys quit, and walk-ons walked off. Those who stuck around would be the rocks, the St. Peters that Coach would build his church on. I was in this group, as were many of the key members who would eventually become the 1994 Rose Bowl champions.

The UW coaches brought in a new attitude and a new language. The terms "you" and "your ass" were interchangeable, and they always spoke about competing. If I had a dollar for every time the coaches said the word "compete," I'd have paid for my entire four years of tuition in one season. A common phrase was, "(Insert player's name here), your ass needs to compete." Or, "Your ass ain't competing." Compete, compete, compete.

The players couldn't help but include the word in our everyday vernacular—if a player was too slow in getting dressed, we'd admonish him for not competing; if he was taking too long in the bathroom, we'd say that his ass literally wasn't competing.

"Compete" covered a wide area of meanings. It meant a player had to try, to battle for every ball, and to never give up on a play. It also meant to concentrate and not make mental mistakes. It meant to show up on time and be where you were supposed to be in your everyday life.

MIKE DEVRIES/CAPITAL TIMES

We didn't often get to see this big a smile from Coach Palermo during practice.

The coaches spoke often about the importance of a competitor possessing confidence, and they had no small supply themselves. I'd say that their confidence eventually trickled down to us, but the main thrust of confidence has to generate itself from within. It follows that if you spend a lot of time working hard, you should and will feel good about your chances for success. Inevitably, from these good feelings, confidence will result.

The coaches' premise was that we'd be confident if we worked harder than our opponents, and they drove us hard accordingly. Many of the coaches were intimidating, none more than outside linebackers coach John Palermo.

Palermo was a big guy with a loud voice that he used often. He wore a permanent sneer under a two-day beard growth. After almost every play, it was common to see him charge the field and scream at the top of his lungs at one of his players. He was the "get in your face mask" style of coach.

One practice, freshman outside linebacker Tarek Saleh, who would eventually become one of the best UW players ever at the position, was struggling and had made a mistake. Coach Palermo flipped out and ran at him, yelling. Instead of listening with his hands on his hips and his head down, Tarek just ran away from Coach Palermo. He was furious, yelling and chasing his player around the field, with Tarek dodging him the best he could. The rest of the team did the best we could to hide our laughter. While Palermo was upset with Tarek, he had to give him credit for his elusiveness.

Offensive line coach Bill Callahan was another intimidating guy. Years later, Callahan would become head coach of the Oakland Raiders and lead them to a Super Bowl berth. After that, he became the head coach at Nebraska. Coach Callahan was rather small in stature, but had the voice of a giant, which allowed him to fit in with the big offensive linemen he coached. When he spoke, he had the wild-eyed look and mannerisms of a crazed combat veteran. Though he was half the size of his players, he had no problem getting in their face.

One day, he challenged the toughness of a 300-plus-pound guard. He swore at him and challenged him to a fight. There was a slight pause in the practice routine as players stole glances to see whether it would happen. It didn't—the player went right back into the drill and business carried on as usual.

Coach Callahan made famous the "step and jolt" technique of blocking. In step and jolt, the lineman steps strongly and firmly plants his feet, then shoots an arm out in a "jolting" motion to anyone trying to get by him. During the team talent show, several players got big laughs doing the step and jolt demonstration to represent Callahan. He put together a physical offensive line that took pride in their toughness.

Coach Russ Jacques was the offensive coordinator. He was a short, balding, friendly looking guy who joked around a lot. I found him instantly likeable and very different from the rest of the coaches. Instead of trying to intimidate you, he tried to put you at ease. I instantly took to him because of that. If he raised his voice, it was usually for a good reason.

Coach Jim Hueber, the running backs coach, was an overweight man with a booming voice. It seemed so strange that a man shaped like a pear could be of any help to some of the fastest, quickest guys on our team. But he did a good job with them.

One day at practice, Coach Hueber pulled his hamstring while running to tell a player something. Unfortunately for him, it was caught on the ever-present practice tape and replayed often by other coaches during meetings that whole next week of practice. It was pretty funny to see him run and then reach back and grab his hamstring as if he was shot. Watching the tape in multiple fast-forwards and rewinds made it even funnier.

Coach Bernie Wyatt was the tight ends coach and the old man on the staff. He had a thick New York accent, and his demeanor and look reminded me of detective Columbo. The other coaches respected him a lot and even though he seemed senile at times, going off on incoherent rants, he would throw out some wise old pearls of wisdom as well.

Coach Paul Winters was in his first season as running backs coach, replacing Coach Seeliger, the guy who had facilitated my coming to UW. Seeliger was the only coach from Morton's staff who stayed on with Alvarez, and apparently he didn't fit in. Winters didn't last long either, but he was "kicked upstairs" to an administrative position in the athletic department as his calm demeanor seemed to fit in better there than on the screaming fields.

Coach Kevin Cosgrove, the linebackers coach and future defensive coordinator, was an intense but likable guy who also seemed to have the most fun with his players. Being in charge of the linebackers—a collection of the more psychotic, off-the-wall players on the team—seemed to suit his persona. Coach Cosgrove welcomed more of a dialogue with his players than other coaches. He and his linebackers conversed like fighting brothers. He often leaned on a player's shoulders when he spoke to him.

One day in practice, during a scout team drill in which I was running a reverse against the first-team defense, I felt I was unnecessarily roughed up by our starting defensive tackle Carlos Fowler. I lost my temper and threw the football off Carlos' helmet and almost got in a fight—one I surely would've lost, since Carlos was a fierce competitor who outweighed me by more than 100 pounds. It was rather comedic when I look back on it, and I'm thankful it was stopped before it began. I was sent to the sidelines for a few plays to cool down. As I was catching my breath and slowing my heart rate, Coach Cosgrove stood near me, just looking at me. I sensed this and looked over at him, and a smirk went across his face. He was like the parent who makes a face to get a pouty kid to smile. It worked.

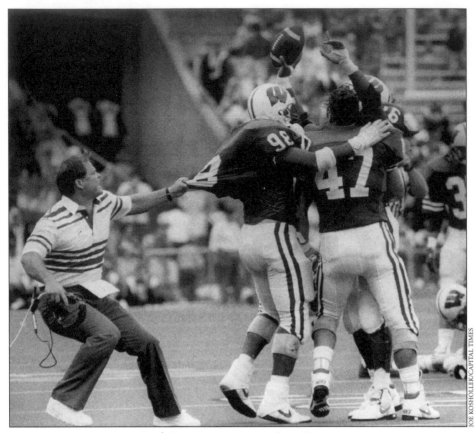

JOE KOSHOLLEK/CAPITAL TIMES

Coach Cosgrove prepares to issue instructions.

Defensive coordinator, and future Iowa State University head coach, Dan Mc-Carney had coached with Alvarez at Iowa and previously played offensive line there. Coach McCarney was a tall guy who spoke with extreme speed and passion, like a dragon spewing fire over his defensive crew. His hoarse voice would waver between encouragement and derision in the same sentence.

He seemingly put his whole being into coaching and was constantly sprinting on and off the field instructing his players. Like a few other coaches, McCarney would wear a rubberized sweatshirt during practice. After a few hours, it was common to see him pull open a sleeve and have a gallon of water pour out.

Coach Alvarez wasn't responsible for a particular position; he would stroll around the field during practice keeping watch over his coaches and players. He would jump in to say something when he saw a correction was needed. Otherwise, he seemed comfortable letting his coaches coach. But there was no doubt who the big cheese was—and Wisconsinites can appreciate that more than anyone.

WHAT'S IMPORTANT NOW

Coach Alvarez was a meticulous planner and very organized. He entered every meeting with a yellow legal pad full of notes. He tried to put together a program based on the best of his experiences as an assistant coach on successful teams.

I was impressed at how Alvarez studied other programs and regularly asked advice of other coaches around the country. I consider him a proud man, but he wasn't above asking for help or advice from others. I thought that showed a genuine commitment to improve the team by any way he could.

Coach Alvarez set forth a team plan known by the acronym WIN = What's Important Now. It was painted on the locker room and office walls, and on all of our playbooks. The main purpose of WIN is to break down large goals into small, manageable plans of action. The WIN principles changed frequently: What's important now? To have a good practice. To learn the other team's tendencies. To train hard in the off-season. To study for finals.

To be a better football player is a generic, common goal. In the WIN system, the goal would be broken down into small, immediate requirements. I need to get better footwork, so I'm going to do rope drills. I need to catch the ball better, so I'm going to catch 100 balls every day. Accomplishing these small goals would lead to the big goal of being a better football player.

The same principles applied to the overall team goals as well. If it was established one week that we needed to do a better job of holding onto the ball, there'd be more strip and rip drills on the running backs. If we weren't being physical enough, there'd be increased contact and more scrimmages at practice.

Coach Alvarez wanted us to be a physical football team. Being a physical player is mental, as strange as that sounds. There are plenty of good athletes who don't like contact, guys who can excel in a flag or two-hand touch football game or on a basketball court, and those guys have no chance of being a football player. What makes them not like contact is psychological, not physical. Oftentimes their bodies are no different than those of football players—no more fragile or prone to injury. But mentally they can't handle being hit. It throws them off their game and they can't function as a football player must. Usually they have low pain thresholds, and a football player cannot succeed if he can't play with pain because you get hurt—a little, sometimes a lot—on almost every play in a football game.

My father always said that what he liked about youths playing tackle football was that the youth had to "grow up" faster in that sport than most others; he literally gets knocked on his back and has to decide to get up and keep playing or walk off the field.

You can be physical regardless of your talent level, and with the talent level on our team a bit below average as we started the 1990 season, we needed to rely on our physical toughness to help us compete.

In addition to setting goals, Coach Alvarez made it a point to control our image and he let us know that we, as the interviewees, controlled the media interviews. He explained that you don't have to answer every question, especially if you sense you're being baited into saying something—which is often the case. He made it clear that it was our prerogative to say, "I don't want to answer that. Next question." If the interviewer persisted, you could just leave. He informed us that the writer needs a story and doesn't want to come back with nothing, so he'll have to take the interview in a direction you're comfortable with to get what he wants. This was eye opening to many of us. For football players who had to follow so many team rules, it was empowering to be able to refuse a request. Alvarez was a master at working the media.

Coach Alvarez didn't like reporters he felt were negative about the football team, and he would refuse to grant them the interviews and access he would give to those reporters he liked. As a journalism student, I questioned the ethics of talking only to reporters who wrote favorable stuff about you. But then again, why should you talk to someone who has written unfavorably about you in the past? Why not make their job a bit more difficult as perhaps their criticism or negativity has made your job more difficult? If an interviewer is biased, why can't an interviewee be?

Coach Alvy spoke often about not flinching. Don't avoid potential painful collisions, take them on. Don't back down from pressure. Don't hesitate. Be deliberate in your actions. The first guy to flinch in a fight is the guy who'll lose the fight.

Coach Alvarez often played the respect, or, rather, lack of respect, angle when attempting to motivate us. "People don't respect you until you smack them into it," he'd say. He preached about respect as something earned, not automatically given. Many actions could be construed as a lack of respect, even little things, like the way an opponent walks around on your home field before a game.

This motivation worked for me. Whenever I thought of someone not respecting me, it got me angry, it got the team angry. Who the hell are they that they think they don't have to respect me? What am I? A nobody? You don't look past me. I'll teach you a lesson. It almost felt as if that was the fuel you could draw upon when you became weary and about to let yourself slip back and flinch. Their lack of respect is your resurrection.

Coach Alvarez figured that a team like ours, which had been buried in a heap of disrespect, could raise itself up on that very heap. Conquer it and plant our flag on it, signaling to all that we were here to defend, to fight, and to let the world know we were ready for battle.

COMMON PRACTICE

I've heard complaints that athletes get to register for classes earlier than regular students, ensuring the athletes will get all the classes on their wish list. The complainers assumed incorrectly this was an example of an athlete perk. The real reason is that athletes are on a restricted schedule because of the time demands of the sport. Since the athlete's restriction is in the service of the university, it makes sense that the university would pay for their classes and grant them priority scheduling of their classes so they're available for requisite practices and games to better serve the university.

Because of daily football practice, players were not allowed to have any classes that went later than 2:15 p.m., which meant the 1–1:50 p.m. classes were the latest you could take. Occasionally someone would get in a 1–2:15 p.m. power lecture, then hustle over to the stadium.

Individual position meetings were scheduled from 2:30 to 3:15 p.m. In our position meetings, we'd review key plays and formations that we were going to emphasize that week. We'd also watch some tape of our upcoming opponent. In the middle of the week, we'd also review our own practice tapes.

I'd love to say that we always had a voracious appetite to learn everything we could, sharpened pencils at the ready for any edge we could get, but it could become quite tedious and especially boring to those players who weren't on the tape much. It was hard to stay awake in the darkened room while the images (lacking audio) flickered on the screen. Sometimes, you'd have to nudge heavy-lidded teammates.

At the conclusion of the individual meetings, we were to suit up for practice and be on the field by 3:30 p.m. The specialists (kickers, punters, holders, long snappers) would spend the first 15 minutes doing their thing while the rest of us would loosen up, play catch, or whatever else you chose to do.

At 3:45 p.m., the whistle would blow and we filed into our stretching lines, offense on one side and defense on the other, facing each other. Each row was a different position and usually you stretched in the order of the depth chart. The coaches would wander around and speak with the players and each other while we stretched.

After stretching, we'd gather in a circle, and Coach Alvarez would talk about the importance of having a good practice and the things we needed to focus on that day. I never heard him say we didn't need to have a good practice that day. Then we'd split off to our individual positions.

One thing you notice at the average practice is how many people are there besides the football team: the equipment managers, the training staff, the film crew, and athletic department personnel.

Several cameramen were positioned high above practice on each side of the stadium. They recorded practice and edited the tapes so they were ready the next day for viewing in position meetings. When we'd practice on the grass field adjacent to the stadium, these guys would be up in cranes. I felt sorry for them on particularly cold, windy days.

The equipment managers supplied and monitored the footballs, our pads, and other equipment used during practice. They also set up cones and pads for particular drills.

The student trainers held crates of water bottles for the players' use all throughout practice. Some guys would insert the nozzle to the back of their throats and suck the water down. Since I have something of a phobia about germs, I mastered the waterfall technique.

These trainers were great, very helpful, enthusiastic, and supportive. My cousin, Sarah Kennedy, was one for several years and I loved having a friendly, familiar face around those confines.

Sarah also told me about the nicknames the trainers gave the players: "Pig Pen" for one player who wasn't overly concerned about hygiene, "Drakkar" (named for the cologne) for the player who was overly concerned with hygiene. Even I wasn't spared. They called me "Plywood" in reference to their discovery, while stretching me at times, of my stiff hamstrings and lower back. I was never able to bend down and touch my toes, quite rare for a skill player.

More than half the trainers were women, and I always wondered how they felt about being in the mix of it with all these guys. If a player had a cramp or something, one or more of these trainers had to attempt to stretch his leg, which probably equaled their body weight. They were witness to some pretty profane stuff— loads of swearing, constant launching of snot rockets, spit, and sweat flying all around them. The smell wasn't grand either. A few of my teammates used to have gastrointestinal issues quite often at practice, and would "release" near female trainers, then look at me and walk away. An innocent man framed for a crime he didn't emit.

I hated seeing players throw the bottles back to the trainers. Everyone knew that it was nothing personal; the players were just taking out their frustration on whoever was near. I knew it was a thankless job so I tried not to do that to them.

While the surrounding staff had no picnic, the folks who had it toughest were the players. The Camp Randall turf in the early '90s was notoriously bad. It was like playing on concrete, but not as soft. Each day you dragged your aching body to practice, you could feel every joint start to inflame, as if the joints intuitively knew you were near that dreaded turf. Anterior cruciate ligaments, if they had a mind of their own, would've just torn themselves and saved their owners the effort.

We'd only practice inside if it was raining heavily, lightning, or we had really strong winds. Somehow, the turf in the indoor practice field in the McClain Center was worse than the Camp Randall turf. The McClain Center field was only 90 yards long and it felt a bit cramped when our whole team was in there. There was always the risk, for receivers and defensive backs, of getting so focused on catching a long pass that we wouldn't notice the padded walls of the building quickly approaching. It's one thing to get clotheslined by a strong safety and another thing to be blindsided by a few tons of concrete wall.

If at all possible, the team practiced outside on the grass practice field next to the stadium. The practices were run in five-minute increments, or periods. Depending on the day of the week, the practices were anywhere from 18 to 26 periods. Equipment managers would blow a horn at the end of every period and replace each numbered sign that kept track of the time.

When you were in a zone and having a good, focused practice, the time cards seemed to fly out of the manager's hands. But we often swore the coaches had secretly added time to each period, or that the equipment manager forgot to switch a card and was purposely trying to drag out practice.

One day, at a particularly slow practice, I was standing next to teammate Robert Nelson, whom I dubbed the "Dennis Leary of the team" because he was always angry and insulting people. Robert said to me in his typically pissed off tone, "I'm so ready for this practice to be over. Right now." I saw that we were only at period 8, 16 more to go that particular day. I tried to cheer him up and replied, "Hey, we're already at period 8." He looked over at the cards, then back at me and said tersely, "It's not enough!" and he stuck his middle finger at the clock. The laugh was a nice tension breaker. And then we went back to work.

The first two to four periods were for individual position drills. I had never played wide receiver in high school, which was both good and bad. Good, in that I didn't have to unlearn any bad habits or lazy techniques, and bad, in that I hadn't developed or worked on specific wide receiver drills before and had quite a bit of ground to gain on those who had.

The wide receivers would do catching, blocking, and line of scrimmage release drills. It may seem strange for wide receivers to do blocking drills, but we do have to block every time there's a running play. Our blocking is very similar to playing defense in basketball. Because you're out in the open field, it's unwise to physically engage or leave your feet to go after someone. It's much better to simply keep your body in front of the opponent and allow the running back to make a cut in either direction off of you.

Coach Norvell liked to do physical drills and so we did one blocking drill that lined up two players who would take turns pushing each other back and forth over 10 yards or until the whistle blew. This was known as a leverage drill as the player who got lower than the other had an easier time moving his opponent. I was pretty strong for a receiver and my background as a linebacker in high school gave me confidence. I always made sure to jump up to the front of the line when we did this drill.

Wide receivers also did line release drills in which two players would face each other, one playing receiver and the other playing defensive back. The defensive back would do his best to jam the receiver and not allow him a clean release off the line. As receivers, we used swim techniques, swatting the opponent's shoulder with one arm to move him to the side a bit and then "swimming" the other arm over the opponent's turned body to get past him quickly. We also used quick lateral foot and head movements to get the defensive back to commit to one side or the other and then we'd go the opposite way. I was not as good at these drills and didn't jump so eagerly to the front of the line. It's very important for wide receivers to get off the ball as quickly as possible, especially when a defensive back, in man coverage, has walked up right in front of you. It behooves the defensive back to make contact with you right away to either gain control of you or at least knock you off of your route. All pass plays are about timing, so the receiver cannot let himself stray from the route or he has very little chance of having the ball thrown to him.

We also did route running drills. Precise route running was essential to getting yourself in the right position to have the ball thrown to you. I quickly learned I had to run great routes to have any chance in college. In high school, many of us got away with sloppy turns and no head fakes because we were usually just faster than our opponents. In college, that wasn't the case.

Sometimes the wide receivers would actually have a chance to catch balls, usually thrown by Coach Norvell and a graduate assistant. Sometimes they'd bring out a contraption similar to a baseball pitching machine, except they'd put a football in it to be shot out at us. We would have to run toward the machine and catch the ball. The ball's velocity from the machine wasn't much different than passes from our quarterbacks.

After individual drills, we'd join the quarterbacks for the next several periods. Here we ran routes and worked on the timing of the passes with the quarterbacks for a couple of periods.

The next three to four periods, the defensive backs would join us and we'd run routes against them. This was all done one-on-one. There were lots of verbal taunts and challenges that occurred between the receivers and the defensive backs. Typically, a starting receiver would go up against a starting defensive back and so forth. It was really exciting to have such a great view of our team's top players going head to head against each other.

It was a high compliment to me when one of our top DBs would decide to stay on the field when it was my turn to challenge him on a route. Early in my career, the starting DBs would walk off the field and a reserve would jump in. It was a bit embarrassing but at the same time it gave you a much better chance of success.

The matchups were usually equal: a starter would take on a starter, a walk-on would take on a walk-on, and so forth. But as I got older, it bothered me a bit when a starter would walk off as I came in, especially if the player was younger than me. If a player did this, I would usually yell to him to get back out there. If he did, I made sure to put forth extra effort to show him up. If he didn't, I tried to find a way of getting him back later in practice with an extra hard block or push off on a route.

All eyes were on you, and as a receiver, you didn't want to drop a ball in these situations as the catcalls would be merciless—not to mention the verbal haranguing from Coach Norvell. Drops happen, but you want to minimize them as much as possible and that's why you have to turn up your focus in these drills. Especially when you have a defensive back pulling, pushing, and grabbing you the whole time.

I believe these drills favored the defensive backs, as they basically just had to stop you from making a catch, whereas a receiver has to run a proper route, timing it right with the quarterback while fending off the defensive back, then make the catch and try to get more yards after he has the ball. Of course, the DBs countered that we had the advantage because we knew where we were going and where the ball was likely to be thrown.

To start the drill, Coach Norvell or the offensive coordinator would grab my jersey or rest a hand on my helmet and call a play. I'd then sprint out to one side of the field and execute the play. Receivers would split up equally, as would the defensive backs on each side of the field. When a play on the right side was going on, the player on the left was getting the next play for the left side. This provided for almost non-stop action, and the energy was high.

Coach would often give me plays with shorter routes—10 to 12 yards or less—as I didn't have burning speed like some of the other receivers. The astute defensive backs picked up on the fact that us slower guys usually got the short routes and the fast guys usually got the long routes and they "cheated" their alignments accordingly. I noticed many players would only drop back a few yards as I ran my route, knowing I was going to stop and they'd be in position to get a good jump on me and the ball, increasing their chances of getting an interception.

As Coach Norvell was running through the possible play calls in his head, I sometimes tried to influence his choice. "Coach, let's go longer on this one," I'd say. He'd look at me and then call a hitch and go, an excellent play for me. I'd stop and turn at about 7 yards; the defensive back would assume it was another short pass play and rush forward. The quarterback would fake the throw, as I simultaneously spun out of the cut and sprinted down the field. The quarterback would loft it up a bit ahead of me and, when all went right, I'd get a nice easy catch while the defensive back tried to regain ground. If I made a great play, I looked to see whether the coaches and other players saw it. If I didn't, I'd sprint back to the end of the line and hope they'd missed it.

After one-on-ones, the team would split into first- and second-string offense versus scout-team defense and first- and second-string defense versus scout-team offense on separate ends of the field.

This would go on for the rest of practice except for the last two periods, when the first- and second-string offense and defense would scrimmage each other. The coaches would also emphasize certain situations here. Red zone offense and defense one day and long yardage situations other days.

At the end of almost every practice, we would have to run sprints, a drill in which you run as fast as you can for a designated yardage. The coaches would yell, "We're going to be a good fourth quarter team—when the other team is tired, we'll be fresh." Sometimes we'd run the length of the field, sometimes half the field, sometimes in 10-yard increments. The coaches would usually allow us to take off our helmets, our shoulder pads and jerseys. But there were several times after a loss or a bad practice we had to keep on our full gear during the sprints.

I usually would finish toward the front in these sprints because I was pretty fast relative to the whole team. Then, too, my legs were fresher than a lot of the key players' legs because I usually didn't participate in the last few periods of practice when the starters scrimmaged each other. Juiced that practice was almost over, I ran hard and seized any opportunity I could get to stand out in the competitive atmosphere of the practice.

After we finished with our running, Coach Alvarez would address the team about how he thought the day's practice went. Then other coaches or administrators would address us with any special announcements and then would finally "bring it in."

This meant we'd all gather in a circle on the field our outstretched arms forming a pyre of differing lengths, widths, and colors. We'd close in on each other, getting swallowed in the sea of teammates, pressed against the sopping wet backs of other players, and we'd all unanimously yell a particular chant like "victory" or "four quarters" or "Michigan." It was nice to feel teammates who'd been competing with each other and banging into each other for three hours rest their arms on your shoulders and all come together as one.

CHAPTER FOUR:
GAME DAY

Fridays before home games would be short, one-hour walk-through practices. On Friday night, the starters and key reserves stayed at the Inn Towner hotel near Camp Randall Stadium. They would go to a movie and then be back at the hotel for lights out. The team would eat breakfast at the hotel then take a short bus ride to the stadium.

The other half of the players who didn't stay at the hotel were on our own, but we were to report to the stadium by 10 a.m. for a 1 p.m. Saturday kickoff.

I recall walking to the game in my only suit and tie, required attire, at 9:45 a.m. and passing balconies crowded with beer-drinking fans. I usually walked with a few other players. Our dapper attire contrasted sharply with the fans around us who were wearing red cowboy hats, red-and-white striped overalls, and "Fuck 'em, Bucky!" T-shirts. Sometimes they'd cheer as we'd pass, assuming correctly that we were players. One particular balcony offered a cup of beer on the end of fishing line asking, "Do you want to hit that?" We passed but said maybe after the game.

The tailgating at UW football games is legendary. The smell of bratwurst and beer, the sounds of radios tuned to pre-game analysis, and the sight of almost every available lot on campus full of RVs with awnings spread over red-and-white-clad fans drinking beer and eating barbeque off the grill. It looked like so much fun. I couldn't believe all those people were gathered to watch my team play. I was honored to be a player and wouldn't have switched places with anyone else, but I also looked forward to when my playing days were over and I too could drink beer and eat brats for breakfast on game days.

We passed by the orange-and-white sawhorse barricades and the stadium security personnel who guarded the entryway outside the McClain Center. The security guys must've recognized us because they let us pass through without checking our identification. They wished us luck and opened the door for us.

SUITING UP

One look at the UW locker room and there is no doubt about the team colors. Everything is red and white. Red carpeted floors, benches, and lockers. A white wall adorned with a large red "W" and red lettering against a white sign with inspirational sayings and team slogans.

On game days, the locker room was laid out in pristine condition. Upon entering, you felt like you should genuflect in the cathedral-like surroundings. Freshly vacuumed floors, newly wiped mirrors, and sweet-scented bathrooms signaled that something special was at hand. Each locker was set up with military precision. Shoes, game-day programs, and laundry bags sat on the benches in front of each locker. Hanging above them, our jerseys were draped in all their quiet, shiny majesty. Our helmets were polished to buff out the scratches.

The players filtered in, and I noticed their many different preparation styles. They moved about in various stages of dress. Some got fully suited immediately. Some would dress half-way and take a break. Others would wait until we were just about to head out of the locker room. Some listened to music blaring through their headphones. Some sat in a trancelike state, envisioning a game yet to be played. Others occupied their time reading through the game-day programs. No one did much talking.

I usually dressed in my game pants and gray T-shirt, and sat by my locker reading the game-day program. A player would get profiled each week. I always looked forward to reading the questionnaire filled out by the spotlighted player, with questions like what his favorite songs were. A lot of guys picked heavy metal or rap songs. I don't question the bravery of anyone on the team, but no one ever admitted to liking Elton John or Madonna. Almost without fail, the favorite meal was steak. The pick for most impressive person varied a bit, but most guys usually mentioned their parents, historical figures, or a legendary football player. A couple of guys chose Coach Alvarez. Not many guys used this questionnaire as a practice in sarcasm, like I hoped they would; however, I do happily remember center and world-class partier Cory Raymer's response when asked to name the one thing no one would guess about him. He wrote that he "enjoyed a beer every now and then."

I recall the first time I got dressed in my full game-day uniform. All players, especially linemen, have extra-tight jerseys so as not to be "holdable." You don't want to give an opponent something to hang on to. My jersey was so tight, I initially didn't think it would fit over my T-shirt, much less my shoulder pads. After struggling and straining to the point I almost broke a sweat, I managed to get it over my shoulder pads with a teammate's finishing pull. It's an unspoken duty of teammates to help each other in this task. The big linemen especially struggled to pull their uniforms over their pads, and it sometimes took the Herculean effort of several players to get the job done. I had to stand on the bench to get high enough to get over the top of some players' shoulder pads.

Players were able to customize their game-day jerseys somewhat. You could get fitted or baggy sleeves. You could get long or short jerseys, to be tucked in substantially or not at all. A lot of the guys went with the bare-arm look, to show off their sizable biceps, also known as "screams." Most skill players went with bare arms as well but modified it a bit by wearing wristbands and elbow pads. Though the wristbands were mostly for show, the elbow pads were a nice way to prevent turf burn. Receivers and defensive backs are the most likely turf-burn candidates as they dive around for balls at high speeds.

I'd requested a jersey with fitted sleeves, so I could show off my biceps. You don't realize how small your arms are until they're dwarfed by shoulder pads. My arms looked like two pieces of straw dangling from a bail of hay.

My body issues weren't limited to my upper half. As if my butt weren't flat enough, the tailbone pad made it somehow flatter. I tried wearing shorts underneath my girdle for some extra backing, but it didn't help much.

I was pleased that the thigh pads made me look like I had huge quadriceps. My calves were a decent enough size, so I had no problem leaving my socks low to help accent them.

This all might seem a little silly, but it's important to look good in your uniform, regardless of your style. Unlike me, certain guys have great football bodies. A lean, well-proportioned body with protruding muscles is the best. A butt is important; some big guys with muscles don't have butts, which makes for awkward slippage of the tailbone pad.

Some players spend most of their pre-game primping, regardless of whether they're likely to get into the game. In fact, the players who are unlikely to play are probably more likely to primp, as they'll be standing on the sideline the whole time and the uniform will not be "adjusted" much during the game. These players would wait in line and get overly taped up by the trainers just to stand on the sidelines the entire game. I guess if play ever spilled out of bounds, they'd be ready. I remember one player in particular who never played, who would get taped up enough to make a mummy blush.

There were a few players who, as long as their pads were somehow on their body, didn't even look in the mirror. I don't think linebacker Nick Rafko washed his game-day t-shirt more than a handful of times all season. How a player looks in his uniform is trivial once the game has started but can impact some first impressions with the other team—hopefully intimidating ones.

The training room became an ankle-taping factory with the head trainers and the student trainers all tearing, pulling, and circling the tape around the players' ankles. The place reeked of disinfectant and adhesive spray. In the corner, players used an electric razor plugged into the wall to trim any hair left on their ankles before they got taped. I never got taped—it seemed like too much maintenance. The laced-up ankle braces we were issued were sufficient for me. Plus, if you got taped for practice or for games you had to get there early and wait in line, two highly undesirable things in my book.

Murphy's Law came into play when you were finally all suited up; you had to go to the bathroom. To pee, you had to unbuckle your belt, untie your "zipper," and push down really hard on the stretchy girdle to be able to get your member out in the open. All the while you're doing this you are holding your breath because the bathrooms in the locker room were unventilated. There were approximately eight stalls for 100 players. It was foul, and I could try to describe it but unless you're a sewage plant worker, I don't think you'd understand.

At home, the dress was always cardinal red jerseys over white pants. On the road, Alvarez liked us to wear white jerseys over white pants because white makes you look bigger. That may sound silly, but football is a game of inches as they say, and you take every advantage you can get. Alvarez shared with us that when he was an assistant coach at Iowa, head coach Hayden Fry had the graduate assistants paint the opposing locker rooms pink, in an attempt to put the opposition in a passive mood.

It was a surreal experience to look in the large mirror at myself dressed in the uniform of my long-beloved Badgers. The Badgers uniform signified power and status to me. Despite all of my hard work and sacrifice, I somehow didn't feel I deserved to wear that jersey. As a young fan, I'd made my way to the field and saw the Badgers of the past up close. They were giants. Great warriors. Under this hallowed shell, I felt insecure and unworthy to wear the same armor. Not so much a warrior but an imposter. However, as time passed and I paid my dues, I began to feel a sense of accomplishment and pride that eventually filled the chasm so that every time I suited up, I became the Badger I always wanted to be.

WARMING UP

During pre-game warm-ups, I actually got to run routes and catch balls on the field. Everything, the passes, the routes, the pacing, seemed crisper and sharper. Like most reserve players, I dove for balls and made it a point to run sharp routes before the game. I wanted to impress anyone who was watching— the coaches, the other team, and the fans who arrived early to the half-empty stadium. The warm-ups did the job of getting us loose and working us into a good lather of sweat.

The pre-game warm-up also allowed us to check out the other team as they were warming up. How did they prepare? Did they look big? Did they look focused or lackadaisical? Were they confident or were they scared?

After the warm-up on the field, we'd head back into the locker room, where the energy level was now increased. The position coaches met with their players in various parts of the locker room and reviewed the keys to winning the game at each position. For the receivers, it was usually something like attacking the ball in the air, running sharp routes, and taking care of the ball (i.e., no fumbling).

Right before we were to exit the locker room, Coach Alvarez addressed the team. Father Mike, the team chaplain, lead with an Our Father prayer. The players would kneel, hold hands, and mumble through the prayer. Father Mike would close by saying play hard and stay injury-free. It made me think about how noble playing football was to us; we were playing for such a high purpose that we asked God to get involved. It gave me chills to be grasping hands and kneeling in a locker room under the McClain facility, with such a big group of guys, knowing we were all focused on the same goals and were there to help each other accomplish them.

Coach Alvarez would give us a pep talk. The players were in various conditions of anxiety, hyper-awareness, and excitement, and were primed for an inspiring speech. Coach Alvarez delivered. He usually spoke about how we'd worked hard all week to prepare and how we were ready to take on this opponent. We knew what to do and now we just had to go out and do it and have some fun in the process. The other team was in our house, our field, our stadium. Coach talked about the importance of taking care of your house, of your family, and of your fans. One pre-game speech, he intoned, "What do you do when someone comes into your house and tries to take something? You kick their ass!" Now, it was time to go out there and play like a Badger. To represent the great men of the past who'd worn these same jerseys. Ameche, Toon, Krumrie, Vincent, Richter, Hirsch, Schreiner. And to represent the great young men who were currently in the room. Coach screamed that we could win the game and that we would win the game, if we played to our capabilities. He said this before every game, and in all honesty we believed that we had a chance to win every game. It was true. On any given day, on the football field, anything can happen. A previously winless team beats an undefeated team. Underdogs win titles. A small guy tackles a big guy. The beauty and magic of hope.

The players all screamed in agreement and met hands upraised in a huge pile. We made our way out of the locker room and up the tunnel, while individual players smacked helmets and shoulder pads, and yelled encouragement to the team. We walked up the ramp that would take us out of the McClain Center and into the stadium hallway.

At the top of the ramp, before we entered the outside world, there was a sign above the door that read, "The road to the Rose Bowl begins here." Players reached up and touched it before every game and every practice. That sign had been painted at the beginning of my freshman season and was met by the cynics with a chuckle. Wisconsin hadn't been to the Rose Bowl in 27 years. Take heart;

cynics don't wear helmets, they don't wear shoulder pads, and they don't walk through that tunnel.

Walking into the stadium tunnel toward the field was like walking into a crime scene. Our pathway was roped off and lined with supportive fans. Your adrenaline was high, you were a bit confused, and it was very loud. As we made our way to the field, the team's pace went from a bouncy walk to a slow jog. Jogging through the dimly lit tunnel, we'd stop just short of the field entrance. Players could do nothing but hop in place until given the signal to take the field.

The bright red fire truck adorned with cheerleaders and the Bucky Badger mascot drove down the ramp and onto the field. This was our signal and the whole pack of players was released to the crowd. Sprinting out of the shadows of the hallway onto the bright green field and into the huge stadium, I felt my heartbeat moving the shoulder pads that covered my chest. The eruption of the crowd

It's no easy day being on the sidelines.

noise felt as if it could blow you off your feet. *The Onion*, the satirical magazine started in Madison, once ran a guide to cheering at Wisconsin games and one of the tips was something like, "When the Badgers take the field, scream, yell, and act as if it is the greatest thing you have ever seen in your life." I'll say when the crowd responded like this, it was one of the greatest things I'd ever seen in my life.

It's initially disorienting to be in such a loud, bright place surrounded by fans three stories high. The whole team congregated under the goal post in a huge, hopping, loud, crazy mass. Guys in the back would run up and jump on top and "helmet surf" toward the center of the group. When you were on top of the group, it was like swimming in a sea of helmets. When you were one of the guys in the group, you felt a slight push down on your head as a player surfed above you. Coach Alvarez gave the word, and then we'd start to separate our human log jam and spread out onto the field.

Once the team stormed the field, most players who wouldn't be playing in the game had to temper our emotions and settle into our place on the sidelines. The shorter of us stood back on top of the benches to get a good view of the game.

LET THE GAMES BEGIN

It's no easy day being on the sidelines. Those who think you just sit there on the bench and do nothing are mistaken. It's like saying you could relax on the floor of the New York Stock Exchange. You can't help but be constantly involved in the game. OK, there are times when you make sure your helmet is off so you can see and be seen by the girls walking behind the bench. But our coaching staff would sense complacency among the sidelines and give us tasks, yelling, "Come on side-lines! Get this crowd going!" We'd respond by turning around to face the crowd and waving towels and our arms up and down. It seemed to work; especially when important plays were impending, the noise would build as you waved your arms up and down. You almost felt like a rock star, controlling a big crowd like that. It was quite a powerful feeling, and it made us feel more a part of the game.

It's exciting being on the sidelines, watching the assistant coaches all giving instructions and watching the players explain what their opponent was doing to them on the field.

Coach Alvarez and his staff were fiery guys. It was refreshing and affirming to see them during games yelling in defense of my teammates instead of at my teammates like they did in practice. They screamed at officials who made bad calls. You could feel and see how passionate the coaching staff was about the game and us players.

I spent a lot of time giving individual support to my teammates out there battling, wishing deep down I'd get a shot. It served us backups well to encourage and help and support the key players in any way possible because if they started kicking butt and running up the score, we could get into the game. "Oh man," we'd think under our helmets, "if we got into the game, we'd finally get to show our talents to the world and illustrate what a tragedy it is that we've been cast to the sideline all this time." If nothing else, I figured it would be nice to get into the game just to have a clear-cut enemy, to finally get to hit someone other than my teammates. I'd really be able to take my mayhem to another level against a stranger in the wrong-colored uniform.

When we were on offense, I focused on our starting receivers. I listened to the plays being called and put myself in their shoes, intently watching what they were doing right and wrong. I also paid particular attention to the opponent's defensive backs. I tried to figure out what coverage they were in and anticipated the adjustment our receiver would make to his route. I was pretty focused on the game, but sometimes I got tired or distracted by other things happening on the sidelines, or caught up in a conversation with some fellow teammates.

If it seemed we had a solid lead, I would put on my helmet and position myself right behind Coach Norvell. Like a stalker, I'd watch and follow his every move. Stepping over headset cables and around other players, I'd make sure that every time he turned around, I was in his sightline. It was my own form of sub-liminal advertising. I would be willing him with all my might to just send me in on one damn play. In my head, I would scream, "What difference would it make? We're just running out the clock! Do you know how much this means to me? Put me in now! Come on, give me the signal!" For many of us, getting into the game, even if just at the end, made us feel we contributed more to the win and justified our whole reason for enduring all the sacrifice this sport demanded from us.

Back inside the locker room, the mood was, of course, dependent on victory. Lots of loud celebrating with a win and stone-cold silence with a loss. Coach Alvarez would address us either way. We'd gather like we did before the game, and after a victory he'd typically end his speech with "Hey, go out tonight, celebrate, and enjoy the win, but be smart. Look after one another. If your buddy gets in a predica-ment, get him out of there."

We'd shower and get dressed back into the suits. Boxed meals were provided in front of our lockers, because none of us had eaten since breakfast and it was usu-ally about 4:30 p.m. by the time we were done. I usually gave my meal away to a teammate because my parents and I (and my sister Katie when she wasn't too tired from basketball practice) had a tradition of having a post-game meal together.

Outside the locker room, many reporters would be gathered along with media reps and cameras, trying to get interviews with the key players. I walked out and they all checked their cheat sheets to make sure I wasn't someone they should be talking to. I then passed by the media people like a ghost on white as they looked through me to find their interviewees.

DAYS GO BY

The winter after my freshman season, 1991, the NCAA instituted time restrictions, in an effort to combat the vast amount of hours college football players were spending on the sport. It became mandatory that players be given one day off each week and be required to practice no more than 20 total hours per week. This was a pretty good reform. Before this new rule, we were spending 30–40 hours per week at the stadium.

Our coaches chose Monday as our day off as I assume most coaches around the country did. It's a good day to get back to class and take a break from that weekend's game. Of course, this is big-time college football and you don't really have a whole day off. Players were expected to come in and watch film, lift, and perhaps, if you were a wide receiver, get together with a quarterback and catch some balls. The nice part was that you didn't have to do it at any particular time.

Badgermania in progress. Win or lose, our fans were always there for us.

Tuesdays were the heavy days, the practices were a little longer, we were usually in full pads and full contact, and we were installing all the key plays for that week's game. I've heard some teams put in the plays gradually throughout the week, but our staff liked to put them all in at the beginning of the week's practices and tweak them as the week progressed.

We were given thorough scouting reports on our upcoming opponents. Sometimes these were 20 pages long. I was always impressed by the research that went into this—minute details like the percentage of times their defensive secondary was in a cover 2 or cover 1. We'd be given tip sheets on keys to victory, things like "anticipate blitz," "be quick out of cuts," and "execute base offense."

All this information was great, as it made you feel confident, but then you'd realize that the other team had just as much information on us. It all looks like a big chess match, but it really comes down to beating the guy in front of you.

Wednesdays were also heavy days, full pads, full contact, and a little longer practice. This was definitely, "Hump Day." Late in the season, Wednesday practices would be downgraded to shoulder pads and thigh pads with shorts.

Thursday, we would usually suit up in spider pads. The practices were usually a bit shorter and not as physical. However, since we did have some protection on, some guys played as if we were fully suited up, and so the spider pads could make you feel more vulnerable than wearing either full pads or just helmets and shirts. The upside of less padding is that you felt lighter and crisper in your play.

Fridays were typically "walk-throughs," where we'd run through all the key plays and assignments for the game. It was a "mental practice," as Alvarez would say. On away games, depending on the proximity, Fridays were also travel days and the walk-throughs occurred at the opposing team's stadium.

Saturdays were game days, a routine that started about three hours before the game and included the three or so hours the game lasted, and then however long it took you to shower and dress.

Sundays were for working out the muscle kinks from Saturday's game and watch film. Players reported around mid-afternoon and ran for 30 minutes nonstop. (This was a good way to help get rid of a hangover from Saturday night as well.) Some of the guys went at a decent pace while others did a glorified walk. Guys recapped their evenings and discussed their various newly acquired bruises and body aches. No one discussed the game: We knew the next four to five hours of the day would be dedicated to that. You could wear whatever you wanted. This was the only day, aside from Monday, you didn't have to wear your helmet.

After the run, we stretched and then reported for the team meeting. Coach Alvarez would review the game and give his analysis of the positives and the negatives. Alvy was very organized and very thorough in everything he did. He would go through a big hand-written yellow notepad and check off points as he went along.

We'd watch the special-teams clips from the game as a whole team. Different coaches involved in different areas of the special teams would chime in on each play with their evaluations. Sometimes one player's mistake would generate multiple coaches screaming at him. Other times, the coaches would point out when a particular player made a great play or showed extra hustle. It was especially fun when a player made a big hit or shook an opponent because the team would let out a whoop.

Coach Jerry Fishbain, the academic advisor, would make announcements and remind or reprimand guys who were struggling with their classes. He'd mention the major tests scheduled that week and also post them in the locker room. Coach Alvarez usually just reiterated that as far as classes went, we needed to "take care of our business."

After the team meeting, the players all split off into their position meetings and would review the game with their individual coaches. Each player who got into the game would be given a percentage score. The wide receivers got grades in many areas including effort, catches, yards after the catch (YACs), knockdowns (if they had any), and mental errors (penalties, wrong routes, *etc.*).

At the end of the year, Alvy would give out awards for who had the best score in certain categories. As for the most knockdowns award, Mike Tams, a wide receiver who was in on just one play but managed to knock his guy down, asked whether they would be basing the award as a percentage rather than on sheer numbers. He was informed it was the latter.

So that was a typical week as a Wisconsin football player. Some days, practice felt like a loud, rude intrusion on my well-being and on others a welcome respite, a physical outlet for my worldly frustrations.

Can you tell these guys are athletes?
Joe Panos (left) and Mark Montgomery, on top of the hill.

CHAPTER FIVE:
BIG MEN ON CAMPUS

Because our pictures were in the game programs, many athletes were instantly recognizable on campus. If you saw a bigger-than-average guy wearing athletic department gear, you could assume he was an athlete. If you saw a big guy on a scooter or moped, you could assume he was an athlete. Because of the small number of students of color at UW-Madison, if you saw a black student, you could assume he was an athlete. It was almost redundant for these guys to wear athletic-issued clothing.

It seemed every other week, we'd have a new style of Wisconsin Football shorts, shirts, and sweatshirts in our lockers. Every locker came with a laundry bag, and after each practice we threw our football clothes in to be washed. The clothes stayed in the bags and were washed every night. Some players tried to get clever and throw their street clothes in the bag. This turned out to be a bad idea; being washed with Badgers red turned their street clothes a pinkish hue. It was almost like the equipment guys' equivalent of bankers putting exploding green dust in the stolen moneybag so that when the criminals opened it, they were marked.

I chose to wear non-athletic-department-issued clothing whenever I was away from the stadium—part of my attempt to feel like a regular student. Because of my average size, I was almost never assumed to be an athlete. If so, people thought I was a hockey player, which was fine by me because through most of my college career our hockey team was very successful, even becoming national champions in 1990. People knew I was an athlete only when I sat next to other football players, such as fellow receiver Tim Ott, in class.

Donny Gray and I used to tease Ott for his fashion sense. Ott would attend classes—and parties—dressed head to toe in team-issued clothing. He once actually wore his receiving gloves, with the sticky palms, to a house party. He said the gloves made nice beer coozies.

Tim was a high school phenom from tiny Hilbert, Wisconsin. Hilbert won the state championship his senior year thanks to Tim's speed and skills. He was legendary in that small town. He was dubbed "Hilbert's Hope." Tim was a small, blonde, curly-haired kid with the puffy eyes of a boxer. He was a natural coaches' favorite, a hard-working kid. I used to joke that he played with a piece of hay in his mouth. I think Tim was a bit overwhelmed playing at such a big university. His dorm probably had a higher population than his hometown.

BARS

With our time-consuming, difficult schedules, the players liked to blow off steam and so many of us went out drinking together during the week. The team rules were that no players were allowed to go to bars or parties during the season from Wednesday through Friday nights. Of course, some of the younger guys who knew they wouldn't play would go out sometimes but were usually pretty low-key about it. Most players got away with it if they chose to go out. Those few who didn't and got pulled over by cops or issued a drinking ticket, had the triple-whammy of getting penalized by the cops, the coaches, and probably the media.

Madison is quite small, and university news is also city news. The college athletes are town celebrities; so if a player gets in trouble, everyone knows. There's a magnifying glass over the athlete's head.

The most popular athletes at the bars were the football, basketball, and hockey players. These are the revenue-producing, high-profile sports at UW. It's no secret that many underage students get into bars, but they usually have fake IDs. The athletes didn't really have to bother. A lot of bars were owned by sports fans and even if the managers and owners of the bars weren't fans, they knew that having the university's high-profile athletes in their bars would be a good draw. It was also common procedure to scoot the underage athletes out the emergency door should the cops arrive.

Why do athletes seem to consistently show up on the police logs across American campuses? I don't have any specific statistics to say whether or not athletes commit more crimes than the rest of the student body, but I do know if an athlete does have a problem with the law, it will make it into the media. It makes sense on some level: Take a naturally aggressive, trained football player; add a good dose of alcohol consumption, throw in the daily pressures of being a student-athlete, combined with the usual emotions of young adults, and you've got a combustible mixture. You can also argue that the preferential treatment given athletes encourages them to break the law.

It's never a good idea to get in a fight with someone in a contact sport like football or hockey. These players are used to hitting and getting hit on a daily basis. Any physical altercation is much more comfortable to them than it is to most people. These athletes have a high threshold of pain and it's going to take a lot to get the upper hand on them.

There were certain players on the team we all knew we had to keep an eye on. I recall one night standing next to a certain defensive player and a few other team-mates in a bar having a good time. The bar was crowded and a guy bumped this player, causing him to spill his beer. The player just snapped. I and two other guys instinctively grabbed him and positioned ourselves between the player and the unfortunate bumper. I looked over my shoulder and told the guy to keep walk-ing, to get away. The bumper walked away and we calmed down our teammate.

A few moments later, the bumper returned. I saw him before the player did and I motioned for him to get away. The bumper ignored me and walked near the player. The player saw him and raised his fist to strike, saying, "Here we go." The bumper waved his hands and said, "I just wanted to apologize." The player heard nothing and only saw this guy's return as a sign that he wanted to fight. Another teammate and I were holding him back.

I once held a friend's pit bull back when a cat made its way into its view. I remember how tense and trembling the dog felt; despite my firm grip, I could barely hold it back. This player felt the same way. Like the dog, the player was essentially trained to be an attacker. He'd gone pretty far in life by his physical tal-ents, especially his ability to overpower people.

Though the bumper posed no threat, he was not off the hook in the player's eyes. The bumper ignored my suggestion to stay away. Despite our best attempt to interfere, the player managed to land a glancing blow to the bumper's face. Never mind that the player had spilled his beer and mine in the process. The blood from the guy's face and the beer from our cups fell to the floor together. I yelled at the guy to get out of there, and he did. A few of us grabbed our teammate and exited the bar as quickly as possible.

I broke up many more potential fights than I ever got into. A bar is a terrible place to fight. Unlike a boxing ring, a bar is full of sharp objects like tables, chairs, and beer bottles. A former wide receiver turned graduate assistant, Chris Ballard, got hit with a beer bottle in the face one night at a bar and needed 30 or so stitches to patch it up. Chris was a good-looking guy who now has a permanent scar on his left cheek because of one drunk's moment of indiscretion.

Teammates are good to have around to help you avoid situations like that, to look out for you, sometimes more than you know. Apparently, one evening I was having a good time with a few women at a bar. Nothing out of the ordinary, except that a group of guys standing nearby had a problem with it. One of the girls was an ex-girlfriend of their good friend and they felt that they had to protect her in his honor. One of them said, "Okay, he touches her one more time and we jump him."

Luckily, a teammate of mine, Nikki Kemp, overheard them talking about me. Nikki touched one of them on the shoulder. The guy turned around and saw Nikki with a few other teammates standing next to him. Nikki just shook his head and said, "Unh, unh. That's our boy." The guys apologized and ended up leaving the bar under my teammates' intimidating glare. This all occurred unbeknownst to me and didn't intrude on my fun one iota. I guess it was a good thing I let Nikki have the armrest at team meetings. I had no clue it happened until I was told about it at practice a few days later. And they wouldn't have even mentioned it except that they wanted to know whether I got any action with the girl. Teammates, man, they literally have your back.

Several of my friends on the team had what should've been private altercations become public embarrassments. College students do crazy, stupid, and sometimes illegal things. Society mostly expects this, if not outright condones it. But when football players, who are college students, pull the same stunts, it's held up for public judgment and ridicule. I'm not trying to excuse bad behavior, I just want to put it in perspective for those who like to blow things out of proportion in an effort to sell papers and for those who like to gossip and judge, often hypocritically. I understand that the players assume an extra responsibility by being an athlete, but the bottom line is that these guys have just entered adulthood, are away from home for the first time, and, for the most part, are just doing typical college stuff.

There were plenty of girls at the bars, and they knew the athletes hung out there. I'd heard of some athletes involved in various sex acts in the bars. I never received that sort of generosity, but I got a few drinks bought for me and some dates out of it.

GIRLS

I was the only football player and the only athlete on my coed floor, and everyone seemed to know that fact as soon as I arrived. It didn't hurt my high standing with everyone when word spread that football players and their under-age friends could get into a handful of "athlete-friendly" bars around campus.

I certainly took advantage of this, maybe too much, as I soon learned that my newfound campus celebrity had its limits. I once showed up at such an establishment with no fewer than nine underage dormmates in tow. The bouncer pulled me aside and said, "Don't ever do this again." He let us all in, though, which was quite nice of him.

Introducing fellow teammates to women was a bonding ritual at bars or at parties. It was part of being a team player. Some guys were easier to introduce than others. Women don't tend to respond to guys with hats on backwards or who drink beer while chewing tobacco. I remember one teammate lecturing another about this: "Look at you, you're the antithesis of what they want." I don't know who was right but I was impressed that the word "antithesis" was used.

In class once, I was sitting with a group of teammates and a female student passed me a note with her phone number. I had a girlfriend, and so I dutifully declined—but I did pass her number on to the most interested teammate.

One teammate attempted to compliment me and the lady I was with at the time by saying, "Chris here is a great guy. And he always has beautiful women with him." I nervously laughed it off. The girl replied, "Oh, really? A lot of women?" "No," I chuckled. But my teammate continued, "No, really, he does. He's just being modest." Oh well, his heart was in the right place even if his mouth wasn't.

Many of my teammates didn't see the logic in a college athlete having a steady girlfriend. Don't get me wrong, I enjoyed my time when I didn't have a girlfriend in college, but I also knew a good deal when I saw one. Even though I'd explain that my girlfriend, Stephanie, was a catch—tall, blonde, curvy, smart, supportive—and that I felt lucky to have landed her, my teammates weren't buying it. Athletes tend to feel they can trade on their status to have any woman they want, or as many as they want, and many of the guys felt that no woman could be worth giving up the freewheeling dating life of an athlete-king.

One day a teammate sat down next to me in the locker room with a concerned look on his face. After unraveling the tape from my wrist and picking at the residue still stuck to my arm hairs, I looked up at him. He just blurted out, "Man, what you doin' with a girlfriend?" I chuckled, but he was serious. I explained how great she was and how great she made me feel, and that I really just didn't feel the need to see other women.

He shook his head in profound disappointment, as if I'd told him I put a dent in his car. He said, "You know, the other day I sat down to make a list of my girlfriends?" I said that was nice. He continued, "Man, I had to get another piece of paper!" He shook his head, shrugged his shoulders, and walked away feeling confident he'd made some sort of point to me. I was impressed—he wasn't a very good-looking guy. But he was a football player, so I guess it didn't matter. It was also interesting how much better looking the girls who hung around the football players became as we started to win more.

A STUDENT AND AN ATHLETE

My relationships with people once I became a UW football player changed. Some thought it was a big deal and thought more of me. Others were jealous and thought I didn't deserve to be there.

Most male students respected, if not downright admired, my being a member of the team. They realized how hard it is to play at the Division I-A level. Playing college ball is a pretty idealized version of manhood.

A typical conversation with them went something like this: "Hey man, that's cool you're on the team." I'd respond, "Thanks." They'd ask me a bunch of football questions then bore me with the highlights of their high school or pee wee league careers. I'd strain to act like I was interested. Then they'd qualify, "Not that

I was good enough to play for Wisconsin. I wasn't as good as you were, of course. Man, that's awesome." "Thanks," I'd reply. "Seriously, man, good luck. I'll be rooting for you. Can I get you another drink?" Yes, you can, buddy.

Then there were the male students who felt threatened by having a football player in their presence. These guys would try to minimize it by saying that the team wasn't that good, or judged you based on whether or not you were a starter. These kinds of remarks were often intended to influence the interests of a girl. Unfortunately for them, most girls could not have cared less who started. I once dated a girl in college who asked whether I played high school football. I explained that everyone on the team not only played high school football but was likely quite good at it. She seemed sort of impressed.

The part I loved about being on the team was that when I was in the presence of one of these jealous guys or a cocky male student, it worked as a silencer. A guy could parade around campus all he wanted with his shirt off, showing off the abs that he'd worked so diligently for in the weight room, but when it came down to it he was a poser. He never took any hits and never got challenged to prove his strength or toughness in any meaningful way. The real tough guys had to put themselves on the line daily in football practice. Pretty abs and talking a big game doesn't gain you one inch on a football field. They knew deep down they didn't put up and tried to overcompensate with a transparent brashness. Football players, real tough guys, can spot this from a mile away.

On the other end of the spectrum were the "jock sniffers." These were nonathletic guys who loved to hang out with the football players and other athletes. These guys could be found hanging on the perimeter of a group of players at the bar. They usually ingratiated themselves by providing the players with a service: inviting them to parties, introducing them to girls, doing homework, buying drinks or drugs. I tried to stay out of these situations. The jock sniffer wouldn't hang around the athlete if he weren't an athlete, and the athlete wouldn't hang around the jock sniffer if he didn't provide him with things he wanted. Not the stuff good friendships are based on.

Regardless, the admiring attention from the vast majority of students and fans temporarily replaced the daily divots taken out of my self-esteem as a walk-on player.

WALK-ONS

The demographics of a walk-on at the University of Wisconsin: The majority are from the state of Wisconsin and some from a neighboring state. They are usually white. They are usually skill players—wide receivers, defensive backs, kickers, and perhaps linebackers. They are usually freshmen or sophomores, and are typically pretty good students. They are more likely to be successful after their football days are over than the scholarship players.

I was a walk-on, and in big-time college football, walk-ons, or non-scholarship players, are essentially second class citizens in the hierarchy of the team. Walk-ons are constantly competing, especially at the beginning, just for the right to exist. As a walk-on player, I found I had to have a high level of intensity on every play to have a chance to be successful—in fact, just to be average. Admitting you're average is very difficult, if not impossible, when you're a competitive athlete. I couldn't have done that then, but I can now.

Most players, whether they admit it or not, are average. But it's also true that the quality of the team overall usually depends on how good the average player is. The backups, the strugglers, are the heart of the team. All players are striving on a daily basis to improve their status on the team. You know where you stand as a player because it's listed on the depth chart every day when you arrive at practice.

A player's performance, at practice, in the weight room, training room, classroom, is under constant evaluation. Each practice is graded. There's not much peace of mind when you're being graded every day. Players sometimes viewed each other as the coaches did. If a player was in the coaches' doghouse, you sort of looked down on him accordingly, and vice versa if the player was getting praised a lot and in good graces with the coaching staff. Many guys went through both extremes at some point in their careers, if not on a weekly basis.

Young, prideful, successful athletes do not like to be humiliated or embarrassed, yet that often occurred on the practice fields. I think coaches like to keep players off balance mentally so that they're more easily controlled and molded.

Coach Norvell once said to me after I dropped a ball in practice, "You drop every other ball thrown to you." It wasn't true but he still felt the need to say it. It bothered me immensely, not because of the insult, but because his saying it might make a teammate or a coach think it was true and that would embarrass me and make me not drop a ball again.

After you've paid your dues and stuck around awhile, you get support from your fellow teammates. This is the amazing thing and the key ingredient to being able to meet the daily challenges of playing college football. The fellow receiver who is your competition is also your best friend. It's a special camaraderie. No one undercuts his teammate. You help one another memorize plays, critique routes, and recognize defensive coverages.

The stories I hear about the cut-throat business world where people take credit from co-workers and backstab and sabotage…well, that doesn't happen on the football field. The guys on this team lived the adage: "May the best man win."

Here's why we don't mind helping each other out. We're all extremely competitive, and if a player is truly competitive he wants to know how good he is, how he measures up. But if he cheats or even plays against somebody who's not playing at his peak, he doesn't get an accurate measurement on the level of his play. I can sincerely wish the best for my competitors/teammates without giving up my own goals, and many of my teammates shared in this sentiment.

Initially, my freshman year, there weren't even enough lockers in the locker room for many of us walk-ons. While the starters and scholarship guys were in the plush locker room with big wooden lockers, we used old steel crate lockers outside the team locker room in a back hallway. We had to change in an area where other athletes and the general public could potentially walk through—and that happened a few times.

Once, a few girls from the tennis team happened to mistakenly go out the wrong door of the weight room and there were a group of us in various states of our naked glory after practice. Many of us were so tired we didn't have the energy to cover up, so there was a stare-off, so to speak. The girls froze in disbelief and embarrassment, then quickly exited, after a few giggles.

This unfortunate situation was remedied a few games into the season after a few more guys had quit, freeing up enough space so that we were all moved into the main locker room. Our new lockers had big wooden double doors with nameplates, huge built-in carpeted benches in front, and a locked safe inside for any valuables. The locker was bigger than the closet in my dorm room.

There were piles of green towels available at the end of practice for showering. The towels were thrown into a separate bin from the laundry bags and washed every night, thank God. After watching way too many players manipulate those towels into the deepest crevices of their bodies, I hope there was napalm and penicillin in the washing detergent.

The showers, too, were not as sanitary as I would've wished them to be. The large shower room had spigots spaced along the walls with liquid soap dispensers between each one. You didn't want to get a spigot by one of the drains in the big shower room, lest your feet be overrun with a river of your teammates' soapy blood, urine, and snot. Whether you were a walk-on or not, you stayed away from the drainage patterns as much as possible. Like in real estate, which shower you chose was all about location, location, location.

A NUMBERS GAME

No walk-ons had their own jersey numbers, so all four years of my career I shared my number with a scholarship player.

My freshman year, I was number 81, shared with fellow freshman Michael Roan. Michael was a highly recruited tight end from Iowa who went on to become one of the best tight ends in UW football history and to an NFL career with the Tennessee Titans. My sophomore and junior years, I was number 29, shared with Jeff Messenger. They were two really nice, quiet guys and great college football players.

While I would've loved to have my own, sharing numbers did have its perks. My sophomore year, while sharing the number 29 with Messenger, I was standing on the sideline watching our team kick off when, after the tackle, the stadium's public-address announcer said, "Tackle by Chris Kennedy!" My buddies and I on the sideline all looked at each other and a couple of other guys peeked over at me. I didn't know how to react. I just kind of nodded at everyone. Later on in the game, a few guys slapped me on the back while I was getting some water. They were down on the defensive half of our sideline and they must've thought I got in the game and made the tackle as charged. To top it off, my name was not only mistakenly announced over the stadium public address but I also got credit over the radio broadcast of the game.

A good high school friend, Brad Ziegler, was listening while duck hunting and was so elated to hear my name broadcast over the airwaves, he screamed and whooped, probably scaring any ducks away.

While I felt bad to get undeserved credit, Jeff made plenty of tackles that year and the rest of his career, so I imagine he wasn't too broken up about it.

In a way, it was compensation for an incident from my high school playing days. Early in a game my senior year against our rival Deforest High, the referees decided my number 34 jersey had been torn beyond acceptability. I was forced to change jerseys, and Coach Quinn had me quickly switch jerseys with a sophomore standing innocently on the sidelines who wouldn't be playing in the game. Not a fair trade, since I got a brand-new clean jersey and he had a muddy, torn jersey to wear for the rest of the cold night.

He got his due though; neither the media nor the public-address announcer caught on that I was playing under a different number. And so this lucky sophomore had his name reverberated throughout the stadium the rest of the night anytime I made a play. To top it off, the next morning's paper also credited him with a touchdown I'd scored while I was still wearing my original number 34! At least Messenger got credit for his tackle on the official stat sheets and in the papers the next day.

My senior year at UW, I was switched to number 18. I thought this meant I would finally have my own number as a reward for my four years on the team. I thought wrong. I shared it with a scholarship freshman.

Thorough rosters and game-day programs would list all the players, but often the newspapers and other sport magazines only listed one player per number. Usually the scholarship player would be listed unless the walk-on got significant playing time. Since I didn't, I was absent from many rosters, which confused a lot of people including me; I could never explain it to people who knew I was on the team. They would've thought I was a pathological liar if they didn't see me on the field on Saturdays. It was embarrassing, to say the least.

I was dedicating my life to this sport but couldn't even get a simple listing to show I was on the team? Certainly a test of your frustration levels when you work your butt off all week in practice, get banged up, and then open Saturday's sports section to see that you don't even exist. The invisible man in pads.

The psychological strain was harder to deal with than the physical strain. While the walk-ons numbered 30-plus at freshman camp, those numbers dwindled to 20 as the camp ended, and by the end of the first season it was down to around 10. This is an illustration of why there aren't many upperclass walk-ons. It's sort of a young man's trial. Typically, a player is given a scholarship within a year or so. If he hasn't received one by then he usually quits, as the odds are he's never going to get one.

While the walk-on road is filled with many casualties, there are quite a few UW walk-on success stories from my time on the team. Here are a few prominent ones.

Joe Panos – Dubbed "the Big Greek," Joe goes down in history as one of the key members of the 1994 Rose Bowl team. He was the team captain, and the heart and soul of the line and the team. Joe transferred to Wisconsin after one season at UW-Whitewater. He came in as a defensive lineman but was switched to offensive lineman, and that's where he started to blossom. Alvarez liked to make defensive players into offensive linemen because he likes the attack mentality on both sides of the ball. He did the same thing with fellow starting lineman Joe Rudolph, a former reserve linebacker turned all-Big Ten offensive guard.

Panos has a great laugh and he was the pied piper of the linemen. His gregarious personality made the offensive line a cool place to be, like a cult with really big biceps.

After taking the senior football picture on a yacht on Lake Michigan near Milwaukee, we all ate at his family's restaurant downtown. Some guys ordered two or three entrees and Joe helped serve the food. He and his family were great hosts.

Joe dished good advice along with good lamb dinners. Once, I mentioned I was having a problem getting to sleep at night, and he had a solution for me: "Here's what you do, you set a few beers by the edge of the bed. Whenever you have trouble sleeping just down a couple of those babies." Joe swung his hand in a straight line. "Put you right out." I tried it a few times. He was right. I also found out that if you had more than a few, you got put right out too…sometimes before you even made it to bed. That's a different story.

Jeff Wirth – Jeff was an extremely hard-working, disciplined kid from Wausau, Wisconsin. His hair was so blonde it was white, hence his nickname, "the White Rat." The moniker fit because he was tenacious as well. Jeff had a great sense of humor. He called me "Cortez Kennedy," referring to the 300-pound all-America defensive tackle from the University of Miami, who also happened to be black. He found the comparison amusing. Jeff once remarked to non-alcohol-drinking, Mormon quarterback Darrell Bevell that he was sorry that he wasn't able to "get high on life" like Darrell could, and needed a drink once in a while. He also tried constantly to catch Darrell swearing, a Mormon no-no. Darrell would argue he didn't say the alleged swear word, but something that sounded like it; Jeff laughed that off.

Jeff's integrity impressed me, too. One time a teammate, a pretty tough guy, was teasing a female trainer, who was getting upset by it. Though the teammate was kidding, she was hurt. Nobody really said anything except for Jeff, who emphatically said, "Dude, shut up! That's not funny." The guy was a little crazy and I thought there might have been an altercation, but the guy stopped and walked away.

Jeff starred on special teams for a couple of years and then was the back-up fullback to Mark Montgomery during the 1993 season. When Montgomery was ejected, unfairly, for his part in a brawl during the Rose Bowl game, Jeff filled in at fullback for the final quarter and a half to help secure the biggest win in our program's history.

Vince Zullo – Vince and I were low on the depth chart when we arrived as freshman wide receivers. Nevertheless, Vince was always very confident. He was a strong, physical guy who'd played linebacker in high school.

When we were sophomores, at a shorts-and-shoulder-pads practice, Vince was to do a crack block on a linebacker. Vince ran a proper route and was in perfect position to block the linebacker. He came back to the huddle and remarked how lucky the linebacker was that we weren't in full pads. A pretty bold statement for a scout-team receiver to make about a starting linebacker. I think I probably chuckled a little bit.

At a full-pads practice a week or two later, Vince held true to his word and flattened the starting linebacker with a crack block. Put him on the ground. There were sounds of approval from the coaches, the scout-team players, and the starting defensive players…and also the shattering sound of his walk-on glass ceiling. From that point on, Vince became the go-to guy as a blocking receiver. He made it onto several special teams and shined there. I was really proud of him. Vince became a team favorite; he was referred to as the "Italian Stallion."

Vince became known around the Big Ten as a receiver you needed to pay attention to, especially if you were a linebacker on his side of the field. Vince had a nice crack block on a UCLA linebacker in a key play during the Rose Bowl game. It was so fun to see the guy I was standing equal with just a few years earlier, a guy I walked to the stadium with on cold, early morning workouts, make such a big play on national television in front of 100,000-plus fans.

Chad Cascadden – Chad came in unheralded as a high school player from Chippewa Falls, Wisconsin. He'd gotten injured and barely played his senior year of high school. He got himself healthy and walked onto the team as a defensive back.

Chad and I lived in the same dorm, and he would invite me down to watch stand-up comedy videos. He had a ton of them. So we'd sit there and watch while he drank all kinds of different protein powders and supplements.

As a walk-on, Chad was a pain to the starters because he would play hard on "light days" as part of the scout team. He was low on the depth chart his first two years, but after a lot of dedication to lifting and eating right, he gained weight and worked his way onto a few special teams. After some great special-teams play, he moved into the rotation at outside linebacker. He got significant playing time there and contributed many plays in our Rose Bowl season. Chad eventually went on to play for six seasons with the New York Jets.

Chad was always in great shape but often needed help from teammates to get from station to station during winter conditioning. He had a lot of nagging injuries. He once screamed out at a team meeting. His legs were cramping so bad, you could actually see the muscles twisting and contorting. Receiver Michael London commented, "Man! It looks like an alien is going to pop out of those legs." Chad spent the rest of the meeting lying down in the aisle.

I heard a great story about Chad. One night at a bar, a very attractive girl approached him. She mentioned that she went to high school with a current teammate of Chad's at Wisconsin. She attempted to gain favor with Chad by talking sports. At one point, she denigrated his teammate, saying he wasn't as good as Chad was and wasn't likely to stay on the team. Chad didn't like her talking smack about his teammate regardless of how great-looking she was. Chad replied, "Excuse me, but he's a friend of mine. And you're a bitch." And Chad walked away from one of the prettiest girls on campus, who was left speechless the rest of the night. The best part was that his teammate found out about the incident from the pretty girl's friend. Chad never told the player he did it. That's a good teammate. That's a guy with character.

Chris Hein – He came in as a walk-on defensive back from Plymouth, another small Wisconsin town. Like Cascadden, Chris also gained enough strength, speed, and size to be converted to outside linebacker. Chris shined at this new position, quickly being awarded a scholarship and a starting position in his junior season. He quietly contributed solid play to a really solid defense that took us to the Rose Bowl. Chris started in that game and recently received a vote as one of the best outside linebackers of the Barry Alvarez era in a *Capital Times* poll.

STEP-FATHER FIGURES

It's natural for college players to seek a male authority figure. The 18–22-year-old age range is a big developmental time for a young man. The sheer size of many players is misleading—they seem like they're older than they are. In fact, they have just entered adulthood.

As excited as I was to embark on this noble journey, I didn't realize how lonely it would be. I went from having very visible and present father figures in my own dad and Coach Quinn, to rather absentee ones in Coach Alvarez and his staff. Logistically, Coach Alvarez had 100 sons to worry about, along with boosters, recruits, fans, administrators, media, and coaches. Plus, UW is a big campus and it would be nearly impossible to keep track of all the players.

It didn't seem to matter how we acted, as long as we didn't get caught. There was some freedom in that, but I'm not sure all of us could handle it or even wanted it. Even though I knew better, I still bought into the delusion that my coaches would be the good, available father figures I needed them to be.

My own position coach, Jay Norvell, and I just didn't seem to click. I often felt he wanted me out of there, but was forced to put up with me. Like the stepdad forced to accept the kids he wished his wife didn't have. Coach Norvell would yell at me without apologizing, or without clarifying why.

One day in practice, when I ran a 12-yard buttonhook route, the receiver on my outside was running a fly, and the quarterback threw it to him. As I jogged back, Norvell confronted me in front of the whole team, "How many yards is that route?" I paused as I thought it was a trick question. I knew it was a 12-yard route and I ran a 12-yard route. I responded, "Twelve yards." "Then why didn't you run 12 yards?" I did run 12 yards. Or was I going crazy and had I run some other distance I wasn't even aware of? As I was second-guessing myself, Norvell took that time to berate me, "You're not gonna get on the damn field when you don't know the plays!" He turned his attention toward the field and walked back to the sideline.

Teammates and coaches from other positions assumed he was right and I was wrong. A few teammates patted me encouragingly, while a few coaches gave me a dirty look. Stunned, I walked to my friend and fellow receiver Donny Gray and asked, "Did you see my route?" He said yes. I continued, "Didn't I run 12 yards?" Donny shook his head disbelievingly, "Yeah! He doesn't need to be yelling 'bout that. You ran it right." I just shook my head and so did he. It's not like it would ever be appropriate for me to argue about it again and if I did, Coach wouldn't believe me anyway. Like the business adage, "The customer is always right," in football the coach is always right. I made plenty of mistakes but when I did something right I didn't expect someone to scream at me.

I didn't understand it. I was a good, hard-working kid trying to live his dream. Coach Norvell was a young, volunteer coach trying to obtain a permanent position with the coaching staff. We were both trying to make it. How could he not see how alike our goals were? How could he not like me? What had I ever done to him?

I surmised eventually that because I wasn't a standout receiver, I did nothing to make Norvell look good as a coach. He needed a star to hang his hat on and make him look good. Ironically, if he had made me into a better receiver it would've made him a better coach than if he just guided someone who already had amazing talent and would succeed with or without his help. But neither of us got to find that out. Though I feel I could've bloomed with just a little more help from Coach Norvell, as it was my improvement would be solely up to me.

It wasn't only Norvell; all the coaches seemed unappeasable. Make a mistake and they'd jump on you. Make a good play and they still could find something to criticize you about. Make an amazing play and they treated it as commonplace, that's what's expected out of you.

One coach even said to a player during a film session, "Everything's fine. You fulfilled your assignment. Your form and your technique are good. But it's just not violent enough." The coach was referring to a practice play against the player's own teammate.

From my perspective as a young player, the coaches seemed to be the undisputed "experts of manhood." So if you crossed them or did something that displeased them, you were being the opposite of a man.

One practice, due to some injuries, I got in on an end-of-practice scrimmage with the first and second-string players. They actually called a pass play to me during the offensive series and I was excited to have an opportunity to make a play in this "live" (full-contact) scrimmage. They even brought in referees for this one.

I ran the route precisely, spun my head around and located the ball quickly firing toward me. I reached up and snagged it with both hands. I immediately squeezed it to my body, and after feeling no hit from the defensive back covering me, I turned upfield. I was just a yard or two short of the first down, so I stutter-stepped to avoid a tackle and just as I was about to reach the first-down marker, the defensive back reached back and grabbed my facemask. The pull yanked my head to an unnatural position and I dropped my body just before I felt the tendons in my neck had reached their snapping point. I was stopped just short of the first-down marker, but since I was facemasked the penalty yardage would give us the first down.

I hopped up, and despite my aching neck, felt good that I'd made the catch and made a play that got us a first down. Offensive coordinator Childress looked disappointed and yelled to me, "You gotta get the first down. We can't have you stopping short." Coach Childress was right up next to me now and said, "That's a critical play." I replied, "I was facemasked." Childress shook his head and replied, "Doesn't matter," and he walked back to call the next play. Hadn't I gotten the first down anyway, because the facemask penalty was called? I felt frustration for being yelled at for something out of my control and wondered how I was ever going to make it if my best effort wasn't good enough and I was expected to control the uncontrollable.

The criticism was so prevalent that I began to accept it and integrate it into my being. To survive, I had to stop trying to get my self worth from the approval of my father figures, the coaches. This was no easy task as I'd depended on father figures my entire life. Despite Coach Jacques once saying, "If we're not screaming at you, then you should be worried," I still took it too personally and let their criticism affect my play. I think I preferred being ignored. At the very least, I felt I learned more from calm logic than from scornful humiliation, but again I had no control over how I was coached.

Even though I knew pleasing the coaches was virtually impossible, I couldn't completely get past my need for approval from them. I remember the elation I'd feel when I got an infrequent compliment from one of the coaches. One day I'd made a catch in front of Coach Alvarez. I jogged by him to the huddle and Alvarez quietly said, "Nice play, Chris." It was quite insignificant from his point of view, but to me it was life-affirming. I was so thirsty for approval that I sponged up any positive comments I could to provide me the sustenance to continue showing up at practice every day.

I soon realized I was like an orphan. I felt a little betrayed by the whole idea of father figures. Much like the pet that is taken to the farm by the family that can no longer keep him, I felt similarly about my father dropping me off at UW's freshman football camp.

I was a pretty independent kid but I hadn't had much practice supporting myself through tough times alone. My parents, though divorced, were prevalent in my life and I realize how lucky I was to have that. I was grateful that I had parents who made me feel as if I could do anything. Whenever I proposed an idea, the response was usually something like, "Sure, why not?" I shudder to think of all the things I wouldn't have accomplished without their supportive attitude.

There were players on the team who had dysfunctional father–son relationships. I heard the story of one player's father leaving the family when the player was only nine years old. The dad told his son that even though he was moving out, he'd still take him to his Little League practices every Saturday. But every Saturday this player would wait on his porch, watching the horizon for his father's car that never showed up. Eventually after too many Saturdays of his father's unkept promise, he gave up. This same deadbeat dad came back into the player's life his senior year in high school, when the player had gained notoriety as a star and earned a football scholarship to Wisconsin.

I'm aware there are parental types whose knee-jerk reactions to most everything are negative, and I also realize such reactions have a paralyzing effect on their children. They immediately nip the buds of possibility. I'd like to think that if I had parents of the negative sort, I would've taken the risks in spite of them but I'm glad I didn't have to find that out.

Growing up, I can't think of anything I thought I couldn't do, a condition I still carry with me today to some degree. I'm still pretty confident that if I set my mind to something that I can do it, and I have my upbringing to thank for that.

At UW, however, I was outside my parents' safety net and now I'd have to suck it up and be my own man. I guess this is supposed to be a big part of what college has to offer. Football bloodied my nose before I even knew I was in a fight. I began my manhood trying to find out who I was. I was using football as a catalyst. I was learning that manhood was tough and lonely, and I had no choice but to accept it and forge myself into this new image in the cauldron of Camp Randall Stadium.

Coach Alvarez and his staff taught us many things, but in their absence is where I learned to become a man.

CHAPTER SIX:
ONE WIN

Unfortunately, there wasn't a lot to celebrate my freshman year. All the enthusiasm and hope so prevalent in the pre-season waned as the reality of the season played out.

We lost to California at home, 28-12, in a game that we'd been eyeing all through summer conditioning and preseason. With our high expectations, it was quite deflating to lose in front of our home crowd and a national television audience (ESPN covered the game). I think the loss was especially hard on the upperclassmen who were hoping to change the losing ways of old with the new coach. We made so many mistakes in that game. We had a touchdown called back in the first quarter because a receiver was offsides. On the verge of scoring again, we were on the Bears' eight yard line when one of their players intercepted a pass and ran it back for a touchdown.

The team bounced back the next week to beat Ball State, 24-7. Our offense should have scored even more but it made some key mistakes, including failing to score on three tries from the 1-yard line. Our defense played great and almost had a shutout except for one pass play that gave Ball State its only touchdown of the game.

A week later, we lost at home to Temple, 24-18. We were up, 18-14, in the fourth quarter but we allowed Temple to score on two drives late in the game. After the loss, Alvarez told the media, "We are not a very good team." He was right. We never won another game the rest of the year. Our record was 1-10 in Alvarez's inaugural season. We went 0-8 in the 1990 Big Ten race.

I don't know whether I can accurately convey how tough it is to dedicate your life to something and to see how much work everyone around you—teammates, support staff and coaches—puts into something, only to get so little in return.

With the exception of a few games, our team had plenty of chances to win. In 7 of our 10 losses, we were in striking distance of a win in the fourth quarter— a fact our coaches never tired of pointing out. Along with the loss to Temple, there was the Iowa game in which we were down, 12-10, and gave up 18 points in the fourth quarter to lose, 30-10. At Northwestern, we lost, 44-34, but we only scored once in the second half and missed a two-point conversion. This in a game where we made three special-teams errors that gave the Wildcats 21 points.

We could have upset fifth-ranked Illinois at home. The score was 14-3 in Illinois' favor with only four minutes left in the game. The nearly full stadium crowd and our team believed we were due for a huge upset win that would help prove this program was headed in the right direction. But we fumbled the ball for the fourth time and Illinois scored another touchdown to put the game away.

Against Minnesota at home, we were down, 21-3, in the fourth quarter on our own 17-yard line but failed to score because we couldn't cover the one yard we needed for a first down, despite two chances to do so. On the next series, we threw an interception at mid-field, ending any hope of a comeback.

Against Indiana, we were down, 13-7, in the fourth quarter but our defense gave up a fourth-and-one on their 7-yard line during a Hoosiers scoring drive that ate up six and a half minutes. We lost, 20-7.

The marching band cheers as Mike Roan pulls in a touchdown—
something we sure could have used more of that 1991 season.

MIKE DEVRIES/CAPITAL TIMES

We ended the season with a 14-9 loss at Michigan State in which we dropped a pass in the end zone and were intercepted in the end zone on the last play of the game.

Unfortunately, I think we got into a losing rut, and no matter how much we fought it, each week's game brought the renewed sense of "here we go again." We made so many mistakes that we beat ourselves as much as our opponents did. Our offense couldn't move the ball. Our special teams made too many critical screw-ups, and our defense, while the most solid part of our team, gave up some big plays.

On a personal down note, my friend Matt Morris decided to quit the team after our freshman season. He said he didn't want to put so much time into the sport and just didn't have the desire to go through it all again, especially without much guarantee of getting any playing time. It made me question my own situation; I had less of a chance than he did. I had too much to prove yet, but I was jealous of his new freedom. He had no axe to grind, nothing to prove. He could have easily stayed on the team and even played some, but his personal time and life meant more to him. Matt's absence put a hole in the support group I'd built on the team.

To add to the agony, I think we all felt looked down upon by the community, the fans, and our fellow students. Any mention of Wisconsin football was met with a snicker and a headshake, if not in front of our faces, certainly behind our backs. Many players didn't want to wear their letter jackets and football apparel.

It hardly seemed worth the hard work and sacrifice. I highly doubt we were putting in any less time and effort than the guys in Ann Arbor, Columbus, or Iowa City, yet they were having success and we weren't.

The irony is that I truly felt no one was more committed to winning than we were. That's all we talked about and discussed and worked toward. Could all the media pundits and armchair critics make that claim? Could they step out on the field and do any better? Of course not. It's frustrating to have to endure their scorn when they don't have the talent or the fortitude to step on a field and compete like those they criticize. I felt sorry for all of us who limped and bled for the school only to have some fans and students scoff at our efforts. The team played hard and competitively, and never quit despite what the record showed. Yes, we blew some opportunities but we weren't as far behind the leaders as it seemed. I regret that the seniors had to go out like this, leaving a half-empty stadium behind them. I know they all dreamed of quite the opposite when they were freshmen like me.

I remember walking down a hallway in my dorm, overhearing a scrawny wise guy make a joke about how pathetic the football team was. I wanted to slam him against a wall, tell him that I'd do that to him three hours everyday for four months and see how tough he was. It's hard to read newspaper stories and hear people talk about your friends and teammates negatively when they don't even know them. I understand it's a prerogative of fans and the media to feel all the emotions that go along with the team and complain when things go wrong. But at the end of the day, the harsh criticism doesn't help anyone. Simply complaining never turns anything around.

I wish the critics understood what it takes to be someone like Don Davey, a senior captain on the team. He was a Manitowoc Lincoln High School star who wanted to play at and represent his state's university. He had the unfortunate luck to be recruited by a coach, Dave McClain, who died before Don could set foot on campus. He honored his commitment to the new coaching staff and attended UW. Don did all the new staff asked of him and beyond, yet only experienced winning six times in three seasons. Then, as a senior, with another new coaching staff and new hope, he was only able to enjoy one win before his Badgers playing days were over.

That's not to say that he didn't get recognized for his outstanding play. Coach Alvarez and his veteran staff appreciated and knew they had a gem in Don Davey. He was used on a daily basis as an example of the model football player. At team meetings, while reviewing game film, it was common to hear a coach yell, "Watch Don Davey!" Don went full speed all the time. Even when the team had no chance of winning, he would always be throwing himself around the field. That's character. Don won many battles with his counterparts, some of whom were playing for powerhouse teams like Michigan, Miami, and Ohio State, and it gave hope to the rest of us. Don didn't limit his efforts to the field; he had close to a 4.0 GPA as an engineering major. This was no underwater basket-weaving major. (Smart-alecks always use that as an example of easy classes taken by athletes. Is it just me, or does underwater basket-weaving sound hard?)

I don't mean to make it sound like life was like war-torn Kosovo. We still had our fun as football players and teammates. Even though Alvarez had instituted a "no-hazing" order, Don and the seniors still got to have some fun with the younger players and enjoy themselves.

After the season, seniors Greg Thomas, Todd Strop, and Greg Miller hosted a party at their house, calling it "freshman orientation," sort of like the university-sponsored SOAR. The acronym for this orientation would've been more accurately titled SORE. I was one of the brave freshman lambs who were willingly led to the slaughter.

Walking into the orientation party, our hands were grabbed and taped to a plastic cup. We were told this was the last time that cup was to be empty of beer for the rest of the night. The entrance fee was to down a shot of tequila and a healthy-sized beer bong. Sustenance was provided in the form of badly barbequed meat and stale potato chips.

We played the "running tapper" game in the backyard. A senior would pull the handle on the beer keg and exclaim that not a drop was to hit the ground. We freshmen stood in line waiting for our turn to fill our cups under the tap, then marched to the back of the line and drank the beer before it was our turn at the keg again. I was all too happy to let any upperclassmen cut in front of me to fill their cup and take a bit of a break. We repeated this process until the keg was finished. The seniors cheered and we freshmen were congratulated for "competing"; we were accepted as members of the team.

The seniors then led us in some bar hopping and treated us to some more fun. Those of us in attendance got exactly what we wanted: some playful abuse with an underlying current of respect and camaraderie. And as young men, we were learning that bonding when the pressure was off paid dividends when the pressure was on.

I felt so strongly about Don and his senior classmates that I dedicated a speech to them in one of my classes. I spoke about how much I admired their valiant efforts in the face of sure defeats. Many of them fought, sacrificed, and played their hearts out on behalf of the university. We were all Badgers, and they were our older brothers. They taught us younger guys how to commit to the unknown with all our hearts and compete to the very end. So, even though the 1990 senior class will go down in history as a one-win team, their efforts contributed to the future success of the UW football program and deserve to be recognized as such. I've heard they were all sent special rings by Coach Alvarez after we won the Rose Bowl in 1994.

That said, the team was flawed. Our talent didn't measure up to the other Big Ten teams, and the team didn't know how to win games. Weekly, the coaches would point out the little things, the mistakes, the opportunities missed that were costing us big plays and hence, victories. It was frustrating, yet heartening, to see that a few plays could reverse the outcome of a game. Football is a game of momentum. Coach Alvarez explained that the pendulum of momentum always swung back and forth, and you had to wait it out when it was on the other end, make a big play and get the pendulum back on your side, to ride it to victory.

Also, many young players got some significant playing time, taking licks now that would pay off in the future as they became veterans. Freshmen like fullback Mark Montgomery, nose tackle Lamark Shackerford, and linebacker Yusef Burgess all got valuable experience that would pay large dividends for them in the years to come.

The coaches' main task during and after that first season was to instill confidence in us that despite the losses most of the players had endured their entire careers, we had winning potential. A new mentality of confidence had to be instilled, and I can think of no one better at doing that than Barry Alvarez. Our greatest opportunity to win games was to compete our butts off on every down and to minimize mistakes. The coaches were constantly pointing out that with some corrections, our team would be able to win more games.

I recall a lot of talk about an upcoming opponent, the Temple Owls, and their alleged toughness. Alvarez, a bit fed up with it all, said at our team meeting, "Yes, they're tough guys." Alvarez's voice rose. "But hey, we're tough too! Do they have a patent on toughness in Philly?" It was like a lightning bolt going off in our heads. We all knew for a fact that the teammates we were banging up against every day were pretty tough guys, so why don't we just acknowledge and accept that we're tough as well, and go out and show the world that? That was our mentality as we went into winter conditioning.

PASS JUDGMENT

A couple of weeks after the season, the players and their position coaches met individually to evaluate the season together. I was very curious as to what my position coach, Norvell, would have to say about me. I hadn't spent a whole lot of time with him; I was on the offensive scout team while he was with the first two strings of the offense. I was low on the depth chart, but with a few seniors graduating I looked forward to getting a shot at filling the vacancies.

On my way to the stadium for my evaluation, I ran into fellow freshman walk-on receiver Tim Ott. Tim was just leaving his evaluation and said that it was encouraging. He said Norvell told him to keep working hard and that he'd have a shot at earning a scholarship by the end of next year. Tim was pretty excited, and so was I. I considered us to be quite equal in terms of talent, performance, and potential.

Tim was a great guy and friend. Quiet at first, his dry, down-home sense of humor inevitably came through. Tim was small, quick, and tough. He was very likable and received a lot of attention from the coaches. They loved touting him as the man from tiny Hilbert with the big heart. I guess my hometown didn't quite have the panache. Regardless, Tim and I had helped each other make it through a difficult season and I looked forward to us one day overcoming the odds together and playing some ball for UW.

I arrived at Coach Norvell's office. We sat down one-on-one, and it dawned on me that he and I had never done this before. While I'd been in meetings and on the field with him every day, we never had any time with just him and me. The room felt claustrophobic with the both of us in there. Norvell seemed uncomfortable as he handed me a self-evaluation packet. He left the room while I filled it out. The questionnaire asked you to grade yourself honestly on things like skills, effort, and areas of improvement. This is a daunting task because you want to come across confident so you want to score yourself well, but on the other hand, you want the coaches to think you can improve a lot, that you're not satisfied with your play and so you want to score yourself low. I decided to split the difference and gave myself mediocre scores. Honestly, I thought my pass-catching ability was above average, but I was just starting to grasp (pardon the pun) the intricacies of catching the ball, so I had plenty of room for improvement as well. My concentration was usually quite good. I tended to get my hands on the ball, and once I did I rarely dropped it. Hence, I gave myself an above average "hands score."

My speed, and more specifically my quickness, were a bit below average. I often found myself getting tangled up by defenders at the line of scrimmage and getting pushed off my routes. This made many of my routes sloppy, and a quarterback can't trust a sloppy route-runner to be where he needs to be to catch the ball. The quarterback throws the ball where the receiver is supposed to end up, not where he is, so timing is key.

I knew getting off the line of scrimmage cleanly would be my biggest area of improvement. Not only did I need to work on my foot quickness but also my hand quickness. The more I could keep a defensive player's hands from getting on me, the better chance I had of making a clean release off the ball and running a proper, unencumbered route.

I wasn't worried that my 4.7 time in the 40-yard-dash speed was below average for a receiver. This was no excuse for failure, as two of the best running backs of all time, Marcus Allen and Walter Payton, supposedly had below-average 40-yard-dash speeds. Although the first thing you hear about any skill player is his speed in the 40, it's really an overrated measure. How often in a football game does one get to run untouched in a straight line for 40 yards, almost half the length of the field?

What is more important for the skill positions than speed is quickness. Agility, the ability to "shuck and jive," or "juke," is much more effective and useful than straight-up speed. Overall body control with speed is imperative to getting a clean release off the line of scrimmage, as well as making sharp cuts on your pass routes and changing directions on a dime. I planned to work on this by doing footwork drills and boxing the speed bag in the off-season.

I rated my blocking as average. A good blocking receiver is similar to being a good defensive basketball player. It's mostly hard work and dedication, more sweat than talent. You sprint at the defender then sink your hips and mirror his every move. Your main job is to stay between the defender and the ball carrier. It's best to focus on your opponent's hips, as the good ones are "shifty" with their shoulders, feet, and arms. But a player can go nowhere without his torso. I tended to work hard and stay with my guy but felt I could work harder and so I rated myself average. With experience, I knew I could get better at this.

Lastly, I gave myself an above-average attitude score. After all, I was a volunteer player, and how could I have a bad attitude when I'm donating my life to the team… for free? Sure, there were days when I would've rather been anywhere but on the field but all players go through that, and on the average I accepted my tasks willingly and as energetically as I could.

Coach Norvell re-entered the room and looked over my answers. He didn't spend much time looking over my well-considered assessments. I took that as a bad sign. He looked down at his hands and shook his head trying to find the right words. He finally said, "Your skills are far below where they need to be." I nodded my head. OK, yes, some of them, I thought to myself. He continued, "They're just not where they need to be to play at this level." The air traveling out of my stomach made an audible grunt. We stared at each other for a few moments. Was he saying what I thought he might be saying? I was being cut? He was writing me off? Norvell suggested I look into transferring to another school as he saw no possibility for me to play for the Wisconsin Badgers.

I'd never been so crushed in my life and so at a loss for words. I don't think I'd ever had words punch me in the gut before. I was thrown into a place in my head I'd never been. I'd accomplished virtually every goal I'd set for myself at that point in my life. My heart was racing, and my head was spinning. I was lost. I wish I'd said something about how he didn't really watch me all year, so how could he say such things? But I couldn't speak. What did he think about my self-evaluations? I felt degraded at the thought of not belonging there, of not being good enough to be around my teammates and the offices I sat in—a latent fear I'd had since the day I walked onto the team. Every insecurity I'd worked so hard to bury came gushing through my body like bubbles running up a freshly opened soda bottle.

Norvell and I sat in silence for a bit, staring at our shoes. My eyes watered and the blood drained from my face. Coach Norvell said he was sorry. I finally said something about enjoying being on the team and then some sort of pseudo-noble statement like I would work hard until they told me to clean out my locker. Norvell seemed to sympathize and told me that I had a good attitude. He said he wouldn't ask me to leave the team. We shook hands, and I walked out the door, full of hurt, confusion, and emptiness. My world was rocked.

As I walked out, I looked around at the other coaches sitting in their offices. Some were laughing on the phone, some were typing on their computers, and some just passed me by like nothing had happened.

Thoughts raced through my brain. Would these all-too-familiar surroundings now be off limits to me? Could I not enter through the "players only" entrances now? How was I going to tell anyone, especially my father, what happened? I didn't really know what happened. I wasn't sure whether I was to be officially dumped from the team or not. Why didn't I clarify? Maybe I was afraid of the answer. I anticipated the humiliation I'd feel with everyone knowing that I wasn't good enough to make the team. A public failure. How did Tim get such a nice evaluation when mine was so poor? Maybe the naysayers were right and I was wrong. Maybe I wasn't going to live out my heroic fantasy after all. I considered for the first time that maybe I couldn't do whatever I set my mind to. Maybe a will doesn't always find a way. I was a reduced young man.

I returned to my dorm room in a daze and called my father at work. I dreaded having to tell him the bad news but also hoped maybe he could make sense of things. I thought I'd pulled it together as I made the call but the difficulty of hearing my father's upbeat voice asking how the meeting went devastated me. As I started to tell him, tears burst out of me like an erupting volcano. Despite biting my hand and lip to distract myself, I couldn't get a coherent sentence together. The only thing my dad could decipher was my repeatedly saying I was sorry. I told him I didn't know why I was crying like that.

His voice had a sympathetic tone I'd never heard before. "It's okay, you're upset, and that's why you're crying." I regained some semblance of composure and told him about the meeting. My dad asked me why I thought I got a bad review. Trying to answer this question, it became clear that Norvell didn't really know me; he wasn't there to see me play on the scout team and wasn't really qualified to judge me.

My sadness started to turn to indignation. "In all honesty, he's wrong about me. He's underestimating me. He truly doesn't know me."

In that moment, I made up my mind that I was going to prove to Norvell, myself, and everyone else that I belonged on the team. My mission became clear. Crystallized. No more Mr. Tentative. No more "Mr. Just Happy to be Here." I'm here and if I'm going down, I'm going down swinging. Amazing how it all clicked for me in that phone call with my father. He had a great way of letting me figure out things on my own, without spoon-feeding me.

They really were going to have to physically remove me from the locker room to get me out of there. My fighting spirit came back and I recognized myself again, or maybe I was learning who I really was for the first time.

My renewed attitude was given more fuel by my one-on-one meeting with offensive coordinator, Russ Jacques, just a couple of days later. Coach Jacques was older than Norvell, more experienced, and more fatherly. We had a nice conversation about classes and the upcoming holidays prior to my evaluation. It was comfortable. Coach Jacques told me I had quite a few things to work on in the upcoming winter conditioning and that I needed to get to work as soon as possible. He agreed with most of my evaluations of myself.

Coach Jacques ended the meeting by saying, "One thing I know about Chris Kennedy is that he loves football and he has heart. How the hell else could you make it as a walk-on? There's a spot for guys like you on this team. Now, have a great holiday and get to work." This is exactly what I needed to hear. I was ready to fight back. Cue the Rocky music.

WINTER OF OUR INTENT

Under spartan fluorescent lighting inside the McClain Center's indoor football field, a large group of Wisconsin football players congregate from the dark, frosty February morning. Our hair is still messed, and our eyes are half-open and red from the sleep we have missed. We have come to be put through intense agility drills at various stations by the team's coaches. We want to improve, we want to stop losing, and we want to be champions. Sacrifice—of our rest, our bodies, our efforts—was the price to be paid for a ticket out of the bottom of the Big Ten standings.

Coach Alvarez and his staff spoke of the Five Ws: Work Will Win, Wishing Won't. They explained that anybody with a heartbeat wants to win on game day in front of the cameras and a stadium full of fans. But if you haven't put the work in at that point, it's way too late. Who wants to win now, nine months before the season is even to start, as the empty stadium sits under a blanket of snow and the probability is high that no one else outside this cold cavern is thinking about Wisconsin football? Our entire team showed up and answered, "We do."

The coaches were wide-awake and screaming, seemingly immune to the early morning hours. There were six stations set up all over the field, and we were required to sprint to each of them in groups according to our position, rotating through each station. The quiet air of the facility was soon filled with whistles, grunts, encouraging yells, and deriding shouts as we frenetically moved from station to station in a clockwise motion.

At one station, we'd break into three separate lines and start firing our feet in one place in a football stance—knees bent, butt down, back straight, and head up. Upon the whistle, we dropped to our hips and rolled to the direction the coach pointed to. On the next whistle, we were to immediately pop back up and start firing our feet in a football stance. After several whistles, we sprinted past the coach to the line behind him, and the next group stepped up while the others caught their breath.

Another station presented more feet firing, then on the whistle we dropped our bodies face-first on the ground in a push-up position and popped right back up, with our feet moving. Up-downs. Upon a whistle and the coaches pointing, we backpedaled, twisting our hips at 45-degree angles, switching directions with each whistle until we reached the end marker and the next group stepped up to do the same.

My favorite station was "the ropes," a low-to-the-ground contraption with bungee chords connected to steel tubes, forming 10 squares. This was an update on running through tires. We were to sprint through this, keeping our knees high, without getting tripped up. With my narrow hips and knock-knees, my body was made for this drill. I could run through this labyrinth at almost full speed without stepping on one chord. It was the only station where I felt I was as good if not better than anyone else on the team.

The next station had us holding 25-pound weights at the end of our straightened arms while crouched, leaning our backs against the wall. The coaches would blow the whistle and we were to focus our stares straight ahead and hold the squat position. With thigh muscles burning and our shoulders and arms twitching, we were to blink back the sweat dripping into our eyes and focus on not letting the weight lower. It seemed like a torture out of a POW camp, especially as bodies started to drop. After leaving that station one day, Chad Cascadden, a member of my group, had gotten cramps in both legs and couldn't sprint with the rest of us to the next station. As he lay unattended, clutching his legs, the rest of us sprinted to the next station at the sound of the whistle, like Pavlov's dogs. When we got there, we were chastised by the coach. "You never leave a man behind. Get him!" Despite our exhaustion, another teammate and I, both of us smaller than Chad, went back, put his unwilling body over our shoulders, and ran him clumsily back. His cramped legs provided no help, and his dead weight slowed our own bodies immensely as we ran as fast as we could back to the station. We set him next to the drill to watch, as he still couldn't stand without pain, and we jumped in line to resume the drill. Two bigger teammates from the group brought Chad with us to the next drill. No man left behind.

The next station was "box jumps," which worked our vertical jumping abilities, not one of my better attributes. Three different-sized boxes were in place, and on the whistle we jumped up and, hopefully, landed on the box we were in front of. Missing could be painful. Scraped shins, jammed toes, and banged knees were some of the most common casualties. The really ambitious and good vertical leapers lined up in front of the boxes higher than their waists to do their consecutive jumps. This is where my respect grew immensely for how talented and tough my teammates were. My group of receivers and defensive backs were some of the best leapers on the team, and this became an impressively crowded box. Lee DeRamus had a vertical leap of 40 inches, one of the better on the team. With no running start, standing flat-footed and jumping straight up, he could get three feet, four inches of air under his shoes.

A final similar drill had us doing the broad jump, leaping froglike three consecutive times to make it 10 yards. Some of the bigger guys didn't quite get there, and some of the skill players made it 12 yards—36 feet in just three jumps with no running start. Again, I was really impressed by the talent and toughness of my teammates, and I knew I had to push myself even when I didn't want to.

Some of the athleticism I witnessed was truly world-class. In these moments, I appreciated the fact I was around an elite group of athletes. These were not regular college students or regular athletes, but were specially gifted physical specimens.

Standing together at the end of the workout, leaning on one another sweaty and exhausted, we put the finishing touch on the workout. Our hands raised and pointed up toward the center of the group, creating something that resembled the kindling in a bonfire. It was a pyre of different colors, shapes, and sizes united under a common goal, igniting a passion to be better than we were before. We'd gotten through the difficult morning's tasks by working together.

While most of the world was still dreaming in their beds, we were awake and working hard to manifest our dreams. Under the vision set forth by Coach Alvarez, we were going to be the best football team we could be, the best football team in the Big Ten Conference, and the best football team to ever play at the University of Wisconsin. This work was our will to win, and the wishing was over.

NO OFF-SEASON

There are many differences between high school and Division I-A college football. The speed of the game, the size of the playbooks, and the hardness of the hits are some of the first that come to mind. The biggest, though, is the time commitment, and nowhere is that more evident than in the amount of time spent in the off-season.

The term off-season is misleading because college football has no off-season. While there are no actual padded practices, players are at the football facility almost as often during the off-season as they are during the season itself. The winter conditioning is valuable self-improvement time.

Instead of padded practice every day, players are allowed to make gains in other areas—weightlifting, for one. While we did maintenance lifting during the season, we were now lifting four days a week, upping the poundage each week and setting new personal goals on each lift. This is when the young linemen who needed to put on some serious poundage did most of their work.

Undersized players who needed to get more speed and quickness worked on the indoor practice field doing drills. Passing leagues started up with the quarterbacks, defensive backs, and receivers to work on routes, catch balls, and build bonds by catching and defending thousands of passes.

Mental strengthening was also involved. Coaches had piles of game tapes to let players study their own play and that of their opponents. Injured players worked on rehabilitation so that they could get themselves back on the field for spring and fall practice.

My first winter conditioning was dedicated to assuaging doubts—my own and anybody else's. I was a man on a mission and it showed. I didn't miss a weight room session, often rising in the early morning darkness before my first class to make sure I got my lifting in. In a few months, I increased my bench press by 30 pounds. I added five pounds of muscle to my frame.

By attending passing drills with quarterbacks after weightlifting workouts and doing footwork drills on my own time, I became a step or two faster and was dropping fewer balls each day. Now that I was more comfortable and knowledgeable of my routes and our offense, I was able to compete on a much higher level than I did in the fall.

Some teammates started to take note of my improvement. Whereas in the past I'd received virtually no comments during drills, I now was hearing shouts of encouragement. After a leaping grab or a sideline catch before going out of bounds, I'd hear something like, "Kennedy in the house!" I was starting to make plays like a receiver is supposed to do, like the guys were doing who were playing in front of me. In the fall, I had been hesitant to jump in on drills for fear of failure; now I jumped in whenever I could so I could get the opportunity to succeed or to learn from failing.

The acknowledgment from the players I respected made me feel authenticated as a Badgers football player for the first time. I realized that my newfound level of tenacity was what was going to be required of me always if I were to play at the Big Ten level. I was proving Norvell wrong and starting to find my place on the team. My confidence level was surging.

During this time, one of my former high school football coaches, Pat Rice, who had replaced Coach Quinn as Waunakee's head football coach, took advantage of having an alumnus on the UW football team. Coach Rice and some of his players were allowed access to the facilities and were able to watch us go through winter conditioning drills. My sister, who was attending Waunakee, said one of the star players recounted to others back at school how excited he was to see the UW facilities and my locker with my name on it. At times like these, I was proud to be looked up to and to be a positive role model to those younger than me. And it made me want to work harder.

Coach Rice gave me a ride home from practice after his visit. After some small talk, he told me he'd heard about my meeting with Norvell. Rice said not to get down, because the UW coaches just didn't know me like he did. "They don't know what Chris Kennedy is all about." Coach Rice added that I shouldn't let anybody take away my dream. He said I was an inspiration to the younger guys at Waunakee and that I had a lot of people behind me.

Most of the time I had to bear my burden alone, but it was nice to be reminded that I had support, that there were people at various mile markers there to cheer me and hand me water while I was running my life's marathon.

The end of winter conditioning was marked by the football team's version of the Olympics. The "winter" Olympics were similar to a track meet, with additional events like obstacle courses and tug-of-war contests. The Olympics, just another excuse to have a competition, pitted the offense versus the defense in each event.

The coaches took these Olympics very seriously because they were competitions and they put the same kind of pressure on us to win that football games did. And the pressure was often overwhelming, both for the players and the coaches.

I have a disturbing memory of hearing one of the offensive coaches tell us after a preliminary Olympic event loss, "I'm sick of the offense being the red-headed stepchild of this team. No more losing! If that means that you have to leave a little early (in a relay race), then you leave a little early. Is that understood?" In other words, he was telling us to cheat. Winning is important, but I'd never heard a coach admit out loud that it was more important than sportsmanship and honor. I don't think he really believed that, but it illustrates the pressure he was feeling.

Anyway, I ran for the offense in several events and specialized in the mile race. I won the event the spring of my freshman year, which helped to up my profile and confidence even more among my teammates. It was also a nice way to solidify the vast gains in my status on the team. I won the mile again the next year but was defeated my last year. This crushed me. I got passed on the final lap to finish second. Many coaches and teammates bragged that I would win it going away, joking that I, like Joe Namath in the Super Bowl, was guaranteeing a win. I didn't exactly say this but I was too overconfident, went out too fast at the beginning, and didn't run a smart race. I'd let down my other offensive mates, who needed a first-place finish from me to gain critical points against the defense. Winning this race had been one of the few times I was able to stand out on this team full of outstanding athletes, and I'm still upset about the one I lost.

My gains over the winter showed in our full-padded spring practices. I didn't challenge for one of the starting jobs at receiver, but I was competitive. I was stronger and more confident making plays on the field. I had almost no hesitation and just went after the ball and the blocks with full effort. I no longer walked to the back of the line at the start of our position drills.

At the end of spring football practice in April 1991, I went in to meet with Coach Norvell for my evaluation. This time, I had no trepidation at all. I was confident I deserved a spot and that's all that mattered to me. I'd proved to myself I belonged, which is why I walked on in the first place. I didn't need Norvell, or anyone, to agree with me on that.

So I sat down again in Coach Norvell's office like I had several months prior—in a way, a lifetime before. We still had some of the same discomfort with each other as the first time. Norvell looked me in the eye and uttered, "Let me start by saying, I'm impressed by the progress you made. I haven't seen anyone make the kind of improvement you have. You improved in every area. There's a place for you on this football team." Again, Norvell had me speechless, but for a different reason. It took a big man to reverse himself, and I respected Norvell for that. He told me to work my butt off that summer and come ready to compete in the fall. We had a nice handshake goodbye, and I felt pleasantly surprised. I felt vindicated like never before.

I wanted to run through the streets of Philadelphia onto the steps of a courthouse and dance around a little. I settled for a brisk jog back to my dorm. I made a phone call to my father. And upon hearing his voice, I cried again.

CHAPTER SEVEN:
MODEL PLAYER

MY CUP RUNNETH OVER

Though the NCAA is very concerned about drug use, especially performance-enhancing drugs, when's the last time you can recall a college football player being banned for such use? No one during my entire four years was ever charged with taking drugs. While this doesn't mean performance-enhancing drugs aren't being used, I don't think they're as prevalent in college athletics as some outsiders think.

The NCAA and the UW athletic department both perform random drug tests on their athletes. Weighing in at a whopping 166 pounds my freshman season, I was an obvious suspect for taking some sort of muscle enhancement and was "randomly" selected for all three testings that year.

Players selected for a drug test were informed the afternoon prior. The short notice and random timing of the drug tests throughout the year was to combat drug cycling and the use of masking agents.

I, of course, was on nothing and wasn't nervous about the test, but I was put off by the 7:30 a.m. urination appointment. The tests were conducted in the team's training room. We had to fill out a questionnaire that asked us to list the drugs we were currently taking. I listed the one allergy medication that I was supposed to be taking every day but took infrequently. I happened to peek at one of our 300-plus-pound lineman's sheet next to mine and saw he'd listed at least 15 or so drug supplements. I asked him whether it was a cheat sheet for a pharmacy exam. He told me to shut up and explained how lucky I was I didn't have to keep more than 300 pounds of weight on my body in order to play. Touché.

Forgetting that I was instructed not to, I had already urinated that morning at my dorm. So when I was called into the bathroom for my sample, I was unable to fill the cup to the requisite level. I should mention there was also an element of stage fright at play due to the two test facilitators in the bathroom with you, watching you as you go.

The testers were two middle-aged men dressed like TV detectives. Their job was to watch you urinate to make sure you weren't using any special whizzinator (fake penis) devices filled with "clean" urine. I was sent out to drink more liquids.

Defensive back Jamal Brown and I were outside the bathroom drinking from big water bottles when the aforementioned big lineman walked out of the bathroom looking disappointed with his half-filled cup. The sight of this monstrous man holding a little plastic cup half-filled with his own urine caused us to laugh out loud. He looked like Andre the Giant holding a drop of honey. He was not happy, and we stifled our laughs with our mouths on the water bottles.

About 10 gallons of water and 20 minutes later, I returned to the bathroom with a full bladder ready for release. The facilitators had become so good and bored with their jobs that they were almost like game-day announcers calling the action. Upon hearing me start into the cup, one of the guys said, "Oh, yeah, you'll have enough there." The other nodded in agreement, "Yup, should be a good one." I was almost expecting them to cut to a commercial.

Turns out they were only partly right, as I had more than enough. The tiny cup didn't stand a chance to hold all the urine I was spewing. I noticed this as the cup was close to full, and panicked. I nervously asked whether I was to dump some out to make room or whether I was allowed to finish in the urinal. They said the urinal would be fine as long as I had a full cup. I ran over to the urinal careful not to spill and finished up there. The facilitators congratulated me and I exited, thanking them for their services. Ah, the glamour of college athletics.

I left the stadium slightly concerned that my urine might somehow be mistaken with a player who tested positive. How bad would I look, at my size, to test positive? There would be the shame of getting caught combined with the stupidity of obviously not using the drugs effectively.

My worries were unfounded, and I tested negative all three times. Incidentally, I was never tested again for the rest of my four years on the team. I also don't recall *any* player testing positive for anything in my four years on the team and that includes street drugs. I don't know how some players who smoked marijuana didn't get caught. I've heard rumors that it has to do with high metabolic systems clearing the drugs out of one's system expediently. But perhaps the drug-detection program just wasn't as fearsome as we gave it credit for.

This brings me to the question I sometimes get asked: "How many guys on the team used steroids?" I can honestly say I never saw anyone take any sort of performance-enhancing drug. There were rumors and suspicions but no hard evidence to incriminate anybody.

I confess I considered going on some sort of performance-enhancing drug at one point in my career. It was my junior year, and I was depressed because it looked as if I wasn't going to ever play much. I hadn't made much progress on the depth chart since my freshman year and I was highly frustrated by putting in so much time at something for which I was getting so little in return. So I considered performance-enhancing drugs. I'd heard from a bodybuilder I'd met on spring break that one could use proper dosages of steroids, and if you timed the cycles correctly, you could increase your size and speed and not have many ill side effects. Could steroids break me through the glass sidelines?

I didn't know who to turn to. I didn't want to arouse suspicion by asking teammates. I finally spoke to my father about the hypothetical possibility of taking steroids. Instead of giving me a generic "steroids are bad" speech, he laid out a more philosophical point of view. He reasoned that sports are ultimately played to learn something about teamwork, overcoming challenges, and about yourself. You learn something from winning and something different from losing. If you're dedicated, losing and failure often lead to improvement. But what do you learn by cheating the process? If you take steroids and succeed, all you've proven is that drugs work. What have you learned about yourself? That you need drugs to succeed and that you will take drugs to succeed. Learning that drugs are necessary to your success is not the lesson you hope to take with you from your college football experience or from any experience.

So, I decided not to take them. I never made it up the depth chart or played much, but I can live with a peaceful and clear conscience. And that's something using steroids can't improve.

MONEY MONEY

The NCAA rules state that a scholarship player is prohibited from accepting employment during the school year. Nor is he allowed to accept any form of compensation from anyone other than his parents, lest he be held in violation and subsequently be suspended, possibly with his scholarship revoked. Pretty serious rules for a guy just wanting to make a few bucks on the side.

Non-scholarship players, like me, were obviously exempt from these rules and were free to take employment. Since we were putting in 40 hours and more a week as football players, we barely had enough time to stay on top of our football and school obligations, much less take on employment, but the option was still there. Working a job was a little more viable in the off-season, but with winter conditioning and spring football there really is no "off-season" for football players. I can't see how it's logistically possible to find a job flexible enough to accommodate a student-athlete unless there were no minimum or specific hour requirements to the job.

The summer provided both scholarship and non-scholarship players the only feasible time to make a little extra cash. Many players came from low-income households and needed to work in the summer if they wanted any spending cash during the school year.

For the players who did want to work, the athletic department had a work liaison staff to help recommend jobs. The jobs were legit—players weren't getting paid for work they weren't doing as some college programs had gotten in trouble for in the past. The jobs usually involved physical labor at a booster's manufacturing plant or working on the loading dock of a large distribution center. The days of football players being paid and not having to show up for work seemed to only be a rumor, or at least a thing of the past.

Camp Randall Stadium hosted concerts by U2 and Genesis during the summer of 1992, and players who stayed around were offered jobs as "security personnel" for the concerts. I, along with about 20 other teammates, signed up to help.

We were given T-shirts similar to the official security, though we weren't technically trained to do the job. Our jobs were vaguely described as ushers and crowd control. Most of us took this to mean we could wander freely around the stadium, and a group of us planted ourselves by the stage to stay for the whole concert.

At the U2 concert, I walked right up to the edge of the catwalk and watched the show. Anyone who saw me should've known I had no idea what I was doing because real concert security watches the crowd, not the show. A few of us let some attractive girls who approached us into the front section. To my amazement, no one questioned us.

This was the U2 Zooropa tour and it was quite a spectacle—actual cars with working headlights hanging from support poles, explosions of fake dollar bills with lead singer Bono's face on them, and an almost uncountable number of strobe and spot lights.

At one point during the concert, a man with a headset walked right up to me, at the foot of the stage, and told me to tell "my people" that it was all right to let the fans come up to the stage for the next song, as Bono was going to pull a fan out of the audience to dance with onstage. I didn't really have time to respond before he took off.

I should have worked my way around the stage perimeter to tell the security personnel, but I didn't want them reprimanding me for speaking on their behalf, in case it was a problem to let the fans come up to the stage. So I just told the two guys next to me about it. When the song started, the fans from my section and the two next to me came up to the stage, while the other sections were held back. Ooops. A lucky girl from my section was selected to get up on stage and dance with Bono during the song...thanks, in part, to me.

So I got a front row seat to see one of my all-time favorite bands and get paid for it too. Track number seven from U2's album got it right: "Some Days Are Better Than Others."

The summer after my freshman year, I got a job doing data entry for Dr. John Witte, a political science professor and family friend. For $7.25 an hour, I would sit in a room and record surveys of low-income families who were slated to be part of a pilot program for a private school voucher system that then-Governor Tommy Thompson was spearheading. This work would eventually lead to a "welfare-to-work" program that provided Thompson with national attention and an appointment in President George W. Bush's cabinet. The survey job was nice, flexible work that allowed me to basically pick my own hours and attend workout sessions whenever I needed to. One of those rare off-season jobs I could take during the school year.

I stumbled into a work opportunity when, in the final weeks of school my freshman year, I spotted a flyer that read, "ATHLETES WANTED, $25/hr." posted on our dorm bulletin board. The interviews were being held the next day at the Howard Johnson hotel across the street. I was intrigued.

Posing confidently—and having a rare good hair day—as my sophomore season began.

The next day, I arrived at the hotel and was directed to a messy suite full of clothes, sports equipment, and many cardboard boxes. A harried woman working behind a desk in the corner of the room said hello. I said I was there about the job and she looked up at me and said, "Great, come here tomorrow at 6 a.m." I replied, "Uh, that might be a bit early for me, I usually don't get...." She interrupted me, "We pay twenty-five bucks an hour." I said I'd see her tomorrow.

I woke at 5:50 the next morning and at 5:58 I was sitting in the hotel lobby realizing I had no idea what kind of work I'd be doing. Since it was a sportswear and equipment catalog, I figured I'd be doing some sort of testing of sports products and maybe giving my expert opinions on them.

A former UW teammate, Damone Freeman, entered the lobby with a girl and spotted me. We greeted each other and discovered we both were working the same job. He mentioned he'd worked for the company, called Eastbay, once before. He said it was a great gig and asked whether I'd ever done this kind of work before. I replied a bit embarrassed, "What kind of work is that?" "Modeling," he said. I became nervous as I'd never modeled before, and I told him this. Damone reassured me, "It's easy, man, don't worry about it, just do what the photographer tells you." I didn't want to lose out on the money and waste the fact I'd gotten up so early outside of football workouts. I figured I could follow directions, and I never claimed I was a model so they couldn't be upset if I wasn't very good at it.

A few minutes later, the woman from the day before, Diane, and a photographer entered the lobby. They greeted us warmly and led us to a mini-van outside loaded with clothes. They thought it was great Damone and I knew each other. They spoke of how picturesque the campus was and how they loved shooting there in the summers.

The van pulled into the parking lot of the student union, a beautiful old building with a big terrace on Lake Mendota. Diane handed me a sweat suit and told me to change in the van. For the first shot, I was told to run along the side of the building. I did and the photographer took pictures of me and after about five or six short runs they said they had the shot. I hung out in the van while they shot Damone and the girl. For the rest of the day, we took turns doing different shots around the campus. When we finished after five hours, I'd made $125 for a half-day's work. That was what some of my friends would make in two long shifts at their retail or restaurant jobs. It WAS easy money, just like Damone had said.

A couple of summers prior, I'd done concrete flatwork from 5:30 a.m. until 3 p.m. every day in the hot, humid summer and barely made half that amount for a day's work! I was onto something.

Fortunately, the Eastbay Catalog Company came back the next month and asked to shoot me again. I got along great with Diane, who remarked how pleasant

I was to work with. How could I not have been? They used me about four or five separate times that summer. I quickly got over changing in the outdoors and discovered that wearing boxers made things much easier.

Another added perk was that the women modeling with me tended to be attractive and had no problems changing in front of me. I guess we were colleagues and they thought I was a professional who was used to seeing that sort of thing all the time. At 19, to pretend a female model casually speaking to me in her underwear was no big deal, well, that was a challenge. But a challenge I was willing to accept.

In the late summer, the first catalog bearing my pictures came out. The terrifying thought struck me, "What if my teammates see my pictures in the catalog?" I hadn't thought about the end product. It struck me that most of these guys probably would see the catalog since they're athletes. I crossed my fingers that they'd be too busy during the summer to see any of the pictures.

At fall camp, no one said anything the first couple of days and I thought I was in the clear. No such luck. Two teammates, Mike Roan and Ed Primus, approached me with grins on their faces and said something like, "So I'm sitting at home and I start looking through my Eastbay catalog...." I'd feign ignorance and guffaw at the suggestion of it being me. I almost had them believing it but they saw through my forced insistence.

Coach Callahan walked by me at the seminary, both of us in flip flops, shorts, and carrying our playbooks. An intense guy I usually couldn't quite figure out, Callahan had a sparkle in his eye and said, "Saw your pictures in the paper." I said yes. He continued, "I told my wife, 'Hey, look at this cat!' That's great, man." I thanked him and he nodded and kept walking.

One day after practice later in the season, I arrived at my locker to find some of the catalogue pictures taped on it. Sometimes when I caught a pass, I'd hear, "Eastbay's in the house!" Or I'd drop a ball, "That's okay, you still look good!" It was hard to escape my teammates' needling. I justified the work by saying, "Hey, it's a lot of money." This piqued the interest of some of my teammates. Or "I meet a lot of beautiful girls," which piqued the interest of the rest of them.

One day, tight end and team clown Dave Czech spotted me doing a shoot near the stadium. The next day at practice, Czech, who was 6' 5" and 250 pounds, quietly walked up to my locker and, without saying a word, started striking stock modeling poses next to me. I reminded Dave that he was riding a red scooter when he saw me, so who should be more embarrassed?

Eventually, I was approached by some of my teammates surreptitiously. "Hey man, so, uh, you think you could hook me up with that modeling?" They'd look around them. "Uh, well, maybe," I'd respond, "You have to give them some pictures of yourself and then they approve you. I guess you could come with me some day and meet them." I'd shrug. "You know I'd be good," they'd plead. "Come on man, look at this smile!" I saw more guys posing and smiling for me than any teammate should ever have to see.

Apparently, instead of me, Eastbay should've been shooting Cyril Weems, a freshman player when I was on the team. A few years after he left school, he was named to *People* magazine's non-celebrity most beautiful people list.

At the training table one night we got proof of Cyril's sex appeal. He had three soccer girls around him listening attentively to his story. One teammate at my table, which had no women in attendance, saw this and said, "Man, look at Cyril, they listening to every word of his shit…and HE doesn't even know what he's talkin' about."

If my teammates weren't asking me to hook them up with the gigs, they were asking me to hook them up with the models. Though I managed to get a few dates, the models tended to go more for the photographers and/or rich, older guys.

I was surprised to see the interest some coaches had in my "modeling career." One time in the weight room a coach called, "Hey, Kennedy." I walked over as he took a break between sets on the bench press. He said, "How's it going?" I said, "Good, just getting my lift in." He said, "Good. How's the modeling? Saw your ad in the paper. Pretty cute girl." "Yep," I responded. There was a pause and then he said, "So, you getting a lot of…?" I modestly laughed and walked away as he went back to lifting with a smirk on his face.

My father saw the pictures and said that they weren't half bad, though we both agreed that in a few of the pictures I couldn't have looked more uncomfortable if I'd been giving birth to twins. He suggested I could do more if I wanted to. He had an advertising agency and was sent modeling cards, called composites, all the time.

I cut and pasted some of the pictures onto a regular sheet of paper, made a bunch of color copies, and sent them to an agency in town. Within a few weeks, I was getting work from local businesses. The pay standard was $75 an hour and usually the jobs were only a couple of hours.

The minimal hours and good money were a perfect supplement for a busy college kid like me. It sure beat having to work some of the typical low-paying jobs that most students had during the school year, especially athletes who, because of the time demands of their sports, would have trouble trying to keep a regular employment schedule.

I booked a job with a store called Borman's that ran a half-page ad in the back of the front section of the Sunday *Wisconsin State Journal*. One particular shot had me wearing golf apparel, hat and all, and for several months. Hence I was dubbed, "Chi Chi" (Rodriguez). I also wore an assortment of UW sports apparel in the ads. In Madison, every department store has to have some UW gear in stock. These ads didn't escape my teammates and usually ended up taped to a bulletin board the following Monday.

Unfortunately, I also did not escape notice by Paul Winters, the athletic department's NCAA compliance coordinator. Winters called me into his office one day and informed me that I had to stop doing the ads. NCAA rules stipulated that amateur athletes were forbidden to endorse products and receiving any sort of payment for these services. He cautioned that he would have to report my work to the NCAA and that we risked having to forfeit games. He instructed me to stop immediately. Winters' paranoia was not unfounded. Badgers fans know that the school was sanctioned by the NCAA several times for violations that were nearly as trivial—athletes were getting discounts from a local shoe store, for instance.

I reminded Winters that I was a walk-on, a non-scholarship athlete, so the modeling work was helping me pay for school. I argued that modeling work was analogous to working at any job, granted with better pay and better looking women. I also reminded him that since I'd yet to actually *play* in any games, there wasn't much of a danger of us having to forfeit any games.

Winters suggested that if I wanted to make an appeal to continue I should write a letter to the NCAA asking for permission. He said he'd make sure it got in front of the right people. I wasn't about to get off the modeling gravy train so easily, so I put my journalism degree to use, researched the rule, and wrote to the NCAA.

The NCAA rulebook is probably rivaled in size only by the Mexico City phone book. I drafted a simple letter defending my right to gain employment as a non-scholarship athlete. I made it clear that I was being hired not to endorse products but to display them. My dashing good looks, not my "fame" as a player, were being used to sell the merchandise. Winters approved the letter and sent it off to the NCAA. Word came back within two days that I was cleared to continue my modeling work. Chris Kennedy 1, The Man 0.

I like to think that because of my efforts, handsome, non-scholarship athletes around the country are now free to model department store apparel, footwear, and funny-looking golf hats. I'm sort of the Rosa Parks of non-scholarship athlete catalog models. If they want to erect a statue in my honor, I've been practicing a few poses for the occasion.

SOPHOMORE HOPE

The summer conditioning workouts before my sophomore season were well-attended. Many players stayed in Madison over the summer to prepare for the fall. Despite our 1-10 record, we were confident that we were getting better as a team and were anxious to turn things around.

We went through an intense fall camp at Holy Name. There was plenty of enthusiasm and optimism. Many experienced players were back. Many players in my class were now in their first year of eligibility and would be challenging seriously for top spots at their positions. I was not one of them. I focused on improving my skills and fulfilling my role as a scout-team player to the best of my abilities. The incoming freshman class was ranked higher than any in recent years. We set our team goals. Win a conference game on the road. Win two preseason games. Manageable, realistic goals. We arrived on campus for our first game ready to play.

We opened the season with three straight non-conference victories, already tripling our win total from the year before. We drubbed Western Illinois, 31-13, at home. Then we beat Iowa State at home in a nail-biter, 7-6.

Coach Alvy, giving a little motivational talk.

The Iowa State victory was thrilling because we won it on the last play of the game by blocking the Cyclones' field-goal attempt. This was huge for the team; even though we still made plenty of mistakes and squandered many opportunities, we found a way to win a game at the end, not lose it like the season before. On this momentum, we then beat Eastern Michigan, 21-6, the next week.

No doubt, things were on the upswing around Camp Randall. The coaches emphasized and celebrated every instance of success they could. Posted in the locker room was a big Xerox copy of the Associated Press top 25 list showing Wisconsin had garnered three votes. A team needed around one hundred to crack the top 25, but this was progress!

I began to see tangible body changes among my classmates this season. After only one year of a college weight-lifting regimen and training table diet, these guys were bulging and thickening on a daily basis. Whole new men were being created out of these teenage forms and shaped into college football players.

Conference play started with a 31-6 loss to Ohio State that began a five-game conference losing streak. That streak included a heartbreaker at home against Iowa, 10-6. The Hawkeyes scored with 44 seconds left on a 14-yard pass to win the game. The stadium was at near capacity and had been going bananas the whole game until that play.

The homecoming loss to Indiana, 28-20, was also a tough one. We were up, 20-0, going into the second half but gave up four unanswered touchdowns to let it slip away from us. We knew we were a good team that could compete against anybody, but we just couldn't seem to put together a game in which the offense, defense, and special teams all played well.

Despite the slide, we rallied to win our final two games of the season against Minnesota and Northwestern. Against the Gophers, we won back Paul Bunyan's Axe, the trophy of one of college football's oldest matchups. The thrilling 19-16 victory in the Metrodome was cinched on Minnesota's last offensive play of the game. Defensive back Melvin Tucker smacked Gophers tight end Patt Evans, who dropped the ball in the end zone. Just like in the Iowa State game, we found the way to win at the end!

The team sprinted over and snatched the axe from the Minnesota sideline and ran around the Metrodome field to the cheers of the Wisconsin fans. For us, the axe symbolized cutting through the losing ways of the past and entering a new era.

We now had four wins, the most any team had at UW since the 1986 season. Not the most impressive statistic, but things felt like they were a changin.'

We ushered in these new times when we returned to Camp Randall the next week to finish the season against Northwestern. The Wildcats jumped out to a 14-0 lead before our offense woke up and scored 32 unanswered points. The defense kept Northwestern out of the end zone for the rest of the game. Final score: UW 32, Northwestern 14.

We were in a confident, festive mood. Many of the players, myself included, stayed out for the famous "fifth quarter" performance by the marching band. At one point, I grabbed a female band member and danced the polka on the 20 yard line. Teammate Theo Carney donned Mike Leckrone's band director hat and conducted the band through a song. This was the kind of fun I'd imagined having as a Wisconsin player. Being under the lights, on the Camp Randall field, dancing in front of the student section with my teammates, getting a little silly, was really cathartic. And it was a great way for the 10 seniors to finish their career in Camp Randall.

We finished the season 5-6, achieving one of the best turnarounds in the 1991 college football season. Amazingly, with just one more win, we could've qualified for a bowl game. I never did get into a game.

What a difference a year makes. The confidence on the team was surging. But while we were pleased with making progress, no one was satisfied with the record. We had no plans of slowing down. This was not a team that planned on losing anymore.

All season at team meetings, the coaching staff would point to the countless "what-ifs": What if this player hadn't tripped, or what if our quarterback had checked to his second receiver, or what if the tackle hadn't missed this block?

If certain plays had been executed properly it would've made the difference between winning and losing the game. With some minor corrections, our team could've easily gone 7-4 and headed to a bowl.

At team meetings, the coaches always pointed out if a player made a great block. I remember them rewinding and playing over and over a block Chuck Belin made by diving after a defender. Chuck didn't even end up making contact but his effort forced the opposing player to retreat to avoid the hit, which allowed our back the necessary space to get by him and score. The coaches made their point, that little things have a huge effect. A full effort is always well spent.

The team was focused on how possible it was for us to be a bowl team. We knew we had enough talent on the team to do it, and we knew that the recruiting classes the coaching staff was bringing in were top caliber. The team was more than primed to have a winning season and go to a bowl the next season.

I'd made huge gains as a player in the off-season. We were a young team and at one point during the season, I was listed on the depth chart for the kickoff team. The coaches decided to put the Pit Bulls—the special teams scout team—as the kickoff team for a few games. They figured by throwing us a bone, we'd play harder in practice and they wanted to send a message to the current special teams' starters that guys were hungry for their positions. They figured right. I know for me, and many others on the scout team, just a couple of plays a game would be all I'd need to keep fuel in my tank to endure another season on the bench.

Just before every game, I'd try to signal to my parents in the stands that this would be the game I'd get in. I was confident. Looking back, I remember how I felt such an air of invincibility. I wish I could've bottled it to drink in years to come. I really believed I could run through a brick wall—or at least a wall of players on a kickoff return.

At the time, I had never been bigger, faster, stronger, or better prepared to play football in my life. I still believed that anything was possible.

The coaches inexplicably stopped putting us Pit Bulls on the depth chart after a few games, virtually ensuring we would not get to contribute on game days as we hoped. Emotionally deflated, we returned to practice duty-filled but disappointed.

During the season we had some great individual performances. We had one of the best cornerbacks in the nation in Troy Vincent. Troy was named an all-American. I had the privilege, if one could call it that, to play against Troy every day in practice. Because I was on the scout team, I played against Troy more than our starting receivers did, as they spent the majority of practice playing against the scout-team defensive backs. I played against Troy more than wide receivers at other Big Ten schools who only played against him once a year.

You'd be hard-pressed to find any receiver in the country who had more frustrating practices than me. I can probably count on my hands the number of times I caught a ball against Troy in the hundreds, maybe thousands of plays I ran against him in practice for two years. Not many NFL receivers have had a lot of success against All-Pro Vincent either, so I'm fine with that fact.

Troy was a nice, quiet guy who was a team player. Though the spotlight naturally found him, he didn't seem to have much of an interest in it. Agents started hanging around outside the locker room because of Troy. I never saw any players speak with these guys, but somehow we knew they were agents. I think it was the prevalence of gel in their hair. I considered exploiting their interest in Troy by telling them they'd have to go through me to get to him. For the effort, I wouldn't mind a few "improvements" to my Pontiac 6000 and a steak dinner. But I couldn't sell out my buddy.

Troy and I had a forestry class together. The class was lead by a stout, German professor who would periodically shout futilely at the construction workers outside the building in German to hold down the noise. One time, he picked up a piece of wood in the class and mimicked the construction workers by banging it on the wall. We also made our own toilet paper in the class. After spending most of the class period trying to make one square, I ended up with something that resembled a large, lumpy spitball.

Anyway, Troy and I got to know each other a bit as we studied for the final together. I definitely enhanced his knowledge of forestry, which has undoubtedly contributed to his long career in the NFL. I'm sure he plans on compensating me for my help at some point. He's the current president of the NFL Players' Association, so I'm sure he's up for negotiating something. If he is not, I've got a whale of a spitball waiting for him.

TRYING TO GET YOUR QUARTERBACK FROM THE MACHINE

For several years, our quarterback situation was a source of controversy. Senior Tony Lowery had started most of the 1990 season as well as the previous one; however, our offense was the weak link of the team. This, coupled with the coaching staff wanting to build for the future, thrust true freshman Jay Macias in to replace Tony for a few games during the 1991 season.

I was standing next to Jay when he was told he was going into the second game of the season against Iowa State. Jay was a laid-back Southern California kid. When he was told by the coaches to get ready for the next series, Jay just said OK and put on his helmet. He grabbed a ball and started to warm up. Another receiver and I found an open space on the sideline and helped him. The other receiver caught his throws, and I caught the receiver's throw back for Jay. (Quarterbacks don't usually catch balls while warming up so as not to risk jamming a finger on the catch.)

From my close proximity, I watched Jay's calm demeanor deteriorate as player after player came up and, rather intensely, told him not to be nervous. After about the fifth guy got in Jay's face, I felt the need to step in and shoo them away. I reminded Jay to just go out there and play like he knew he could. His eyes were noticeably bigger as he nodded and jogged onto the field.

After shaking off the rust, Jay was unimpressive in his debut but showed enough potential to garner significant playing time the rest of the season. Jay lead the team to Alvarez's first Big Ten conference victory against Minnesota. Although he was only a freshman, Jay was considered to be the front-runner for the starting QB position the next season.

Lowery's benching was a sign to many of the upperclassmen that a new team was being formed underneath them and they were being nudged out. If the captain and senior leader was being replaced, they were soon to follow if they hadn't been demoted already.

Robert Williams, the starting running back when I first arrived on campus just a little over a year earlier, was eventually side-by-side with me on the scout-team huddle the whole season. Many of us felt bad for him and marveled that he stuck it out. Robert had gotten caught for shoplifting prior to the season. He wasn't a bad guy, he just did a stupid thing, and perhaps the coaching staff was punishing him for it.

I recall at the end of our last home game and his last ever, he got in on one play. While many of my teammates and I were on the field celebrating a victory against Northwestern, Robert was simply hugging his father by the sidelines. He'd reached the end of his road, and it certainly hadn't ended the way he'd hoped. There was something powerful and sad about the moment. It was nice his dad was there to help him through it as much as possible.

There were many changes. On the coaching staff, a few assistants from our freshman year were replaced. It was the last season for our offensive coordinator, Coach Jacques, who was under fire for the offense's lack of productivity.

Every time a new coach was brought in, the players wondered how they'd get along with him. The guys who were in good graces with the former coach were suspicious and nervous they wouldn't have the same relationship with their new coach, while those who hadn't been on that coach's favorite list had a new source of hope.

Player personnel went through much change as well. Many of the upperclassmen, players brought in by a different coaching staff, didn't fit in with the current staff's scheme. Since many of these players were still on scholarship, it made for a difficult situation. Some were flat-out told they should consider transferring, while others tried to hang onto their jobs as the barrage of talented new recruits challenged them for those jobs.

The resentment between the older players toward the new coaching staff was understandable, as some of the guys who were demoted or asked to leave were their friends, teammates, and roommates. Now they were among the casualties of the many battles of big-time college football.

BIG-TIME PROBLEMS

Changes were taking place all around us, right down to the "Ws" on our helmets. The traditional block-style letter I'd grown up seeing was replaced with a curved-motion W. Having always imagined myself wearing the traditional emblem, I didn't like the new W. To me, in some way, it was the equivalent of changing the colors of the American flag. I guess I did get to wear the old block-style letter on my helmet, if only for a year, and I am lucky enough to have a picture of myself in it.

The word was that Alvarez was in on the new helmet design and stood to profit anytime it was used on merchandise. I doubt this was true but we players felt Alvarez was a shrewd businessman and I think we liked to imagine that he wielded as much power over the business world as he did in our world. Besides, changing the team logo gave Alvarez a chance to put his mark, literally, on the program.

At the time, I thought it was opportunistic and didn't like the profit motive being so apparent—as if the multi-million-dollar television contracts and the merchandising industry devoted to Badgers sports paraphernalia was ever subtle to begin with. Ah, youth is full of idealism. It doesn't take a genius to know that money makes the college football world go round. Eighty-thousand-seat stadiums need to be filled.

I'll not get into a great debate here, but the idea of amateurism in the multi-billion-dollar-a-year industry of college sports is the height of contradiction. The notion that athletes should somehow remain amateurs amid the gold rush going on all around them, maintaining their purity while others profit from their efforts, is laughable. When the almighty dollar takes precedence over student-athletes—and it does—at our institutions of higher learning, well, something's rotten in the state of Kansas.

The woes of the UW athletic department while I was in school were no secret. Nearly every audit and opinion determined that there was only one way for the athletic department to get out of the red, and that was for the football team to win.

It's no coincidence that schools with the most lax policies toward athletes' academics are almost always the winningest in the country. It doesn't behoove a team to have its players focusing on anything but football. As a result, the athletic departments and the universities have conflicting goals. The athletic departments are businesses dependent upon the bottom line, and the universities are about giving degrees.

The NCAA forces the abuses under the table by not allowing any of the financial windfalls produced by athletic performances to be given to the athletes. The athletes, while they may not be getting an education, are neither stupid nor blind. With everyone around them flaunting their affluence, why shouldn't athletes secretly grab what they can?

NCAA, please save your little lectures about the ideals of amateurism. You don't even believe it yourselves, selling athletic exploits for multi-million-dollar TV contracts. Where are your amateur ideals there? You've created a "get what you can while you can" world and then blame the citizens living in it who dare to ascribe to the same values.

There are those who say athletes should feel lucky to be given the opportunity to play, that they should be motivated by the game itself and that should be sufficient. They say that athletes should be content with their tuition being paid, and any compensation they seek is greedy. But I challenge any of those people to play four years under the current college football system and then hold onto such ideals. As a former high school coach of mine used to say, "Real easy to talk about, not real easy to do."

Big-time college athletics have been out of hand for too long. True amateurism would be to let the true student-athletes play on the team. If you couldn't get into a particular institution based on your academics, then you simply couldn't play for that school's team.

The problems of big-time college football are virtually unfixable without a major overhaul of the entire system. No one is willing to shake things up that much, so the NCAA will continue to generate new, silly, soft rules that are impossible to follow in a poor attempt to clean up the mess they made themselves.

Coaches drive nice cars donated by local car dealerships. They are given complimentary country club memberships and draw sizable appearance fees to give speeches at local meetings and events. There's a lot of extra money, besides their salaries, that coaches make, especially seen through the eyes of players who are living on ramen noodles and Old Milwaukee beer. It was sort of jarring when we players realized we would be in violation of an NCAA rule if we so much as took a ride home from a practice in their cars. I have no problems that the coaches get these things. They earn it. They bust their butts. It's not unusual for them to be in the football offices from 8 a.m. to midnight every day during the season. It's just that there is such a disparity between all their earnings and the players' poverty.

Sadly, it appeared that players' interests, or even doing the right thing, was overshadowed by the big-money bottom line. The players quickly realized that this sport of football we'd all started playing in our backyards and neighborhood parks had turned into a much bigger deal now. It turned into something we didn't even recognize.

With all the money involved, there's inherent pressure on the coaches and the players to perform. When things aren't going well, that pressure mounts further and the result is the ugliness in today's big-time college football: payments to players, steroid use, fraudulent tests, alcohol abuse, police altercations, and cheating coaches.

The individual player's importance is directly related to his performance on the field. Often if a guy is playing well, he's a golden boy. If he's playing poorly, he's in the doghouse. Worse, if the player is injured, he's persona non grata. For players who have been in the spotlight their entire careers, becoming suddenly insignificant is quite an emotional blow. It causes him to try to play as soon as he possibly can, at the risk of his physical and mental well-being. This is big-time college sports, and the behemoth waits for no one as it swallows players in its large shadow.

While I felt special to be on the team, I knew that as a lower depth chart dweller, I was expendable. It was hard to watch last year's golden boy get replaced and sometimes demoted to the scout team. I remember one running back telling me, "Man, how's coach lookin' right at me and call someone else's name?" Welcome to my world, I thought. "You and I gotta break outta here man, get the ball, score, then spin the ball in the end zone, like, shoulda been there the whole time. Know what I'm sayin?" Yes, I did. I imagined greatness in my mind every day.

In my room, I'd listen to Van Halen, get inspired, and picture myself making a leaping catch to score the game-winning touchdown. I'd imagine my family and friends celebrating in the stands. I imagined my post-game interview in which I'd be humble yet proud.

In my imagination, the length of the depth chart and the many barriers that kept me from the field ceased to exist. I'd drift off during a slow lecture, and imagine myself making routine plays, not even scoring, just making a tackle on a special teams play. Or throwing a nice block on a running play. Coach Alvarez would praise my hustle to the whole team. This feeling would buzz through my body and I bounced across campus to the stadium.

Of course, the reality set in once I got around the coaches and other players, and saw how average I was in their eyes. My football-playing experience was nothing like what I ever imagined it would be. It was always better to be a Badger in my fantasies than it was in reality.

It was the world of more than half the guys on the team, actually. The majority of the players on the team were the tryers, the strugglers, the attention seekers. Less than a quarter of the players on the team start, and the remaining three quarters are delegated to supporting roles.

I understood and accepted it, but I didn't love my role, which was to get the starters prepared and provide a proverbial breath down the back of their necks to keep them in some sort of concern about their job. I knew that while Alvarez cared about his players, his primary concern was for the team as a whole. So, a player must look out for himself as much as he looks after his team.

I started running into conflicts of interest, as do all student-athletes. As a non-scholarship athlete, I was at the university to be a student first. I was a good student who maintained above a 3.0 GPA my entire college career. I was on the academic honor list every semester. Had I played the requisite snaps, I would've been a shoo-in for academic all-Big Ten, which is something I would have been very proud of.

Keeping up my grades, however, required me to put limits on my commitment to the team. I felt that to be in the good graces of my coaches, I should spend as much time as possible at the stadium, watching films, lifting weights, and catching passes from anyone who would throw them. I did want to improve, but I had to find a balance in my life so I could also spend as much time as possible learning, studying, and preparing for exams. I did the best I could do to dedicate myself to both. While football inspired me more in the short term, I knew that academics were more important to my future.

Once, in the off-season, I skipped an "optional" passing drill to attend an exam review/study session for a test I had the next day. The teaching assistant was leading the review at the behest of many of us in the class who were struggling with the material.

I felt animosity from my position coach Norvell, who called me into his office to discuss my commitment or lack thereof. Our relationship was strained. He questioned my dedication to the team. I said that just because I'd attended legitimate study sessions for an important test, it didn't mean that I wasn't committed to the team. The fact is that players have to take tougher classes and larger course loads in the off-season to keep up with the University's academic requirements. If I didn't keep my grades up, there would be no point in my being at school—and then I wouldn't be on the team at all.

You only have so many hours in a day. While I believed I needed to put in as much time as necessary to improve myself as a player, I was a human being and a college student first, and had to allocate my hours the best and most efficient way I could.

I lived with the contradiction of wanting to just be a regular student with less stress and worry, yet also wanting to be set apart, somebody more special than the regular student. I ultimately decided that being a regular, non-player student would make me feel more worthless than being a relatively unknown player on the team.

This was, and still is, a problem with college athletics today, and I bow to any student-athlete who was able to, or even tried to, perfectly balance his academic and athletic commitments. I know in my heart I tried to meet all my obligations to the best of my ability and take care of all my business. I don't know how I graded out in the end, but I deserve an A for effort.

TEACH A MAN TO FISHBAIN AND
HE'LL LEARN FOR A LIFETIME

Coach Jerry Fishbain wasn't technically a coach but the academic advisor for the team. He was the guy who monitored all the players' class scheduling and attendance. He was a 60-ish, sincere, businesslike guy whom I always liked. We got along well because I was a good student and he never really had to deal with me. If I didn't show up to class, it was on my dime and at my expense in every way.

They have plaques in the football offices that indicate the football academic Honor Roll every semester. For every semester I played football, my name is on the plaques. If it sounds like I'm bragging...I am. Come on, I hardly ever saw the field, let me have some glory. There were probably about 15 to 20 guys every semester with a GPA that was 3.0 or above.

The athletic department loved to advertise guys like Don Davey, who graduated with something like a 3.8 GPA—in engineering, no less. It's extremely difficult to find the balance between school work, football practice, and a social life. Don Davey was a freak of nature. Using him as an example was like using Lance Armstrong as an example of what all cyclists should be.

So much is on a player's mind, especially for starters. Where would your attention be if you had to go from being worshipped on Saturdays by more than 80,000 people, appearing on national television, and having your quotes and face printed in newspapers on the weekend, to then sitting in a lecture hall Monday morning and try to focus on theories about supply-side economics?

I took pride in being a good student and had a genuine yearning to learn. I liked to think of myself as a renaissance man; as someone who could participate intelligently in a comparative literature class on Goethe, then two hours later be growling and crashing into a mass of bodies. I wanted an extreme intellectual and physical exertion, to stretch both of them to the limits. I felt this made me a more complex, interesting person, so I was vigilant about keeping a well-rounded life. I feel that I did all right overall, and some other guys seemed to as well but most of the guys had trouble finding that balance.

There were the guys on the team who never went out, who basically lived football with some school thrown in and that's it. No social life or a very limited one. Athletes can sometimes find themselves distant from the regular student body because of their busy schedules. An athlete really has to put forth an extra effort to integrate himself into student life, and some guys just didn't have the energy or drive to do that.

There were also guys who really lived it up and put their social life first. The coaches hated these guys and they usually didn't last very long.

I found many of my professors and teaching assistants to be quite helpful. My journalism 351 (radio journalism) professor, Dave Black, allowed me to do one of my two required weekly stories on the football team during the season. I still had to interview, get audio, and edit my stories like everyone else, but I had a nice "in" each week by interviewing players or coaches.

Of course, I had a little fun with this, as did the interviewees. I once interviewed my friend and teammate, Scott Nelson, about a game and he kept responding with things like, "That's the worst question ever" and "I'm not going to answer that" or he'd just laugh and not respond. I'd usually counter with questions like, "Why does your breath smell so bad?" and "Who on the team do you have a crush on?" Very serious journalism. But seriously, I think it's a testament to professors being understanding and non-judgmental about the athletes. I appreciated them knowing I was incredibly busy and yet not assuming I was a rock-head just because I was an athlete.

Coach Fishbain was prone to temperamental outbursts at team meetings. He had no patience for players who just wanted to slack. While he was short in stature, he had the voice of a giant. At one team meeting, he read from reports he had been getting from various teachers about some players on the team. "Doesn't show up to class! Haven't seen him!" Coach Fishbain would bellow. "This is bull-shit, guys! You're better than that!"

Tight end Todd Van Roo once shared with us a message Fishbain left on his home answering machine. Todd, in a dead-on Coach Fish vocal impersonation, said, "Yeah…is the Phantom there? This phone tag we've been playing is BULL-SHIT!" Todd capped it off with a typical Coach Fishbain hand wave.

Coach Fish would also monitor the mandatory tutoring sessions that players attended in the McClain facility. The emphasis on tutoring may be why, as far as I can recall, during my tenure on the team no UW football player was declared academically ineligible to play.

A scholarship player could get a tutor or be in a tutorial group for every class he was in. In the first few years, when most of the players were fulfilling general degree-requirement classes, it was common to have many players in the same class and have big tutorial groups. Walk-ons were also allowed to attend any tutorial session as well.

I took full advantage of this for my Portuguese class. I needed three semesters of a language other than Spanish, and I'd heard Portuguese was similar. In addition, I was advised that there was a great Portuguese tutor in the athletic department named Mary Schill and that many other players took the class as well.

Her tutorial sessions were held in a McClain Center meeting room one night a week or more if there was a test that week. I attended virtually every session as did the other football players and a few other athletes, female soccer players, hockey players, and basketball players. I also got to meet Ken Stills, a former Badger and Green Bay Packer who had retired from the NFL and was back at school trying to finish his degree. It must have been humbling for this guy I'd watched on TV to be putting his nose in his notebook, trying to study for a quiz.

The athletes of the various sports all shared an instant camaraderie. It was a great way to get to know each other, and if you ever needed a ticket to one of their sporting events, you had a nice in, to boot. I made this deal with a hockey player to get him tickets to a few of our games in return for tickets to a few of his games.

The tests and drills Mary had us do in these tutorial sessions were harder than the ones we got in class. *A classe era muito fácil para mim.* In translation that's "the class was very easy for me." I got straight As in the class all three semesters, which was one reason I liked it.

I also enjoyed flirting with the female athletes and really liked my teammates in the class. I probably should've just stuck with Portuguese but I was applying for the School of Journalism and had other requirements to fulfill.

Rich Thompson, our kicker for a couple of years, was from Oklahoma and spoke Portuguese with a drawl. He had a dry wit and would always crack up the class. My favorite times were when the teacher would speak only Portuguese at him, hoping for a response back in Portuguese. Rich would have a really intense look on his face while he was listening, and then when it was his turn to speak, he would just shake his head and say, "Sorry. Not a word." Or she'd ask him a question, and he'd turn his head and look at me with a deadpan look on his face, like "You catch any of that?" I should mention that Rich actually ended up doing pretty well in the class.

One of my other favorite players in the class was offensive lineman Chuck Belin. Chuck was a 6' 3", 320-pound black guy who wore glasses and spoke softly. He was the nicest, gentlest guy on the team, I swear. He listed the *Wonder Years* as his favorite TV show in the game-day program. It takes a brave guy to write that.

As I got into the School of Journalism and took more specialized classes, I had no other athletes in my classes and so I no longer got this tutoring. Since the NCAA was reducing the number of scholarships available, I had no hope of getting an athletic scholarship. Fortunately, heading into my final year I was awarded an academic scholarship through the School of Journalism, courtesy of the Madison Advertising Federation.

I'll always look back on those tutoring days like a little boy in a wistful, nostalgic narrative. I got by with some great tutoring and a little help from my friends.

LOCKER-ROOM LEADERSHIP

The media gave our 1993 Rose Bowl team a nickname, "the lunch pail gang." To me, being the lunch pail gang meant that we believed work was the important thing and spoke for itself. When you know what's important, bragging or calling attention to yourself stands out as the nonsense it is. Coach Childress once said, "Leave your egos at the door and let's go to work." The leaders of the Wisconsin Badgers football team had that attitude and the rest of the team followed. After all, if the best players on the team don't make a big deal out of making a play, how silly do other players look if they do?

A team is a many-splendored thing. There are leaders on the field, and there are leaders off the field. Sometimes they are the same, and other times they are not. You don't have to be the best player to be a leader. A team is a social family in many ways, and so everyone is important. From its limited exposure to the team on game days, the outside world wouldn't understand the dynamic within the team. It may seem to the fans that the only important players are the ones playing, and playing well, on Saturdays. This is not true. Some guys are important to the team because they keep morale up through humor, intelligence, and generosity. Our team had many of those guys.

Even though he wasn't a starter at his defensive back position, Korey Manley was an inspiration to both walk-ons and scholarship players. Korey earned a scholarship through his exemplary work in practice and then on special teams during his sophomore year. He became one of the best special teams players in the entire Big Ten conference. Korey was from Fond du Lac, Wisconsin, and at an undersized 5' 8" tall and 170 pounds, was never given a look coming out of high school by any Big Ten team. Korey was an excellent student and a really likable guy who had a great sense of humor.

One day after a long practice, as many of us slowly removed our gear in front of our lockers, Patrick Tompkins, a defensive starter and scholarship player, addressed Korey. "Man, I don't know how you can do it." Korey asked Patrick to clarify. Patrick said, "How you guys [walk-ons] can do this…for free! Man, I couldn't do that." Korey answered, "I do it so that one day you don't have to ask me how I do it, because I will be on scholarship." Patrick just shook his head and said, "Well, I respect you guys. I really do." Korey inspired a lot of us with his work ethic and his pleasant, affable demeanor off the field. It was nice for me to hear scholarship guys say they respected what walk-ons were doing; to get respect is an integral part of being considered a valuable team member.

Tom Browne, a black player from Milwaukee, was another former walk-on turned scholarship player. Tom was awarded his scholarship in front of the whole team at Holy Name my freshman year. I remember how he cried and how every player from his class walked up and hugged and congratulated him. While he didn't play much, his fellow receivers looked up to him and respected him. Tom was a tough competitor on the field but one of the most mild-mannered guys off the field. You might have assumed he was a librarian instead of a football player. His even temperament, likeability, and popularity garnered him the nickname, "the President."

One of my personal inspirations was a walk-on defensive back one year ahead of me, Bernie Caputo. I met Bernie during summer conditioning before my freshman year. He was small, about 5' 8" and 170 pounds. Not an ounce of fat on him. He was quiet, kind, and intense. He always wore a white T-shirt and shorts splattered with paint. He worked out incredibly hard. He was the definition of scrappy. I respected him immensely.

When I first spoke with him after a workout, I told him that I was a walk-on. He just shook his head and said, "It takes a special kind of person to be a walk-on." The statement was simple, truthful, and powerful, much like the guy who said it. Bernie kept to himself mostly. He was well liked and respected, but quiet. Because he and I shared a bond of being walk-ons and Madison-area kids, I was a bit closer to him than many others on the team.

Bernie was a madman in the weight room, and whenever I got the chance to lift with him, he was a great workout partner. It was the highest compliment when he said he thought I gave a great effort on the field or in the weight room. He had a good sense of humor and enjoyed discussing politics and current events. I always wanted him to lighten up in front of the other guys on the team, so they could see that side of him.

Humor is a key ingredient in stress relief and in survival in a competitive atmosphere like big-time college football. Humor creates bonds and breaks down barriers. All work and no play makes a team of dull boys. I particularly appreciated the guys who rose above their own problems and mustered up the energy to entertain and lift the spirits of their teammates.

After a particularly hard practice, Haywood Simmons, a backup defensive lineman, would stand in front of a bunch of downtrodden players at their lockers, hold his hands up and ask loudly, "Who thinks they have faster hands than me?" Upon hearing no answer, he yelled again, "WHO thinks they got faster hands than me?" Someone would answer something like, "I'd kick your ass." Haywood would smirk and say, "Well, step on up then." Then he'd move his big frame in a Muhammad Ali dance, naked, and you couldn't help but laugh through your exhaustion.

In the take-yourself-too-seriously world of college football, our team could always count on Nick Rafko to keep things in perspective with his fun-loving presence. Nick could light up a room with his goofy grin. Whether it was his impeccable impersonations of coaches or actor Bill Murray, his impromptu dances, or his slick observations of particular locker smells, Nick made it fun to be on the team. I remember him doing a hip-hop dance after an interception in practice that had even our no-nonsense coaches laughing—only Rafko could do this.

Nick had an interesting background. His sister was Kai Lani Rafko, a former Miss America. It was richly ironic that Nick, who didn't seem to own a razor or hairbrush, would have a beauty queen for a sister. Nick owned a practice jersey that reportedly hadn't been washed all season as some sort of demented experiment. Kai Lani would be interviewed at nearly every game by some network reporter. Nick would re-enact these predictable exchanges with uncanny imper-sonations of both his sister and the brown-nosing reporters.

After we lost to a good Washington team, I remember how refreshing it was for many players to hear Nick re-enact the futility of playing against the Huskies' 6' 8", 360-pound tackle, Lincoln Kennedy. Nick said that, after exhausting himself trying to get around this mountain of a man, he just started doing swim and rip moves on Kennedy. Even though they had no chance of working, he reasoned, at least he wouldn't get yelled at for bad form on the game tapes.

When Joe Panos was sitting next to Nick at a team meeting, with his sleeves rolled up over his large biceps, Nick took note. He exaggerated his glances at Joe's arms and his own, and those of a couple of smaller players around them. He began to sing in a high-pitched voice about Joe's arms, "One of these 'screams' is not like the other, one of these 'screams' is not like the rest…." Nick would move his finger like it was a bouncing ball between his arms and Panos' arms. Joe just shook his head and couldn't help but laugh, as did many others. Joe then rolled his sleeves down to shut up Nick but Nick wouldn't let him roll down the sleeves. "No," Nick protested. "Let the 'screams' breathe…it's OK, let 'em breathe." Then Nick would fan them for him.

Nick and his crew would have legendary nights out on the town, and when a guy would return to the locker room the next day resembling the Grim Reaper, Nick would smile big and put his arm around the guy. "It's OK," he'd say. " It'll get better. You just need to come out with us more often."

It's also important to note that Nick's humor was never mean and never at the expense of anyone. He was always polite and treated everyone, walk-ons, stars, young players, and student trainers with an equal amount of respect. Outside of the team, he was equally respectful to training-table workers and maintenance folk. Sometimes other players wouldn't be, and it was nice to see a well-liked guy such as Nick showing them how to act. That was another reason Nick was such a great team leader, more off the field than on it.

Watching the news one summer night at my mom's house, I saw a local news report that Nick Rafko was killed in a car accident in his home state of Michigan. I was shocked and devastated. It didn't seem possible that a guy that happy, that full of life, could be associated with something as dark as death. Nick was 23 years old and had just graduated a couple of months prior. The truck his buddy was driving went off the road and struck a tree, killing them both. They'd been out on the town and were driving home, undoubtedly after a night filled with laughs.

I tried to make sense of Nick's accident by calling some friends to discuss it. None of them were home, and I left messages to call me. I got ahold of my dad and as I told him the news, I broke down uncontrollably.

Nick had graduated and moved back to Michigan, and I was moving to

Chicago, so it was unlikely I would have seen him much anymore. But Nick was one of those guys I looked forward to bumping into at games and alumni events. I couldn't think of a better guy to share a beer with and have some laughs about our playing days. I wanted to know what he was doing, what kind of job a guy like him would have. I felt bad for all the people who wouldn't get to know Nick. He would've been an amazing dad, husband, and neighbor.

A bus was chartered for any players living in Madison that summer to go to Nick's funeral. I signed up but backed out on the trip at the last minute. A 16-hour round-trip bus ride and a day spent at a funeral were too macabre for me to handle at the time. I didn't want to see the gregarious Nick Rafko in a casket. Despite this, I regret not attending. I wish I would have gone to show my support to his family and my former teammates in attendance. I did write his family a letter explaining how much I thought of Nick.

I still try to follow Nick's example of using humor as a key ingredient in getting through challenging times. I strive to get as much enjoyment out of life as he did. I haven't yet, and I'm not sure I'm capable, but I'm trying.

Tragically, Nick isn't the only member of this team no longer with us. In 2004, wide receiver Aaron Brown was killed in a car accident along with his girlfriend. Their little girl, who was also in the car, miraculously survived the crash. I was home at my mother's house for Christmas when I read the story. Aaron was kind, a good athlete, and I never saw him lose his cool despite tough circumstances. Aaron was a nice-looking guy, undersized, skinny legs, but hard working and tough. He was poised, upbeat, and friendly.

He was working as a mentor with youth groups at his church. It's sad, especially for those kids, because they lost a great mentor. I just hope someone else can step in to take Aaron's place, and impart to them the same spirit he would have. No easy task.

Nick, Korey, Haywood, Tom, Aaron, and many other guys inspired and bolstered the team by being not only good football players but good people. Fun guys to be around, guys you wanted to be on a team with. Good teammates. They made the hard times easier to endure by inspiring the rest of us and making us laugh. Their effect on the team often escapes the eyes of the fans on game days, but their teammates treasured the benefit of having them on the team. One should never underestimate that the overall dynamics of a team depend on the people underneath those jerseys and helmets. Character counts, regardless of where you are on a depth chart.

CHAPTER EIGHT:
SCOUT'S HONOR

It's been said that college football teams are only as good as their scout teams. It isn't hard to argue that football is a team sport. Whether on offense, defense, or special teams, there are always 11 players from each team on the field. The players who are not on the field are almost as big a factor in winning and losing as those who are on it.

If you're not on the first or second string at your position, you're on the scout team. Being a scout-teamer is a dirty, thankless, yet necessary job. Scout-teamers are the sparring partners of college football. So it ends up that the third- and fourth-string offensive players spend the majority of practice playing against the first- and second-string defensive players and vice versa.

Our scout team competed, to quote a phrase oft-used by the Alvarez staff. We scout-teamers understood that the best way to serve ourselves and our defense was to play our hardest. If any of us slacked off, the defensive coaches would get on us just like they would their own players. We played to win at every practice, even though we almost never did win. Playing against the starters is a nice measuring stick for your own talent. I enjoyed comparing how I fared against our starting defensive backs with how wide receivers for a team like Michigan performed against them.

I remember looking around at our scout-team huddle and counting a few high school all-Americans. I realized how talented the players were on this team. I wished this would have been my high school team.

The scout team's purpose is to give the starting defense a good "look" at what they'll see from an opponent. We would succeed sometimes, and score on our defense or at least move the ball significantly against them.

Unfortunately, when you make a great play the defensive coaches scream at their players for letting it happen and then they run the same play again. This is bad because now the starters are pissed and they know what play you're going to run. Sitting ducks have better odds.

I once got unnecessarily roughed up by defensive tackle Carlos Fowler in one of these situations and lost my temper, slamming the football off his facemask. Luckily for me, a couple of players grabbed him before he could respond, and I was pulled away by a player and an assistant coach before Fowler could kill me. I apologized after practice, and Fowler told me not to worry about it.

As receivers, we do lots of sprinting along with many abrupt stops and starts. Even the very best conditioned receiver gets tired. There were usually about five or six receivers on the scout team, so we could replace each other every few downs. With injuries and such, however, we could be down to only a few guys to take all the reps. These were long days to say the least.

We scout-team players got to play against greats like Brent Moss every day.

Scout-teams are mostly made up of walk-ons and young scholarship players. Walk-ons tend to get more repetitions, as they want to prove themselves, and happily jump in. Scholarship guys tend to feel demoted by being on the scout team and sit back sulking a bit.

Eventually though, the scholarship guys realize they must prove themselves like everyone else or they will not play or move up the depth chart like they want to. Some never get over the fact they're no longer stars like they were in high school. They can't deal with it, and so they end up quitting or transferring to another school. Others take the ball and run with it, so to speak, and get themselves promoted.

Admittedly, some older players let the younger guys take more reps on the scout team as they want them to earn their place on the team like they did. I'm embarrassed to admit there were some practices where I just didn't want to be there and let the younger kids take more of the reps. Since coaches review practice tapes every night, I realize my lack of reps impressed no one and was a good reason why I didn't play much on Saturdays.

I played on the scout team all four years; the last two were the most difficult as I realized that I'd never get off the scout team. I used to argue with my good friend and defensive scout-teamer, Phil Chavez, that being on the offensive scout team was more work because the starting offense can execute without the defense and would do so on light practice days like Thursdays and Fridays, while the defense needs the offense to perform the plays they react to. Phil tried to convince me that getting blocked by Joe Panos or trying to tackle Brent Moss would be no day in the park either. Regardless of who was right, no scout-teamer had it easy.

It took me a while to accept, if I ever truly did, my role as a player who would help the team during the week but would stand on the sidelines on game days. To compound the problem, 10 scholarships were eliminated in my final two years, the most likely time for a veteran walk-on to earn one.

I got into the rhythm of being a veteran scout-team player. I knew to "butt up" with the defensive players but to never take them down. I knew how to go at a good speed and give a good look but not to show them up. This helped the starters and me get along well, but didn't help my playing chances or allow me to impress the coaches very often. The coaches knew this happened a lot and even had a term for it, "brother-in-lawing." Don't get me wrong, brothers-in-law didn't slack off, they played hard and fulfilled their roles, but they didn't attempt to go above and beyond them.

Other players went against this idea, hoping to take advantage of their time on the field by trying to outplay the starters. These guys were called "Thursday all-Americans." This referred to the day of practice where the team scaled back the hitting, practiced in shorts and a helmet, and polished up for the game on Saturday. These "all-Americans" would give full effort and cause trouble for the starters. This pissed the starters off and sometimes the coaches weren't too impressed with it, but other times they were. Some of those guys got elevated to special teams because of their standout practice performances.

Upon further reflection, I should've been more of a T.A.A. than a B.I.L. I just didn't want to be seen by the starters as one of those guys who "didn't get it." Turns out what I didn't "get" was playing time.

Other times, my feelings would vacillate. If a young starter or key backup was on defense, I would flare up a bit as I was jealous and prideful. I'd be damned if

I'd let a younger player come in and push me around. I'd put in too much time to let that happen and would hit those guys extra hard whenever I got the chance just in case they thought they were better than me.

Sometimes I'd just feel privileged to be on the team and jump into any role necessary to help us win. If that meant pushing the starters hard during the week to get them ready for Saturday, then so be it. I sought to make the starters feel that they would have an easier day on Saturday than they did playing against me all week.

Having little successes in practice against the starters can keep you motivated and give you a reason to gain some confidence. I had the privilege/unenviable task of running pass routes in practice against our all-America defensive back Troy Vincent for two years.

Troy had long arms and a 4.3 speed in the 40-yard dash. When he walked up on you at the line of scrimmage, it was nearly impossible to get off the ball if he got his hands on you. And if you were lucky enough to get off the line on him, Troy could catch up to you in one or two strides. Once in a blue moon, I would catch a ball while he was defending me. That feeling of excitement was akin to a young boxer landing a punch on Mike Tyson and causing him to buckle or a young defensive lineman sacking Brett Favre.

Even though, by and large, being on the scout team is a thankless job, Coach Alvarez talked about how every player had a role on the team and that your duty was to fulfill your role to the best of your ability. If everybody did that, we'd be successful. I take great pride in the fact that I fulfilled my role to the best of my ability and that my contributions, no matter how small, helped my team to win a Rose Bowl.

GRADUATE ASSISTANCE

The scout teams are led by graduate assistant coaches better known as GAs. They are usually college coaches in training and have many of their tasks dictated to them by the position coach they're assigned to help. The GAs would fill out stacks of manila envelopes with diagrams of the opponent's plays and formations. At practice, these cards were then used in the scout-team huddle to show us what plays we were supposed to run against the starting units.

We had about six or seven GAs, all of them in their late 20s or early 30s. They could be more informal with you than the regular coaches. It wasn't unusual to bump into one occasionally at a bar. The good ones end up being big brotherly advisors for the players on topics ranging from improving your footwork, to girls, to the best way to cure a hangover.

Early in my career, I was having trouble getting a clean release off the ball when defensive backs would walk up on me at the line of scrimmage. Since my speed wasn't very threatening, many DBs could line up close to me without much risk of me beating them deep. It's imperative that receivers get off the line quick, and this is done with deft moves, quick hands, and quick feet. I struggled to do this with the moves taught by Coach Norvell, and I was frustrated.

One practice, Coach Lance—we rarely used last names when referring to graduate assistant coaches—saw my struggles and pulled me aside. He made me perform release drills against him over and over. He would line up inside of me, outside of me, and directly in front of me and I would have to adjust and get by him in each formation. Finally, he spotted what was happening, "You think you're driving your feet, but you're not. You're keeping your head straight, so the defensive backs have no reason to backpedal when you drive at them. Take a look." He demonstrated my faulty technique back to me. I was picking my head up and just assuming my feet were going where I wanted them to go but once my head stayed up, my feet stopped firing. I was fooling no one but myself. Once I drove my head at my opponent properly, my feet followed suit and also kept firing. Now, defensive backs had to respect my moves and that allowed me to get separation from them on my cuts and my releases off the line of scrimmage, and hence, get the ball thrown to me more often. Thanks again, Lance.

The GAs usually gave good advice off the field too, pushing us to succeed. I happened to strike up a conversation with an attractive female track athlete outside the training room one day after practice. We spent an inordinately long time flirting. In the meantime, GA David O'Keefe, a.k.a Irish, had walked by us several times, giving me the thumbs-up signal. When he passed by us later, and he noticed we were still in the same position as earlier, he said, "Christ, Kennedy, just ask her out already." Though embarrassed, I now had to address the issue and it forced me to ask her out. She said yes and we ended up dating for a while. Thanks again, Irish.

On another occasion, the morning after my 21st birthday, I showed up to Sunday practice with a hangover bad enough to make me give up drinking only one day after I was legally able to do it. I had gone out on the Saturday night after a home game. There was a custom at State Street Brats bar that you kiss the Gnu head hung on the wall on your birthday. Just as I was about to do so, a buddy told me that just the week before one of the wrestlers had put his bare butt on the moose. "Avoid the nose area, kiss it high," my friend advised. The plan was for me to do 21 shots. I cannot actually say that I hit that number because if you've ever tried to do 21 shots, you know that your ability to count is seriously impaired about halfway to the goal.

I vaguely recall making it to last call, going to an after-bar at a fraternity, then meeting up with a group of girls I knew. I swear I won an informal dance competition with a feverish Denny Terrio imitation, and then things got foggy.

Some of the girls I was with lived near the Langdon Street frat house, and I woke up in their apartment staring at an unfamiliar ceiling. I was lying on the couch fully dressed with a blanket over me. As I groggily woke up, I heard the girls giggling and saying things like, "He's alive! I could just see the headline: UW Football Player Dies in Girls' Apartment." "How are you feeling, sweetie?" one girl asked. "Like death…but worse," I responded. I thanked them for their hospitality and went home. I still had a few hours before I had to be at the stadium for our Sunday practice.

Sam Veit, one of my roomies, asked me how my night went and I told him it was fun and that I didn't feel too bad. Sam didn't drink and didn't really go out, so he just laughed at me and read the paper. I poured a bowl of cereal and read about the previous day's game. I was actually feeling pretty normal. But after finishing the bowl, I felt dizzy and sick to my stomach. I nervously stumbled to the bathroom and relocated the newly ingested Sugar Smacks, along with some of the drinks from the previous night, into the Madison sewer system. Next thing I knew, I was on the floor using some spare toilet paper rolls as my pillow when Sam woke me to tell me it was time to go to practice.

I made it to the stadium and recounted some of the night to my teammates. What I'd forgotten, they happily filled in. I was not feeling any better and didn't want to throw up in front of the coaches, so I decided to skip the requisite 30-minute run in the McClain Center. Some of my teammates covered for me during roll call while I stayed down in the locker room.

I thought I was busted when GA Bob Carsky came walking through the locker room and saw me lying against my locker with a sock placed over my eyes. Instead of scolding me, Carsky helped me to my feet and told me to drink as much water as I could. He told me to go sit in the sauna to sweat out the alcohol. He said he knew it worked. I felt awful sitting in there in that suffocating, hot sauna, drinking ice water while my pores flowed like water faucets but his advice got me functional again. I was able to shower and get myself to the team meeting. He said nothing to the coaches about it. Thanks again, Carsky.

MOREMEN AT QB

Quarterback Darrell Bevell joined the team in the winter of 1992. New offensive coordinator Brad Childress had coached Bevell at Northern Arizona for Bevell's freshman season two years prior. Darrell, a Mormon, left college football for two years to do missionary work for the Church of Latter-Day Saints.

While others worked in locales like Africa and the Caribbean, Darrell's mission took him to the faraway, exotic land of Cleveland. It's fun to picture Darrell, with his flat-top Johnny Unitas haircut, wearing a skinny tie and black pants, being chased out of doorways in the ghettos of Cleveland. Perhaps this experience helped to serve him well as a Big Ten quarterback, though.

Suffice it to say, Darrell was not your typical college football sophomore. At 21 years of age, he was already as old as some of the team's seniors. He was engaged to be married and he purportedly didn't swear or drink alcohol. Darrell was also undersized at about 6' tall and 170 pounds. By contrast, the other quarterbacks both weighed more than 200 pounds: Jay Macias was 6' 2", and Jay Samala was 6' 5".

The quarterback is the leader of the offense, and usually the entire team, and I had my doubts that someone so different from his teammates could get them to follow his lead. Darrell wasn't one of the guys and didn't exactly fit in right away. Since Darrell was brought in by a new coach, he seemed like a coach's pet. Because of his personal beliefs and the restrictions of the Mormon Church, Darrell didn't hang out much with the players outside of practice. He was viewed as aloof by most of the players, some of whom even called him "Childress' son."

The new offensive coordinator, Childress, and Darrell were very similar guys. Both came across as intense, fierce competitors and very particular guys who focused on winning and not much else. The two had a nice chemistry, which is obviously important in the quarterback–offensive coordinator dynamic, but it was questionable whether the whole team would mesh with them.

Coach Childress had some very interesting stories and a peculiar speech delivery. He'd walk around during the prepractice stretches, clapping and chanting,

HENRY KOSHOLLEK/CAPITAL TIMES

The new offensive coordinator, Coach Childress, dispensed the hard facts about football.

"Stretch those hammies [hamstrings] it's a little greasy [wet] out here today." When he wanted you to play hard, he said you had to play with "some shit on your neck." He talked about the cold, hard truth of the college football world: "Guys, this is a what-have-you-done-for-me-lately business." He mentioned that you were to leave your ego at the door, you were going to get yelled at, and to just deal with it.

One major reason for the initial chasm between Darrell and his fellow team-mates, especially the wide receivers, was his knack for getting hysterical after a dropped ball or an incorrectly run route. In Darrell's defense, he was hard on himself as well and just wanted to win, but his offensive mates didn't appreciate the advertising of every little mistake they made, especially by the guy who was supposed to be their leader. I understand getting on a guy about loafing but mistakes sometimes happen to those giving their full effort as well, and you need to know not to show up a teammate in front of everyone.

Scott Nelson, an upperclassman safety and one of the defensive leaders who witnessed his shenanigans during voluntary winter-conditioning drills, had a talk with Darrell. Scott had pulled Darrell aside and said something to the effect of, "When you get to the point where you never make a mistake, then you can act like that. Until then, cut the theatrics." Scott had spent three seasons on the team and was a holdover coveted by Alvarez and his staff. He'd already been through a lot and was setting the tone for the mutual respect and trust this team would become known for. Do your job, support your teammates, and play your hardest. No attitudes allowed. That's what made a guy like Scott Nelson a leader.

The fact that Darrell realized he needed to change and started to become more encouraging toward his teammates, showed he also had what it took to be a leader. Off the field, he joked around more, and he relaxed and bonded better with his teammates. By that next fall, he'd situated himself as one of the team leaders, a hard worker who wanted to win, and was there to help his teammates do the same.

Being a member of the team taught me that leadership isn't just given to you because you hold a title. Senior. Coach. Quarterback. Leadership must be earned, and you earn it by showing your followers that you have their best interests in mind, that you're competent, and that you respect them.

I also learned something about our team that winter. We wanted to change things, and we were willing to work to make the changes happen. That directive came from the top players, and the rest followed suit. The overall attitude was inclusive and infectious. We were all in this together, and together we would achieve great things.

RACE YA?

By my calculations, our team was approximately 59 percent white, 38 ½ percent black, 1 ½ percent Hispanic (Jay Macias is the one and my good buddy Phil Chavez, who is half Mexican, makes up the half) and 1 percent other. The other was reserved for Jason Levine, who was one of those guys who was hard to place. Jason was dark-skinned with a Jewish last name and a Midwestern accent. He was a good friend of mine. A great, soft-spoken guy who seemed too nice to be as good a football player as he was. But I still couldn't tell you his true ethnicity.

We did have one Jewish player, Michael Brin, a fellow wide receiver who was a couple of years younger than me. He was a good-humored guy who joked that he was a hero in the Jewish community for his athletic prowess.

Speaking of the Jewish community, the Towers, a private residence hall, became an optional living quarters for scholarship players. The Towers, which normally housed a large proportion of Jewish kids from the East Coast, was now infiltrated by football players who wanted out of the dorms and into the prime State Street location. While scholarship players still had to live in dorms their first three years at school, they could now choose between university dormitories — the Towers, or the Regent, another private residence hall right across from the stadium.

Generally, the black guys hung out with other black guys and the white guys hung out with other white guys. There was no forced integration, and so when guys of both races did hang out, it was genuine. What's most important is that we were being true to ourselves. If we can accept each other for who we are without going through the charade of false friendships, we're truly respecting and accepting one another. That's how our team did it.

A Big Ten college football team really is a melting pot. Where else are there situations where guys from so many different backgrounds come together on one team and work to achieve a common goal? Other than football, I'd say in a military platoon, but that's about it.

Not only are there racial differences, but economic, geographic, political, religious, and philosophical differences as well.

Economic. The majority of players on the team came from middle-class backgrounds. Very few were rich and very few were poor. Alvarez used to say, "I can win with two-car garage guys, but not three-car garage guys." Middle-class, working-class, but not rich. Our 1993 championship team was known as the "lunch-pail gang" after all.

Geographical. A few of the players were from big cities like New York or Chicago but the majority came from relatively small towns. Half of the team was from the state of Wisconsin, which Alvarez wanted. When Alvarez first took the head coaching job, he said, "The hands and feet might have to come from somewhere else, but the heart needs to come from the state players."

Religious. Like a lot of students at the university, the players tended to not attend religious services of any kind. But most were raised Christian.

As a lapsed Catholic who was curious about getting back into religion, I looked into the Christian organization called Athletes in Action. I'd heard of them when I was younger because they had a basketball team of former college players that would get clobbered by the UW basketball team in an exhibition game every year.

A.I.A. had a program on our campus, and I would see flyers advertising meetings every so often. I found out that backup Jay Simala was an active member and so approached him one day to ask him about it. Jay, who was from Indiana, was a very nice guy and in his southern drawl told me, "Well, Chris, I don't know what your relationship is with the Lord, but I know it's helped me." I've attended Catholic school and church most of my life, but I still get nervous when people casually mention the word, "Lord." Regardless of my apprehension, I attended a meeting held in a small room at Union South. Jay was the only other football player and there were about 10 to 12 other athletes in the room, half of whom were female soccer players. Apparently, the women's soccer coach, Greg Ryan, was a fervent Christian and spoke often about religion during practices and games.

Jim Bakken, a former UW athlete and NFL player who was now in his 50s or 60s, was the keynote speaker. He had some job in the athletic department with a fancy name but I don't know what he did other than wear red blazers and hang around shaking hands with everyone. Anyway, he gave a rather incoherent talk about how "the devil was out there, you better believe it, brother." Everyone was nice enough but I knew this wasn't for me, and I regretted using my free night attending the function. I'd have to defend myself against the devil using the same techniques I used dodging strong safeties.

Political. During the 1992 election, again like most college students, many of the players didn't vote. I do remember some talk about most of the coaches being Republicans and the players being pretty evenly divided between the two parties. But this didn't really have much of an effect on the team as no one really mentioned it.

Religion and politics, like at most dinner tables, were not discussed much in the locker rooms either.

I can say from my point of view that despite a few hiccups, the race relations on our team were quite good. I think a big reason we all got along was that we were just too busy with important things, like surviving the schedule of a student-athlete, to be concerned with unimportant things like the color of our skin. We quickly realized that we needed each other for support, regardless of whatever differences we all had, and that working together strengthened the team. We were all in the same boat and the constant rough seas of big-time college football were colorblind.

I was in the minority as a white receiver. Having come from a high school with one black student, the team was my first real close encounter with black people, and I learned quite a bit about the black player's world. I learned about "morning ash," what the black guys called their skin when it got really dry and turned a grayish, ashy color. This explained why almost every black guy was always putting on lotion at his locker.

Another problem was the serious lack of Madison barbers who could cut black people's hair properly. Considering Madison's black population is about 4 percent, that's not much of a surprise. A lot of the black guys on the team cut each other's hair; now if that's not trusting your teammate, I don't know what is. Also, it seemed to really hurt if someone swiped his fingers across your freshly shaved 'do during a meeting.

One time during my sophomore year, I got a ride from a black teammate of mine, Chuck Belin, to our Portuguese tutor's house on the west side of Madison. Chuck had an older car, and we stopped for gas. Chuck pulled into the station and mistakenly parked at one of the full-service pumps. The gas station attendant notified us of that over the intercom. I just chuckled as we got back in the car and Chuck swung it around to one of the self-service stations. Chuck, normally a pretty jovial guy, was visibly upset.

"How does he know I don't want full service? Who is he to judge?" I said that the attendant was probably just reacting to the sight of two college kids pulling up in an old car. Chuck felt it was racially motivated, and I tried to convince him it wasn't. I didn't want my buddy to feel bad, and I really didn't think it had anything to do with Chuck's skin color. But then again, I hadn't spent my life being black, and in this case we saw the world differently in large part due to skin color.

The only time in my four years I remember any racial tension among the team occurred over the music played in the weight room. The strength coaches allowed players to bring in their own CDs and play them in the five-disc changer system.

The white guys, especially the big lineman, typically preferred heavy metal and hard rock music. The black guys typically preferred rap and R & B. Not to say that none of the guys crossed over, because they did, but in general that was the case. Since the linemen were usually in the weight room more than anybody, they got their music choice most of the time.

One day, a few of my black teammates complained that they were tired of the rock and replaced it with rap music. This angered a few of the white guys who were working out. Words were exchanged, and a white guy and a black guy almost got into a fight over it. Teammates and the strength coaches had to step in.

Coach Dettman, the head strength coach, said he had the solution. From then on, half the music was to be rap/R & B and the other half hard rock/heavy metal. The five-disc music player would be set to the random mode. If there were any more problems, there would just be no music in the weight room. Case closed.

That ended the strife and I'll be damned if, after some time, a few white linemen couldn't throw down rap verses on the spot. I also remember Patrick Tompkins, a black defensive lineman, yelling out, "Hey man! Put in some of that NirVANa!" Ah, ebony and ivory working out together in perfect harmony, side by side on the bench press and squat racks.

On a side note, I want it to be known from this day forth that I, Chris Kennedy, initiated the current student section phenomenon at Camp Randall that takes place between the end of the 3rd quarter and beginning of the 4th quarter.

Let me 'splain. It was 1992, and the Irish-American hip-hop group House of Pain came out with its self-titled debut compact disc. I read about the group in a student newspaper. As an Irish-American and as someone who liked to work out to both hard rock and rap, I rushed out to buy it the first day it was released.

I loved it, especially the song, "Jump Around," and brought it into the weight room to play it. Most everyone, both black and white guys, liked that disc and especially that song. It became sort of an official team anthem. Special-teams standout Korey Manley requested to borrow the CD so he could play it when the team traveled to the next game. Some guys began calling Camp Randall "The House of Pain," especially where opponents were concerned. We started to play it in the weight room before and after games and at parties. I recall a house party where the song was played and everyone at the party was jumping up and down. The floor was moving up and down, and I swore that we were all going to crash onto the floor below us. Fortunately, that didn't happen.

Under the song's hard rock/rap melodies, black and white teammates put aside any petty differences and united our UW football team, the same way that song now unites our fans. That's something to jump around about.

I guess I'm sort of the team's version of Martin Luther King, Jr., and Mahatma Gandhi. I think they were wide receivers too.

WEIGHTING GAME

Our weight room was housed under the practice field in the McClain Center. It was right next to the training room, which was right next to our locker room. The weight room was expansive and pristine. It was nicer than any health club weight room I'd ever been inside. It was a barrage of red, white, and mirrors.

The strength coaches sat up on a raised platform next to the disc player. One section of the weight room housed the hang clean area. This is the section where guys would hoist up big, heavy, bouncy, plated barbells, competitive-weightlifter style. This area was filled with chalk dust, screaming, and bandaged knees.

The other areas had room for bench, incline, and shoulder presses. There were many dumbbells, squat racks, and cardio machines as well.

Usually the big linemen were the only guys on the cardio machines, as the skills players spent most of their time sprinting around the field every day. The machines were a great way to drop a few extra pounds the big guys might be lugging around. Some liked it more than others. One day while exercising on a Stairmaster, center Brian Patterson read the standard warning on the machine and yelled to head strength coach Dettman, "Hey, Coach, this machine says right here, if I experience any dizziness or fatigue, I should stop!" Dettman shook his head, Brian shrugged, and I laughed.

I remember reluctantly agreeing to spot Mark Montgomery, who was bench-pressing a weight I couldn't even squat. My encouragement was genuine when I screamed at him to push it up, as I didn't want to be responsible for his chest getting crushed as a result of my inability to return the bar to the rack without his help.

Each position had its own records for different lifts and running events in the off-season. I had no shot at any of the records. The wide receiver bench-press record was held by Mike Tams at something like 375 pounds. I was about 100 pounds below that. The only record I had a shot at was the 300-yard shuttle record held by former receiver Lionel Crawford. His time was 43.8 seconds.

On the test day during my senior year, it was about 100 degrees on the Camp Randall turf but that didn't hamper my enthusiasm about potentially breaking the record. The deal was that every player ran two 300-yard shuttles—60 yards back and forth five times, touching the end line with his foot each time to avoid disqualification.

I ran my first shuttle in 43.0. We were given two minutes to catch our breath, and I was sucking in huge mouthfuls of air and trying to slow my heartbeat down before the two minutes were up. Many teammates gathered to encourage me as word spread that I had a shot at breaking the record.

On my second sprint, I ran so hard that my vision was obstructed by the sweat and wind blowing into my eyes. I crossed the finish line as the coach read off: 43, 44, 45. A group of my buddies cheered and told me that I crossed at 44, which would put my average at 43.5, a record for wide receivers and the second fastest ever on the team. I took their word for it; I didn't recall hearing anything other than my gasping breaths and pounding heartbeat. Several guys were hugging me and patting me on the back; I felt like I was going to faint.

Two teammates, Jason Levine and Terry Glavin, helped guide me to a drinking fountain. I buried my face in the arc of water and drank in between heaving breaths. A cold rush went down my spine, rested on the back of my neck, and the room started to spin. I don't recall much after that other than throwing up into the water fountain.

The next thing I knew, I was lying against the wall, as assistant strength coach Dave Ellis held a cold towel around my neck. He told me the team had gone back to Holy Name and that he was going to drive me and another player, who'd also suffered heat stroke, back in a van. I was embarrassed but took comfort in breaking the record.

Coach Ellis said it was close but that it wasn't official yet. He said, "Regardless, that's the way to leave it all on the field, Kennedy. Really nice work."

I returned to the seminary in a white van. All the guys asked me whether the rumors were true that I had to have an IV put in. They weren't. A few said that it was bullshit that I didn't get the record—Coach Dettman had me at an official combined time of 44.0. I really didn't care; I felt Coach Dettman was a fair and honest guy. I was proud to have challenged it and to have given it my all. I was also proud that my teammates saw it and acknowledged me for it. "Dang, you ran like an all-American today," a fellow receiver told me.

Though it would've been nice to get a little notoriety for myself and have my name up on the board outside the weight room for all to see, the most important thing was that my teammates knew I gave it my all.

READY FOR BACKUP

With age comes wisdom and new perspective. Typically, the hazy hopes of youth dissipate while the cold front of reality sets in. As I made it past the halfway point of my career, I had a strong sense of the poverty of my efforts. Despite two full years on the team and my third year of summer conditioning, I'd yet to step foot on the field during a game and I didn't seem on track to get any serious playing time in the near future.

Checking the depth chart at the end of spring practice in my sophomore year, I noticed that another walk-on and I were listed below an incoming scholarship freshman. Despite my two years of effort, this kid was already ahead of me on the depth chart, and he was still a senior in high school! Potential doesn't mean anything; the only thing that matters is what happens between the lines and between the whistles on a football field. How is anyone supposed to feel in that situation? Even more depressing was that the slot was on special teams, the one place all reserves feel is the best opportunity to get on the field.

Of course, the high school kid in question was being brought in on scholarship and so the coaches were invested in him. As a walk-on, I knew the only investment in me was my own time. Even so, I had seen several highly touted scholarship players come into the program and fizzle or just plain bomb. I also saw a number of non-scholarship players step into key roles, and some of them were subsequently given scholarships. I'd mistakenly believed I knew who my competition was, but it turned out the staff already thought more highly of an absentee. This was an experienced coaching staff, though, and I assumed they knew talent—or in my case, the lack thereof. Obviously, I hadn't shown enough potential.

I assumed that I would move up the depth chart as I got older and better but with the talent level on the team at its highest point in years, I didn't see much potential for a change in my circumstances. By the way, that scholarship player, while highly skilled, showed an overall lack of enthusiasm for the game, spent the year on the scout team, and quit the following year.

The fall of my junior year, I reported to Holy Name Seminary in a less-than-optimistic mood. Faced with the reality of never getting a real consideration from the coaching staff, I seriously contemplated quitting.

These feelings of hopelessness, compounded by my maternal grandmother's impending death from cancer, and by the departure of two of my closest friends, fellow walk-on receivers Tim Ott and Donny Gray, caused me to take a leave from the team.

I remember Donny telling Tim and me over the summer that he was quitting the team. Donny was just too exhausted with the schedule and wanted to pursue other interests in his life. Tim and I were upset but understood; we'd been contemplating the same thing. We all hugged, said our goodbyes, and promised to stay in touch. Donny wished us luck, from the bottom of his heart. He knew we needed it.

Then that fall at Holy Name, I stopped by Tim's room to hang out after one of our practices. He was sitting on the bed leafing through the team program. He looked up and said, "I'm not in here." I laughed it off because, of course, he was. Tim said nothing in response but just looked at me and clarified, "I'm out of here." I was shocked and silent. Then I noticed his bags were packed. "My roommate's coming to pick me up," he continued. "I just can't do it anymore." My heart sank, but my head understood exactly what he was saying. I knew it would do no good to try to talk him into staying, especially when I was barely able to talk myself into it.

I carried one of his bags for him and walked him to the entrance. On our way to the front door, I noticed some younger players joking around down the hall. These guys didn't know Tim or me that well. I wondered how Tim leaving could be so small to them while it loomed so largely for me.

We hugged goodbye and wished each other luck. We said we'd definitely stay in touch. Since we'd already lacked communication with Donny from just the summer, we also knew it was highly unlikely we'd keep our promises long. We were both tough guys and didn't allow any tears. I knew Tim was gone. I wish I would've thanked him for his help in keeping me afloat the previous two years but I was too thrown by the circumstances.

Tim jogged out to his roommate's beat-up car, jumped in, and they sped off. The dust kicked up and faded away, much like his once-hopeful plans of earning a scholarship and playing wide receiver for the University of Wisconsin. I had spent time with Tim every day, but I only saw him a couple of times before he left school. Once he left, I never saw him again.

Two days and four practices later, I went in and spoke to Coach Norvell. I'm sure he assumed I was also quitting as Tim and Donny recently had. The third musketeer to fall. I told him I needed some time. I told him of my grandmother and my lack of focus. He asked whether I was quitting, and I said I wanted some time to think about it. He thought that was fine. "Just be honest with us," he said as I left.

I packed my bags and left Holy Name Seminary, like I'd fantasized about the previous three years. But because of my restless mind, there wasn't the sense of relief I thought I'd feel.

I spent some time alone in my apartment to try to figure out what I wanted to do with my life. I'd played football for 10 of my 20 years. Who was I if I wasn't Chris Kennedy, the football player? Could I just be a regular student? Could I just go drink and sit in the stands and watch the games? I doubted it.

I thought not only of the consequences in my own life, but how my quitting the team would affect my family, friends, and support community. I now realize how many ghosts I created, false groups of people I supposed were really concerned about everything I was doing. I put the weight of the world on my shoulders, or rather, the weight of "The Only Waunakee in the World." I imagined all the disappointment I'd create in so many people.

I spoke to my mother. She was supportive as usual and said she stood behind whatever decision I ended up making. She wanted me to be happy. My mother and I went out to visit my dying grandmother. I remember driving out to her house, thinking I should be at practice right now and wondering what period they were on. Then I felt guilty and angry that the sport was overpowering my thoughts even as a very special person in my life was about to die.

My grandmother was in a virtual catatonic state, propped up in a wheelchair and fed by a hospice worker. My grandfather walked over and shouted that her grandson Christopher was here. Her mouth slipped into a bit of a smile, and she made a small noise. I knelt down beside her as my grandfather said she was excited to see me. I sat with her for awhile and held her hand. She wasn't able to have any conversation and she looked worn out. I kissed the wrap on her shaved head and said goodbye. She died shortly afterward.

My grandmother was one of the people in my life who really gave me confidence. She treated me like a king my whole life. There wasn't anything that she didn't think I could do, and I guess I mostly believed her. She would sneak me candy, and if I were punished in her presence she made sure to give me a hug later on to tell me it was OK. I was lucky to experience such unconditional love.

In some way, I hoped seeing my grandmother would provide me some profound answers about life. Maybe it would make me see that football was a silly thing to obsess over and make it easy for me to quit. But I was just as unclear, if not more so, after visiting her.

My father caught wind of my leaving camp through the grapevine. I didn't know how to tell him. He called and asked me to meet him at Country Kitchen for dinner and I agreed. As we sat in the booth, my life felt much like the skillet scramble plate I tinkered with. I tried to explain my dire situation, my virtually hopeless future with the team, and my lack of interest in football.

When I hit similar rough patches in the past, I'd fall back on my friendships on the team. Specifically, Tim and Donny, who were now gone. I told him I just didn't see how I could continue. So many of the guys in my boat had left or moved up the depth chart and were playing.

My dad listened and told me I could leave, and he would understand. But he countered that I'd already put so much time in and made it through the first few years. The toughest part was over. There was nothing at this point that I hadn't already been through. The team was on the verge of a breakthrough and I'd helped get them to that point. He reasoned that I should stay and help them get over the hump, and then reap the rewards. He was right. I'd put a lot of work into the team, and I believed that I could continue to help the team. Whether I was appreciated for it or not, I would accept my backup role and continue to battle for a playing spot, regardless of the odds. My dad somehow got me psyched up again; he was always great at that. I returned to camp the next day. I made it through the rest of Holy Name and the 1992 season.

I still had my bouts with depression during the season. On the scout team, I didn't jump in on as many reps at practice as I once did. There was a whole new crop of younger players who wanted to prove themselves, who were full of hope, as I'd once been. I drifted back to let them share the workload. I considered it part of their initiation.

Coach Childress addressed the team one day and equated that the way you do things reflects your character. He told us to pretend we had to sign our name on every play. After each play, you'd ask yourself the question, am I proud enough of that performance to put my signature on it? Does that performance represent who I am? It sounded familiar to me because that's what Coach Quinn was trying to instill in me every day in practice.

I watched myself on the practice tapes at our daily position meetings and I was embarrassed by how listlessly I was practicing. I wasn't competing. I was a self-fulfilling prophecy. It's no surprise that I re-injured my shoulder during this period of time. Like Coach Quinn always said, "Those not giving a full effort on the field are the ones who are going to get hurt."

TRAINING ROOM BLUES

The training room is one of those deceptive places. It's a nice place to visit, but you wouldn't want to live there. Sort of like Florida. It looks good from the outside, like a day spa. Everyone looks so comfortable walking around in shorts and bare feet. They don't have to practice. They get stretched out and worked on by female trainers. There are heating pads for your back and a whirlpool for your aching body parts.

However, once inside, the injured player realizes the attention focused on him is as much to get him out of there as it is to really fix him. If your ox gets a broken leg, you get it fixed so he can keep working for you, not because you're concerned about his pain.

The rehab schedules are always lengthy, always start early in the morning, and are often grueling. The injured athlete is also expected to be doing some sort of rehabilitation before, during, and after practice. He spends more time at the athletic facility than the healthy athlete.

In addition to the physical pain, there's the mental and emotional pressure. The injured player naturally stresses out over losing valuable ground, as well as the very real possibility of sliding down the depth chart the longer he is out. Competitive, fast-paced college football waits on no one. The coaches seem to ignore you if you're injured. You feel powerless about your injury and how quickly it will decide to stop causing you pain. That seems to be more up to a higher power. It happened by accident, and now you've got to deal with it. You can rehab as hard as you like, but you can't really cure yourself.

When you're healthy, you can control things more. If you want to get stronger, you lift weights and get stronger. If you want to get faster, you do speed drills and get faster. But with an injury, it seems time is the main factor and you can't affect that. The futility of your efforts can be overwhelmingly frustrating.

Coach Alvarez often mentioned that he didn't want a lot of guys hurt. In his experience, losing teams tended to have more guys on the injured list than winning teams. It's not a chicken-or-egg argument; it's more of an illustration that when things are going well and morale is high, guys don't stay on the injured list long. But when morale is low, guys are less rushed to get back into the swing of things and will stay in the training room.

Let's distinguish between being injured and being *injured*. College football players play with a high tolerance of pain. This isn't curling. This a collision sport, where big, strong, fast guys slam into each other. They are trained to take you down.

A player basically gets hurt on every play, whether it's a small-yet-painful injury like smacking your hand against someone's helmet, or an elbow to the neck that steals your breath, or landing with the football penetrating your rib cage. Just the grind of cutting and running on artificial turf can leave your socks bloody from a torn toenail (I learned it usually takes a full season for a big toenail to grow back in).

I once bruised my ribs in a practice when I went up to catch a pass; my body fully extended, I took the full brunt of the strong safety's shoulder pads attacking my mid-section. My shoulder blades were the first thing to hit the turf, and I momentarily lost my breath. I felt a cold shiver surge through my body. When the pain set in about two seconds later, I felt as if I'd been hit with a sledgehammer. Bruised ribs are almost untreatable and so for the next month I had to take short, shallow breaths because if I inhaled too deeply, a sharp pain shot through my body almost to the point of shock. Sitting down on the toilet and going to the bathroom caused almost dizzying pain with each push. I was surprised there wasn't blood in the bowl when I finished, as other players said had happened to them after taking some major hits. There is no way to get a good night's sleep on bruised ribs, as any movement immediately woke me to remind me that I was not healthy. Yet, such things never show up on an injury report. They are just the basic collateral damage from playing a contact sport. The helmets and pads aren't for decoration.

Upon getting really rattled by a hit, your initial reaction isn't of retaliation or anger but of disorientation. First, you do a mental scan of your body: Can I move everything? Does anything feel "wrong"? Can I get up? If you get the right answers to those questions, you enter back into the noisy world and carry whatever residual pain with you to the huddle, ignore it, and refocus on the next play.

When you do have a more serious injury—a broken arm or leg, a torn knee ligament, a dislocated shoulder—you do the same mental scan, but something in your body prevents you from getting up. You become accepting and serene about it in most cases. Well, that happened, you think to yourself. Hope this heals fast.

I remember a practice when Theo Carney was tackled and landed awkwardly with one hand getting pinned under him. He arose with a scream, and I noticed his pinky finger was pointing down and off to the side, as if it were hanging by threads (ligaments, I guess). He still had his gloves on when a few trainers crowded him, isolated the hand, and tried to pop the finger back into place. It seemed a bit painful for Theo, and I remember Patrick Tompkins yelling encouragingly, "Come on, Theo, let 'em pop it back in, man. Fight through that shit, baby!" It's the only thing a teammate could do, understand the pain, be there for him, and support him through it. They got the finger back in its proper place, taped it to the neighboring finger, and Theo was back playing before the end of practice. I'm sure Theo felt it in the morning.

All players really feel the pain the next morning after the adrenaline is gone and they're left with the dull and sharp pains from the previous day's practice. The muscles, the joints, and the connective tissue of the body all take such a pounding during a typical football practice. Sometimes you have to pull one leg out of bed to get the other to follow. Many guys on the team downed aspirins or painkillers every morning as commonly as their Wheaties. Many players looked like the Michelin Man, with ice bags bandaged to their joints as they hobbled home after practice.

It's easy to skip classes when you can barely move your cramped legs. As a receiver, I always found my fingers got jammed a lot and they'd be so swollen that when I made a fist, a swollen digit or two stayed bent hovering behind the others. I found taking notes almost impossible as I couldn't grip a pen without wincing. This is as good an excuse as any to borrow notes and arrange for study sessions with the best-looking girls in your class.

The injury I got when I was a junior was the first semi-serious one of my college career. My left shoulder, which I'd severely sprained at the beginning of my junior year in high school, was re-aggravated during a practice scrimmage. While being driven into the less-than-forgiving Camp Randall turf, my elbow planted hard and my left shoulder slid out of place. A hot-then-cold surge went through my entire body, and I knew I'd hurt it significantly again. I stood up and was able to snap it back into the joint but not without eye-watering pain. I walked right over to a trainer and explained what happened.

You forget when you're healthy how miserable it is to be hurt. The immediate pain is one thing, but when it's worse the next day you know it's bad. I had to sit out a few practices, which didn't please my coaches or me much. What good is an injured volunteer worker (a walk-on) if he's not working? Next!

The head trainer, Denny Helwig, mainly dealt with rehabbing the starters' injuries, so the student trainers helped me with my rehab. They were very sweet and competent, and treated me well.

Every day, an injured player list is posted in the training room with the type of treatment to be done that day. The injured player would be given a list of exercises and hot/cold treatments to be done: Chris Kennedy = Cybex, whirlpool, stretch. The list also mentioned how much, if any, practice you could do. Chris Kennedy = No practice or running only, no contact, or light contact. It's no secret players are asked to return to practice, and want to do so, as soon as possible and probably return before they should.

I was instructed to return to practice after only two days of rehab, due more to the impatience of the coaching and training staff than to the recovery status of my injury. Athletes want to play, want to progress, and want to compete. So obviously, I was not opposed to giving it a shot—who wants to risk looking like a baby by saying he's too hurt to play? But I also knew I was not ready.

I tried to play, but sure enough, after a few plays the pain was too restricting and I had to take myself out. Every time I hit with my shoulder, it felt like an anvil had been dropped on it.

It's almost impossible to rest a shoulder while playing football. You can't do any significant weightlifting, catching, or tackling. I had to sit out for a couple of weeks and my shoulder, despite my daily rehab, just wasn't getting better. I was frustrated and felt more worthless with each day of practice I missed. I watched guys in the weight room through the glass while receiving treatment, and I was jealous they were building up their muscles while mine atrophied. I questioned whether I'd ever be healthy enough to lift weights or play pain-free.

The coaches and the training staff grew increasingly frustrated and seemed to feel I was prolonging my injury just to spite them. It was mental, emotional, and physical hell.

As a last resort, I was scheduled to see the team doctor, who decided that a cortisone shot directly into my shoulder would be the best option. He said it wouldn't do me any more harm since the shoulder joint was already pretty messed up and it would decrease the pain in the joint, which would allow me to return to practice. I just wanted the pain, the rehab, and the stress to be over with, and if this shot would do it, fine with me.

The doctor administered the shot after the next practice. I went into a small room and lay down on a table. The needle was much longer and thicker than the needles I was used to seeing. As he inserted the shot right into my shoulder joint, it made an uncomfortable popping sound. The pain was more dull than sharp. Once the needle was firmly in place, I felt a distinctly warm solution slowly spread throughout my shoulder. The solution cooled after a few seconds as it continued to spread down my arm.

The doctor took out the needle and patted my other shoulder. He told me to just lie there for a while and relax. He mentioned the joint was tighter than he thought it would be, which suddenly made me wonder whether I had been misdiagnosed and whether I really needed the shot.

The shot put me into more of a daze than I thought it would. I felt really relaxed and lethargic. I remembered seeing kicker Rich Thompson in the training room a year earlier, and I stopped to chat with him. He was usually a real gregarious guy but that day he was just in a trance. I asked him what was wrong and he said, "I just got a cortisone shot. I'll talk to you later." Now, I understood the effect he was under.

A senior teammate saw me a few moments later and tried to strike up a conversation. I apologized that I was out of it due to the cortisone shot. He told me, "I would never let these guys give me a cortisone shot. They're just painkillers, man. They're not helping nothin'." Now, I felt duped, stupid, and guilty. Why was I taking the risk of sacrificing my body for the rest of my life for a team that saw me as essentially disposable? I was ashamed for not standing up for myself. For not respecting myself enough to wait. I rationalized that I did it for the team, even if my sacrifice went unnoticed. After all, I felt that most of what I did went unnoticed anyway, so I guess I was used to it. Besides, the deed was now done and I had to make peace with it.

I can attest that the shot worked. I returned to practice the next day, and my shoulder was now virtually pain-free for the first time in more than a month. It was so great to not be nagged by that damn shoulder. Maybe it was a false sense of security, as the shoulder joint was probably just getting worse. But I couldn't bear any more time spent in the training room, college football's purgatory.

GLADIATORS

Football games don't get cancelled due to weather, and football players don't stop playing due to injury.

A football player must accept pain. Both on the field and off the field, pain must be accommodated. Bruises and turf burns will meld into your skin and become fixtures there. Your fingers will balloon and break. Your alarm clock announces new and familiar aches each morning.

To play at a sufficient level to succeed, a player must commit himself completely to the moment. He needs to be ready and willing to make a full effort in the face of whatever comes his way; anything less, and he risks failure and injury.

A game is the sum of individual plays, individual battles. The team with the players who win the most battles is the winner. Yet when it comes down to it, the game is not about winning and losing. It's about participating fully in these battles. To not back down, to not flinch despite the expected pain, is the sign of not only a competitor but a gladiator. Being a competitor has nothing to do with talent. It has to do with embracing and embodying a warrior's mindset.

College football players have faith, they believe in something. No one puts himself in harm's way just because of a game. The players are fighting for something: Respect. Honor. Fame. Reputation. The opportunity to become something more than what they are.

Courage is stepping onto the field with your pads on, chinstrap buckled, and mouth guard squeezed between your teeth, come what may.

Many times in life, the unsuccessful, the average, the mediocre are content to shirk the hard task. They make fear their personal dictator and, like water, take the path of least resistance. College football players don't do that. They must be hard. They have to try on every play. Pain is sure, and of little consequence. Only the game is important.

Rarely is one given the opportunity to do something grand, something great. But it's not rare on a football field. It's there waiting on every blow of the whistle and snap of the ball.

Good football players don't hesitate. They don't flinch. To fight to win a game is a worthy battle, supported by stadiums of fans and millions of television viewers.

I often feel my current life doesn't present the clear-cut challenges it once did when I was a college football player. It's harder to determine which battles are worthy to be fought and which are to be abandoned. I search for the nobility of a good fight. My college football experience has trained me to come out swinging when the bell rings.

CHAPTER NINE:
JUNIOR WINCE

Facing the biggest hurdle in my college career, I sought inspiration and found it in a letter my father gave me after I graduated from high school. He mentioned in the letter that I would be tried and tested like never before in my life. This was where I was going to need "huge courage to overcome any personal insecurities" that may arise on my path. I was questioning a lot about myself, but I realized that the only way through adversity was to put my head down and plough through it.

I decided I needed to take more pride in how I played regardless of whether or not I was recognized for it. I had myself to answer to, and that was more important than anyone else's opinion. I rededicated myself to embracing my role as someone who'd help his team get ready to win on Saturdays.

My own personal yo-yoing was congruent with the team's fortunes. We started the season at 4-2 including an upset of 12th-ranked Ohio State.

One of our losses was an away game against the defending national champion Washington Huskies. Surprising many in the college football world, it was a good game and we played them tough. We lost, 27-10, but showed we could compete on the road against the nation's best.

The real test came the next week when we took on a bowl-winner from the previous season, Bowling Green, at home. We just couldn't start the season 0-2 and still expect to turn the program around. This was a game we needed to win to establish that we were a better team than we were in the past. Alvarez knew it and locked out the media at practice that week. No outside distractions.

We were confident going into the Bowling Green game, and we proved why. Our offense scored 39 points, and our defense created six turnovers and held Bowling Green to 18 points. The Falcons had played Ohio State the week before and lost, 17-6. Bowling Green's coach said after the game, "I thought Wisconsin controlled the line of scrimmage against us better than Ohio State did."

A good thing, because we played the Buckeyes a few weeks later in Camp Randall. We were heading into the game with a 3-1 record. ESPN was going to televise the game nationally and Jesse Jackson came to speak to the team at practice during the week to inspire us.

Jackson told us we were lucky to have the opportunity to work together across racial divides to accomplish something and urged us to carry that on after football because America needed that. He ended the speech by having us all repeat, "I am somebody."

We had Saturday's game to prove that we were somebody. Both UW and Ohio State were physical teams and OSU got the better of us in the first half, jumping to a 10-3 lead. But we steeled ourselves for the second half and scored 17 points. OSU brought the score to 20-16 and got the ball to the UW 23-yard line. On a fourth-down call with 2 minutes left on the clock, safety Reggie Holt tackled OSU quarterback Kirk Herbstreit before he could get a first down and our offense took over and ran out the clock. The 70,000-plus fans at the stadium and the national television audience witnessed the upset on a beautiful, sunny day. A UW victory over mighty Ohio State was truly something for Badgers fans to celebrate.

Our optimism was hard to contain. A bowl game was virtually a lock, and we started fantasizing about which bowl games we'd go to. Greed sets in mighty fast.

As our success caused a stir around the state, the four complimentary tickets each player received for each home game suddenly became a major issue. Attendance was starting to reach full capacity. It was great to witness and exactly what we wanted to have happen. But it meant that game tickets, once easy to get, were becoming scarce. Former bosses, relatives, and students called and congratulated me, and then asked for tickets. Two of my tickets were reserved for my mom and step-dad, Vern Endres, and the other two were usually given to relatives. My father had his own season tickets, and my sister had student tickets. Plus, most students wanted to sit in the famously lively student section and not with the parents and relatives in the player section, even though they were better seats.

There was a rule that three of the four comp tickets had to be for a relative and the fourth could be given to anyone. This was to help prevent any sort of ticket scandal. If you needed to get extra tickets, you could borrow them from fellow teammates. It was usually best to get extra tickets from younger players from out of town, as they'd be less likely to use all four of their comps.

After our impressive 3-1 start, we lost to Iowa, 23-22, as they put together the winning drive in the last four minutes of the game. We beat Purdue, 16-10, the next week and then went on a three-game losing streak, dropping road games at Indiana and Michigan State, and a heartbreaking 13-12 loss at home to Illinois on Halloween.

We'd lost focus on what was important—playing football, practice, and taking one game at a time. Knowing we had better get our act together, we recommitted ourselves to our next game.

We were to play against Minnesota at home. All week, the coaches talked about how getting the Paul Bunyan's Axe trophy back the year before was a big turning point for our team. The Gophers and the Badgers had been playing each other for more than 100 years, one of the oldest rivalries in college football, and the reward for winning the game was an eight-foot-tall wooden axe. The handle of the axe was imprinted with the score of every game since the late 1800s.

It was exciting for us to sprint to Minnesota's sideline the year before as they were forced to stand aside and watch us snatch the axe from their possession. It got passed from player to player as we made a lap around the stadium. The coaches emphasized that we needed to keep it in our football offices for the next year.

The team had a very focused, intense week of practice. At the end of a couple of practices that week, Coach Alvarez had former players come back and address the team on the importance of winning the Minnesota game and keeping the axe. At the end of Friday's light practice, Coach Alvarez told us we'd practiced well and were ready to win the game.

Emboldened to redeem our once-promising season, we stormed the field ready to explode against Minnesota. Our offense established its dominance by amassing 411 yards and 34 points, and scoring on four long drives. Wide receiver Lee DeRamus caught two touchdown passes, running back Brent Moss ran for 137 yards, and Terrell Fletcher ran for 85, chewing up Minnesota's defense.

Our defense was relentless, allowing Minnesota to score only six points the entire game. The UW defense sacked Gophers quarterback Marquel Fleetwood six times, and our cornerbacks intercepted two passes and recovered a fumble. At the end of the day, the axe was ours again: final score, 34-6.

Once again we paraded around the

MIKE DEVRIES/CAPITAL TIMES

Parading with Paul Bunyan's Axe.

stadium with our trophy. I was able to briefly hold onto it. It was surprising how cool it felt to hold onto a big piece of wood; I really felt like I had a piece of history in my hand.

My teammate Bryan Jurewicz and I were both dating girls from the same sorority at the time, and we attended their formal dance after the Minnesota win. I remember we spoke about bowl possibilities. Many of those in attendance congratulated us and joined in on the speculation. The Freedom Bowl against USC seemed like the most interesting matchup. It would be the same pairing as the 1963 Rose Bowl game. I was excited by the prospect of playing in the sunny California weather. It was like a dream. We drank and danced the night away. The song "Freedom" by George Michael came on and whipped us into a frenzy on the dance floor. Everything felt fresh and new, and the world was full of possibility.

The team went into our final game of the season against the Northwestern Wildcats in Evanston, Illinois. With our record now at 5-5, we needed only one more win to be bowl-eligible for the first time in nine seasons.

Coach Alvarez addressed the team that week about the bowl-game experience. He said that as a player at Nebraska and later as a coach, the bowl experience was one of the best things about college football. Coach said it would be one of the most memorable events in our lives. He brought in a bunch of his bowl rings he'd received as a coach and a player. Coach said that the bowl was for everybody: "Every swinging dick goes along." That was good news to all my scout-team brethren.

Wisconsin is legendary for a supportive fan base that travels to watch the team, or at the very least seems to come out of the woodwork of any city where the team is playing. That, combined with Wisconsin having not appeared in a bowl-game in almost 10 years, made us a very attractive team. In fact, two bowl game representatives were in the Dyche Stadium pressbox in Evanston ready to hand us invites right on the spot if we won the game. (Yes, the Freedom Bowl was one of them.)

The stage was set and clear-cut for us to win. Although we hadn't won a road game all season, we were optimistic. We had everything to play for and Northwestern, with a 2-8 record, seemingly had nothing to play for…and, on the flip side, nothing to lose.

The weather was drizzly, cold, and sloppy, and we played accordingly. Our defense struggled all day with Northwestern's big quarterback, Len Williams. The Wildcats marched 80 yards on their first possession for a touchdown and 76 yards on their third for another score that made it 14-0 with 14:47 left in the first half.

In the second half, Williams and the Wildcats continued to have success moving the ball against our defense. Especially devastating was an 80-yard scoring drive in the fourth quarter that put Northwestern ahead, 27-25.

Our offense couldn't get the ball in the end zone or make big plays until the fourth quarter. Even our kicking game was off, as we missed two field goals from 25 and 40 yards and failed to recover a blocked punt. Despite our lackluster play, we were still in great position to win the game in the fourth quarter.

With about a minute left in the game, down by two, our offense put it together. Bevell connected on passes to receivers DeRamus and Dawkins. We had moved the ball down to the Northwestern 27-yard line, well within Rich Thompson's field goal range. Coach Alvarez decided we'd run one more play to the right. The yardage didn't matter much; we just needed to get the ball spotted on the right hash mark to make it easier for our kicker to nail the winning field goal.

Ah, the best laid plans. The handoff exchange from Bevell to running back Jason Burns was foiled by a blitzing Wildcats linebacker. The ball hit the turf, and a Northwestern defender recovered it.

The Wisconsin fans and sideline looked on in stunned silence as the Northwestern players and fans hysterically celebrated. I begged the field to materialize a yellow penalty flag or for anything that would give us another chance. There were none.

Northwestern got the ball back on offense and simply let the remaining 40 seconds run off the clock. We looked on powerlessly as the final gun sounded. Northwestern fans stormed the field and jumped on the goal posts. End of game. End of season. End of career, for the seniors. The bowl invites stayed in their envelopes.

There was an inhaled quiet among the players and the fans. No blaming or

Coach Alvarez keeping the sidelines pumped up.

complaining or crying, just an eerie quiet. It hit me that there would be no cavorting and dancing in the California sun for a bowl game against the USC Trojans. It had seemed to me we were destined to go, and I was confused and upset and very disappointed.

Despite this, I felt lucky I'd at least be back the next season to give it one more shot. But I felt bad for the seniors. They would leave their playing days behind, like the nine classes before them, without going to a bowl game. With the bitter taste of "almost" lingering in their mouths for eternity. Perhaps I was just being melodramatic, but it felt that tragic to me.

Our team finished, like the previous season, with a record of 5-6. Perhaps it was a sign of progress that the year before the 5-6 record was viewed as somewhat

151

successful, whereas this year it was viewed as a huge disappointment.

The Northwestern game felt like a sucker punch to the gut, and the team carried that achy, nauseous feeling with us throughout the off-season. The sting lingered into the winter conditioning, where the team's intensity signified that we didn't plan on failing anymore.

THE AMBASSADOR

I was a Madison-area kid. I was clean-cut and well spoken, and I enjoyed any notoriety I could get. I wanted to feel like what I was doing was important, like I was making a difference in the world. All this combined made me a perfect candidate for the team's philanthropic assignments.

Various youth organizations, like the Boy Scouts, made requests to the football office for players to come and speak at their meetings, awards ceremonies, and conferences. Periodically, I would be chosen. I'm sure these groups would have preferred the starting quarterback or running back, but no one ever seemed disappointed when I showed up. It was nice to feel so important, so revered in these settings.

Because Wisconsin is a football crazy state with only one Division I-A team, Badgers players are celebrities in Madison and across the state. The adults who welcomed me were always very appreciative, and the kids were usually wide-eyed and excited to see me. It was such a juxtaposition to go from Mr. Important at one of these functions and then head to practice where I was essentially an invisible player. I didn't know which one was really me.

Typically, I'd wear my jersey to these functions. Sometimes the football office would arm you with a highlight reel and Wisconsin football knick-knacks to hand out. I usually spoke at one of these functions about hard work, setting goals, and never giving up. Some days when I didn't feel like practicing, the enthusiasm I gleaned from these groups gave me the inspiration to dive back into it all.

The most memorable presentation I gave was at my alma mater, Waunakee High School. Coach Rice asked me to come and speak at the Waunakee youth football program orientation, and I was happy to oblige. I had played in that youth league and knew how much it would have meant to me to have a Badger come and talk to us.

I wore my Wisconsin jersey, of course, and made the trip to Waunakee after a Tuesday practice, the longest and toughest of the week. I was surprised to see hundreds of kids and their parents in attendance. Looking at the way these young guys lit up when they saw me made me realize I was a role model for them, whether I felt like one or not.

I told them how lucky they were to be in the Waunakee football program with such caring coaches. Hopefully, knowing that I had been in their same position years before would help them realize that they could achieve great things. I told them at their age it was most important that they have fun playing football with their teammates.

Afterward, I posed for pictures, answered questions, and signed autographs for the kids. It was as special for me as it seemed to be for them. Moments like this made me feel all my sacrifices were worth it.

Other outings were more serious. Some players visited dying children in local hospitals. The nurses and doctors would say how much it meant to the kids to have players visit them. It blew me away that average guys like us, doing simple things like signing our names on a football, could make them happy. How much more useless can you feel than when a kid needs a new kidney to stay alive and all you can do is hand him a foam Wisconsin football?

Seeing a bald little kid in a hospital bed, hooked up to ominous machines, was devastating to many of the players. Hearing a little kid calmly and matter-of-factly tell you he has a tumor in his brain slays you to the bone. We realized how unimportant college football was relative to bigger problems in the world. Big-time college football is often over-hyped and made out to be much more than it is, and these trips to the hospital were blunt reminders of reality: Being a good human being was first and foremost.

One of the best things I was able to do with my "fame" as a player was to donate my Rose Bowl championship team plaque to a fundraiser for Niemann-Pick disease. My father's good friend, Gary Vorpahl, had a daughter named Stacey who was diagnosed with the fatal disease at the age of 18 months. My father suggested I donate the plaque, and I happily obliged. I was happy to hear in a thank-you note from Gary that the plaque was one of the top money-makers of the day. I was happy I could contribute in any tiny way, but I felt guilty that they were so thankful when I hadn't really done anything but donate a piece of wood.

Being a player/ambassador was one of my favorite perks during my college career. It's a great program that benefits everyone, and something that is very right with big-time college football.

SPRING BASH

One of the many differences between high school football and big-time college football is the existence of spring ball. Spring football follows winter conditioning and lasts a little over a month. It's very difficult to feel like playing football at the exact opposite time of year, especially in Madison. The temperatures warm up, the campus looks beautiful, and the girls come out of winter-coat hibernation into shorts and tank tops. With so many distractions, it's very hard to focus on football, much less endure grueling physical practices.

While spring ball is hated by the players, it's loved by the coaches. None of the time is geared toward preparing for an opponent like in the regular season, so the coaches can focus on player and team improvement. This is where the players get the most movement on the depth charts. It's highly competitive, with teammates viciously squaring off against each other to get playing time for the fall. It's not unusual to see fights break out between teammates on a daily basis.

Player anxiety rules the day in spring football. If you're a first-teamer, you're fighting to keep your spot against the second- and third-teamers who are trying to move up.

Every day at meetings, the players are given grades for their performance from the previous practice. As receivers, we were graded on multiple tasks: route running, blocking effectiveness, knockdowns, overall effort, passes caught, yards after catch, and mental errors.

The annual intrasquad spring game is played in Camp Randall Stadium at the conclusion of the spring practices. The coaches split the team in two by holding a draft of the players, and the coaches like to make a big deal out of it.

On the eve of the annual spring football game my sophomore year, the receivers were told to report to a boiler room tucked away in Camp Randall. We reported and waited outside. Lance, our GA, instructed each of us to come in individually. I was about the fourth or fifth guy to go. The others in front of me had come out shaking their heads but saying nothing. I was called to enter.

The room was cluttered and dimly lit. There was a big stein sitting on a table that held candles, a pen, and a stack of paper. Out of the shadows stepped Coach Norvell, wearing sunglasses, a serious look, and black shoulder pads draped with a long cape. He resembled some kind of gladiator-pirate you'd expect to see in a Mad Max movie.

Coach spoke in an exaggeratedly ominous tone. He introduced himself as "The Spirit of Camp Randall." He said he embodied the spirit of this hallowed stadium and Badgers football players from the past. He leaned back his head and shouted my name at the ceiling, then instructed me to kneel down in front of the table. He talked about how special it was for me to be a player on the team. He asked me whether I was willing to accept the responsibility of being a Badger. I responded, "Yes."

He told me that if I was truly committed to being a Badger, I was to sign the promise sheet in front of me. On the promise sheet, there was a list of vows and phrases stating positive claims about commitment and teamwork. My favorite phrase read something like, "There have been many great men to play here before me and many great men will come after me, but right now, it is MY time in history. And I vow, that before I leave, history will remember me as a champion." Your name was to be signed below. I got chills when I read that, and I signed my name on the line.

Coach grabbed a baseball bat and knighted me on both shoulders with it. And so now I was anointed with the privilege of being an official Badgers receiver. I then drank from the sacred cup, which was filled with blood spilled in the name of UW football. The blood of players past tasted very similar to the cherry-flavored Badger Maxx sports drink developed by strength coach Dave Ellis. I was dismissed, and the next receiver entered.

While this resembled a fraternity hazing, it did capture an important component of what I feel is so special about playing football for the University of Wisconsin. I think the phrase "I vow that history will remember me as a champion" captures an equal reverence for the past, the present, and the future.

As bizarre a situation as it was, it began a new thought process for me. I realized I was a part of the university's history now. I felt like I was a part of something bigger than myself. It was both humbling and bolstering to think that I was doing something bigger than just showing up and working hard at practice every day. Now when I walked through the stadium halls and the football offices, I paid closer attention to the pictures of the players of days gone by. I was connected to them.

I read articles about them. One article written by retiring sportswriter Tom Miller, who had covered Wisconsin football for many years, stands out for me. He wrote that his favorite player over all the years was not an all-star and didn't go on to play in the NFL. He certainly wasn't the best to ever come through the program and wasn't even the best on his team. He was a walk-on special-teams player who tore down the field full-speed every time he was on it. There was something about that player's burning passion for the game that was unlike anyone else on the field. Something about the way he put every fiber of his existence into his efforts. Something about him inspired the writer. The player was small in stature but big in heart and tough as nails.

I thought about who that guy was on our current team. I wished it would be me but knew that wasn't the case. I thought of a few. Korey Manley. Jeff Wirth. Chad Cascadden. I started to see the guy, the player, the teammate behind the framed faces that lined the walls. They were no longer staid black-and-white pictures to me, but manifestations of the dreams and desires I knew so well.

It also dawned on me that not every former player was a star; there were players no one spoke of who contributed greatly to past teams. Usually a team is referenced by its stars: "That team was the team with Heisman Trophy winner Alan Ameche on it." It was heartening to realize that players like me, the backups, the reserves, the walk-ons, were also part of the same legacy.

It's a privilege to be a part of the Wisconsin Badgers football team and have that connection to all the great young guys who have worn that jersey. I was affirmed that my teammates and I would also leave a legacy, and it was up to us to determine how great it was going to be.

For the annual spring game, you were either on the cardinal or the white team. Usually, special T-shirts were made up for each team. One year, I was on the white team and we all got "white lightning" T-shirts. Another year on the red team, we were dubbed the "Mean Machine," a nod to the film, *The Longest Yard*. We even had the Ws on our helmets turned upside down to resemble the letter M.

The players always looked forward to the spring game. For many of us who didn't get to play much, it was fun to get reps in a game situation even if it was against our own team. As the team's talent increased, so did the attendance. I saw the most action in the spring game prior to my final season. I was in the game for several series. It was so much fun to get to actually execute my team's plays instead of our opponents' plays like I had to do during the season. All of the reserve players knew a good spring game was a nice launch into summer conditioning and fall camp. The coaches love to watch tape and we knew the coaches would comb through every inch of this footage over the summer to watch for great efforts.

I got to go up against Kenny Gales, our starting defensive back. I ran a nice six-yard stop route against him, got open, and had the ball thrown my way. Unfortunately, it was underthrown a little and I scooped the ball up as it bounced off the turf. Pass incomplete.

I was happy to hear a pass call in the huddle while I was in there during the next series. It showed confidence in me, and I didn't want to disappoint. I was going against a reserve DB on the wide side of the field and felt confident I could get open on the 10-yard out route to the sideline. I sprinted toward him, got nice separation, and spun my head around on the cut to locate the ball. I spotted the ball just out of reach over my head. I managed to get my left hand up in enough time to have it bounce off my fingertips. The play was right in front of my sidelines. I heard several teammates voice my frustration for me and heard a coach yell at me, "Catch the damn ball!"

It was nice to hear my name over the P.A. system, though it would've been nicer to hear, "Chris Kennedy on the reception," instead of, "Pass *intended* for Chris Kennedy."

Too many missed opportunities for me. I felt I gave my best effort and with a few catches might have impressed somebody. But that didn't happen. The only bright spot of my performance came when I gave a nice downfield block that helped spring a touchdown run. I took advantage of being in on a touchdown play, and sprinted to the end zone and started the mob celebration on the running back who scored. Fun stuff.

The spring game was tied into a couple of university-sponsored activities. Preceding the game is the annual Crazylegs 5-Mile Run. This popular race makes its way through the campus and finishes on the field. The race is named after former UW player and Los Angeles Ram Elroy "Crazylegs" Hirsch. Elroy was the UW athletic director for many years and was a Wisconsin football icon. He was a gregarious guy, always smiling, shaking hands, and taking pictures with fans. He always wore a silver crew-cut and a red blazer.

After the game there was the annual Butch's Bologna Bash. Butch is Butch Strickland, a big football booster who owned a meat-packing plant outside of Madison. Butch, who was in his 70s, had thrown the bash since the late 1960s. This was one of the biggest fundraisers of the year for the football team, though there's debate about how much money it actually brings in. Thousands attended the bash, which was held inside the fieldhouse adjacent to the stadium. You could always spot Butch drinking beer and eating sausage with his white-haired crew cut and red blazer—"the Elroy look"—and cheery demeanor. Wisconsin fans are famous for having a good time, and this party was a prime example. The only entertainment needed was good conversation, good beer, and good meat, and it was all served in generous helpings.

The players always looked forward to the bash. It signaled the end of spring practice and the beginning of summer. The cover charge, beer, and food were complimentary for football players. This was a great opportunity for our team to party together and with the other UW athletes. (Alas, Butch threw his final bash in April 2007.)

The coaches rubbed elbows at the event and let loose a bit too. Coach Norvell and I even had a nice conversation there, both of us a bit buzzed and friendly. He was sitting up on a stage with his feet dangling and said sincerely, "I wish you'd caught that out route." I saw a glimpse into the guy who cared about his players. He was coaching the other side but took note of my play. I was touched…and kicking myself inside for not having caught the ball. I wanted another shot so much. Another player came up to me and told me how important it was that I catch those balls. I never realized how much scrutiny one is under on the playing field. All eyes, from the stands to the sidelines, are on the open field and there's nowhere to hide.

CHAPTER TEN:
FIELD OF DREAMS

"In '92, we knocked on the door; it's time to kick it down!" This quote by Alvarez was on the cover of our 1993 summer-workout assignments. It captured the mindset of our staff and our team. We did not view ourselves as a sub-.500 team, and we felt we had to redeem ourselves for not fulfilling our potential the year before.

While most experts picked us in the lower-middle section of the Big Ten standings, one preseason publication picked us to finish fourth! (Personally, I was excited to see my name listed on a depth chart that appeared in one of the national college football magazines.) The reason for the increased recognition was that our team had a lot of returning players with experience.

Our own goals, discussed only among team members, were four in number: Win all of our home games. Win four Big Ten games. Win a Big Ten game on the road. Play in a New Year's Day bowl game.

Looking around at our team, you couldn't help but feel we could play with anybody. On offense, we were deep. Our starting offensive line and a few key reserves had all seen lots of playing time. These guys were the true lunch-pail gang. Do your work, don't brag about it, and grab a beer afterwards. They took pride in their trench work, which was getting plenty of praise from coaches and teammates. A veteran offensive line is the most solid foundation of any football team.

Our linemen were characters, lead by Joe Panos. Joe and his fellow linemen worked out together, practiced together, lived together, and went out together. They were a tight unit.

Cory Raymer was a great center and the kind of guy you'd want to hang out and drink beers with. He managed to be both easygoing and tough. He was once asked why the skill players who score all the touchdowns seem to have all the fun. He disagreed, saying the linemen had their fun by "beating the crap out of 'em after they score a touchdown."

Joe Rudolph was becoming a great guard. He was a very dry, funny guy and very intelligent. "That ain't competin'!" Using the coaches' mantra, Joe said it about anything unrelated to football, especially to someone who turned down a shot or didn't finish a beer. Rudolph and Panos competed to see who could make the most opponent knockdowns during games.

Mike Verstegen and Steve Stark were the other two starters on the offensive line, both a bit quieter than the others, but no less effective. Backup center Brian Patterson stepped in for Raymer for a few games and played well. Brian's play in the Iowa State game earned him the nickname "the Microwave" because he kept the Badgers hot. Brian was another funny guy who made a great drinking buddy and displayed the same combination of being both easygoing and tough.

Tarek Saleh was a freshman when Brian and I were seniors, and we knew him as a fun, loose guy and a great football player, arguably one of the best pass rushers Wisconsin's ever had. On the field at a recent team reunion, Tarek was standing next to Brian and me when his cell phone rang during the national anthem. Tarek quietly answered and got off the phone quickly. Brian and I turned to look at him. Tarek shrugged sheepishly. Brian just kept looking at him and prodded him, "Oh, you're just sooooo busy." Tarek defended himself. "What? It was Illich asking if he should leave the bar and come over here yet." Turns out Tarek wasn't being rude; he was just being a good teammate.

Alex Illich and I became friends in college after we'd been roommates at Holy Name. Alex, at 6' 5" and 290 pounds, always wore a scruffy beard and looked like he was 40 years old when he was a freshman. Alex was another behemoth lineman who would have contributed a lot more on game days but was plagued with injuries his whole career. Alex always cut quite a figure, wearing long black leather coats, gold jewelry, and designer sunglasses. He was an easy guy to talk to, and when Alex laughs, he throws back his head and belts it out.

Our running backs, Terrell Fletcher and Brent Moss, were both good enough to start at any other school in the Big Ten and they complemented each other well. Terrell was extremely quick and shifty, making it difficult for defenders to get a hold of him. Terrell always had a bounce in his step and a smile on his face. It was rare that anyone ever got a solid hit on him, and perhaps that's why he always looked so carefree. On a rare occasion when Terrell actually got hit hard in a game, Alvarez ran onto the field with the trainers to check him out. When Alvarez went onto the field because of an injury, you knew someone very important was down. While the trainers attended to him, Terrell caught his breath and said, "I'm OK, coach…how're the fans doin'?" Alvarez knew he'd be all right; when Terrell bounced up, the crowd roared.

Brent was a compactly built, hard runner who punished defenders. He was very explosive on contact and was always moving forward with the ball. I knew a guy who tried to tackle Brent Moss at the state all-star game and tore his shoulder apart. This was a big guy and a good player. He was like Mike Tyson carrying a football.

Brent had been highly recruited coming out of high school in Racine, Wisconsin. He had academic difficulty entering school and had to sit out a year under NCAA rule Proposition 48, losing a year of eligibility to get his grades up.

Joe Rudolph (63) helps Terrell Fletcher (41) celebrate a big play.

Despite his toughness, Brent was always joking around in the locker room. He'd shadow box you when you walked by and then playfully slap you on the arm. Sitting by his locker, with his head cocked slightly to the side and a mischievous grin, he reminded you of someone hanging out at a barbershop, shouting comments to anyone passing by. A guy wearing new all-white shoes would pass and Brent would yell,

"Hey, nurse? Come back here. Nurse?" The guy would tell him to shut up and Brent would laugh hysterically. "Go make your rounds, nurse!"

Mark Montgomery, the blocking fullback for the Terrell–Brent combo, was now entering his fourth straight year of getting significant playing time. Mark was one of the most muscle-ripped people I've ever seen in my life. He marched to a different drummer. He had no problem delivering impromptu songs in full voice during practice or working on his dance moves on the sideline. After catching a few balls in a row, he'd pronounce, "What's a dropped ball? I've never heard of a dropped ball!"

I've mentioned Mark's habits: He wore shorts throughout the year and drove around campus balancing his considerable bulk on a pink scooter. Fortunately, Mark's large size and craziness allowed him to do whatever he wanted without anyone saying much to him about it.

We were also stacked with two great players at the tight end position, Mike Roan and Matt Nyquist. Mike was the starter and one of the team's best all-around athletes. Mike had been an all-state basketball and football athlete in Iowa. He was the quintessential tight end: great hands, a tough blocker, smart, and agile for his size. Matt Nyquist was a former fullback who had been switched to tight end. Nicknamed "Nitro," Matt played on almost every special-teams unit, filled in nicely for Mike, and took the field when we went into a two-tight-end formation.

Five or six receivers played a lot, and they were led by J.C. Dawkins and Lee DeRamus. J.C. was a solid pass receiver who ran smart, precise routes. He was the only scholarship receiver from our freshman class and went to the same high school as Brent Moss in Racine.

Lee DeRamus was a big playmaker and was born to be a receiver. He was 6' 4", had a 38-inch vertical jump, ran the 40-yard dash in 4.4, and had big hands. There'd be plays in which you swore Bevell was just throwing the ball out of bounds, but Lee would somehow snatch it from mid-air.

Lee was an easygoing guy, constantly smiling and laughing. He seemed to enjoy his life as much as anyone I'd ever met. He was nicknamed "Famous DeRamus" (by whom, I don't know…or it may have come from Lee himself). But the name was just for fun. On the field and off, Lee wanted to have a good time and didn't take himself too seriously.

Michael London, a key reserve, was a high school teammate of Lee's. Michael and I had an acting class together, and he does great impersonations. He was also brave enough to portray Coach Alvarez in a skit performed at Holy Name. Michael hiked up his shorts exaggeratedly and strutted in the confident way Coach Alvarez did. I gave him a B for his imitation, and an A for the balls to do it in front of Coach Alvarez and the whole team.

Michael was one of the fastest and smallest guys on the team. One day, the team was together watching a film of a special-teams kickoff return by Michael. He was speeding down the field, bobbing and weaving, resembling a squirrel sprinting around on a freeway. Patrick Tompkins blurted out, "Man, that nigga's runnin' scared!" and everyone, including Michael, burst with laughter.

Our quarterback, Darrell Bevell, helmed our offense with precision. What he lacked in speed and size compared with other college quarterbacks, Darrell made up for with his intricate knowledge of the game and his great decision-making. He seemed to know where everybody on our team and the opposing team was going to be at every moment on the field. He didn't try to do too much, forcing throws and getting the team into trouble. He was patient, made his reads on the defense, and exploited them where they were vulnerable.

MIKE DEVRIES/CAPITAL TIMES

What quarterback Darrell Bevell lacked in size and speed, he more than made up for in brains.

Speaking of the defense, most every starter was an upperclassman and had been competitive in the Big Ten the last few seasons.

On the defensive line, we had Carlos Fowler, a big guy whose cheeks looked huge squished under his facemask. He was very intense on the field. A 350-mph talker. One of his roommates on the team would often walk around naked in the locker room and Carlos would grab a shoe and threaten, "Put that thing away, dammit!"

Even when he was only a sophomore on a losing team, Carlos was prophetic. "I'm not leaving here without roses, baby!" he proclaimed.

Coach Alvarez started to like what he saw in 1993.

MIKE DEVRIES/CAPITAL TIMES

At nose guard, Lamark Shackerford was the last player in the senior class to be given a scholarship by Wisconsin—a steal, as it turned out, when he was named to the all-Big Ten team. Lamark was a friendly, easy-going guy; it was hard to believe he was such a terror on the field. He had one of the biggest butts on the team, and he knew it. One day, he exited the shower, stood in front of the mirror, and asked all within range, "Look how big my ass is! Dang, that's a big ass, huh?" And no one disagreed.

Rounding out the defensive line was Mike Thompson, a Portage, Wisconsin, native. He had a great "arms raised" tackle celebration that made him look like a conquering gladiator whenever he made one of his many TFLs (tackles for loss). Mike held the school record for most TFLs for a long time. He always looked to me like he should have been riding a Harley to a Metallica concert. Mike was so tough he was rumored to have knocked a guy out in a street fight with a punch from just 10 inches away.

At outside linebacker, we had a steady rotation of Chris Hein, Chad Cascadden, and Chad Yocum, all Wisconsin natives. Hein and Cascadden had been walk-ons but their stellar play on special teams earned them each a scholarship. These two guys started as defensive backs and bulked themselves up enough to become outside linebackers. Yocum was from nearby DeForest. His personality matched his play—straightforward and tough. He struggled with back pain throughout much of his career and had he not, he probably would have been one of the top outside linebackers ever to play at Wisconsin.

At inside linebacker, we had two New Yorkers, Yusef Burgess and Eric Unverzagt. It was said Yusef loved football so much, he even loved practice. One day he explained that a linebacker needs to be like an assassin. Once you were in this mindset, it was easy; you just marked your man and took him out.

Eric Unverzagt, a.k.a. Unvy, always kept the hair on his head and the hair on his face closely trimmed at exactly the same length. He and defensive lineman Jason Maniecki had the thickest accents on the team. Maniecki's family had emigrated from Poland when he was a boy, and Unvy was from Long Island.

After a particularly tough practice at Holy Name, Unvy made the following speech to the reserves and underclassmen: "Hey, it may be tough for y'all to make it trough dis, but you'll make it. We need you. I mean, we [the starters] really need y'all to jump in on da drills...cuz we need da rest." Though no Tony Robbins, Unvy was a sweet guy under his five o'clock shadow.

At the cornerback positions, we had Kenny Gales and Jeff Messenger, two effective, underrated players who did their jobs well and never celebrated themselves. Gales was a junior college transfer who nicely filled a void for the team. He was small and quick, and would usually cover the opponent's fastest receiver.

Jeff Messenger, while a bit undersized, was also very effective. He had a great instinct for intercepting the ball. Though he was sometimes dismissed as being too slow, he was actually deceptively quick. He was one of the best special-teams cover guys Wisconsin has ever had.

I once tried to cover him in practice during a special-teams drill. He was covering the punt and I was assigned to hold him up at the line of scrimmage. My job was to not let him get an inside release on me, so I made it a point to position myself firmly to the inside, thereby forcing him toward the sideline. He managed to make about 10 moves in about a second after the ball was snapped, and before I knew it he was inside of me, leaving me in the dust. I didn't even lay a finger on him, and I was only a foot away.

Our safeties were both fifth-year seniors and the undisputed leaders of the defense, free safety Scott Nelson and strong safety Reggie Holt. Though Scott was white and from nearby Sun Prairie and Reggie was black and from Miami, Florida, these two shared many traits. They were both Don Morton recruits who Coach Alvarez and his staff loved. They were both hard-working guys who spoke more with their shoulder pads than with their mouths. They were both smart, disciplined, and tough on and off the field. They were both incredibly effective and underrated, and didn't care a bit. They were true team leaders.

Scott Nelson was sort of like Superman. He had huge calves and he wore capes. Well, not capes. He did wear glasses and looked like he could be a banker, which apparently he was for a while after graduation. His nice-guy demeanor off the field belied the fact that once he put on the helmet and the uniform, he was incredibly intense. He would throw his body around the field with abandon, punishing the opposition and saving the defense from giving up points. Like Lamark Shackerford, he was the last guy offered a scholarship from his class and also was named all-Big Ten.

Reggie Holt also seemed like a super hero with an alter ego. Off the field, Reggie was a quiet, humble, and sweet guy. He joked around easily and never raised his voice to anyone. But on the field, Reggie made some of the most ferocious hits I've ever seen or *heard*. He had an ability to just pop players on contact. Despite being a bit undersized, he didn't lose a one-on-one battle that I can recall, even when he was up against guys who outweighed him by 40 pounds.

On either the offense or the defense, you'd be hard-pressed to find a weak link or a bona fide star. If our starters had anything in common, it's that they were tough, humble, experienced, and hungry for victory. Mentally, they were disciplined, focused, and smart. Solid enough players on whom to build a winning foundation.

"SHOW 'EM WHAT YOU FUCKIN' GOT"

We started the 1993 season—our quest for respect—with our goals set. We opened the season strong, winning our first three games against non-conference opponents, Nevada, SMU, and Iowa State.

Nevada surprised us, thinking well enough of themselves to talk trash to us on our own field. Their defensive coordinator said he was glad that he didn't have to face a good passing team in the beginning of the season. Our offense heard him, and Darrell Bevell responded by throwing a school-record five touchdown passes against them—two to Dawkins, and one each to DeRamus, Roan, and Nyquist.

Our defense did their own butt-kicking by intercepting the Nevada offense four times in the first half and holding them to six rushing yards the entire second half. Jeff Messenger was voted Big Ten player of the week for his 10 tackles and two interceptions in the game.

This game helped solidify my own quest for respect; I finally got what I'd been aching for my whole career. With a little over a minute left in the game and secure in our two-touchdown lead, Coach Norvell turned and looked at me, looked back at the field, and pointed right at my chest. I'd locked eyes with him many times before, only to have him turn away or point to another player. But this time there was no mistaking it was for me. Before he could reconsider, I was immediately by his side as he grabbed my jersey, pulled me toward the coaches, and some coach—I don't remember who—told me the play. Simultaneously, a teammate was smacking me on the butt and yelling into my ear hole, "Show 'em what you fuckin' got, Kennedy. You waited too long for this, baby." I sprinted onto the field, bursting through the glass ceiling of the sideline, toward the huddle repeating over and over something, like Pro right, 24 sweep, Pro right, 24 sweep, Pro right 24 sweep.

I reached quarterback Darrell Bevell and regurgitated the play, over-enunciating to make sure I communicated it correctly. I found my spot in the huddle—in the back row, on the end to the left. He repeated the play to the team, and I sprinted out to my place on the right side, the strong side of the formation. Since there was a tight end on my side, I had to make sure I was lined up properly, two yards off the line of scrimmage. I looked over to the side judge and pointed at him. He knew I was referring to my alignment and he nodded yes.

I read the coverage. The defensive back in front of me was a bit smaller than I was. He was playing about eight yards off the ball, a cover 3, I told myself. Pro right, 24 sweep was a running play, and my task was to keep the defensive back from getting to our running back. Since the game was winding down and we were running out the clock, I assumed he'd know to run toward the carrier as soon as the ball was snapped. My strategy was to run right at him in an attempt to make him think I just might be running a pass route anyway.

As the ball snapped, I barreled right straight at him. To my surprise, he fell for my trick and started to defend me as if I were running a pass route. Once he saw me start to slow to block him, he realized he was being duped and started sprinting toward the middle of the field toward the ball carrier. I took this opportunity to throw a cut block on him. A cut block is when a player makes it look as if he's going to engage another player up high, by his chest, but at the last moment throws himself at the opponent's lower body. This is not a popular move among defensive players— if they don't spot it, they get their legs taken out from underneath them. The block can also damage knees if they don't defend themselves properly.

Anyway, I threw the block and because he wasn't running all that hard toward the ball carrier, he was able to jump back and keep me away from his legs. This was fine by me as it just put him further away from the play and ensured that if anyone tackled the ball carrier, it wasn't going to be him.

We huddled up lazily for the next play, taking our time to run out the game clock. By the time the referee started the play clock we didn't even have to line up to snap the ball and the game was over.

Though it wasn't exactly crunch time, I was still thankful to be on the field at all. I was struck by how ordinary it all felt. I just executed what I'd been taught. And it all went by amazingly fast; there wasn't much time for a thought to complete itself before I was ensconced in the hurried pace of the game. As an added bonus, it was fun to be on the field with the winning team at the end of the game—it created the illusion I'd been in there the whole time, and the television cameras would capture me celebrating with my teammates.

Exiting the stadium was almost as fun as entering it. Running up through the tunnel right in front of the student section made me feel like a hero. Fans hanging over the sides with their arms out, reaching out to touch you, pounding your shoulder pads as you trotted by, getting excited when you high-fived them. Our team started the custom that after a win, we would take our helmets off and hold them high in front of the student section as we left the field. This was our sign of respect and appreciation for them, and it was greeted with a loud roar of approval.

Right outside the McClain building entrance, a small gathering of families, girlfriends, friends, and fans were waiting for the players. After my first time in a game, I couldn't wait to see my parents' expectant faces as I filed out of the door. My mom had mentioned to my girlfriend before I arrived, "You know he got into the game today." My mom and dad showed pride and joy, but also relief. The 300-pound gorilla wasn't only off my back, but theirs as well. Too many times I'd exited that door happy with the win but also tinged with a bit of sadness because I didn't get to contribute to the game on the field. After I'd played, it was a special moment to share with them—they'd been with me along the whole journey and could appreciate the significance of the moment. It was almost like it didn't happen unless they witnessed it. The fans and NFL scouts may not have taken notice of my performance, but the people I cared about did.

SIX AND OH MY!

We beat Nevada 35 to 17 and I helped contribute to our seventh home win in the last eight games. It was nice to dominate a bowl team at home. The game attendance was over 70,000 and would be the last game of the season at Camp Randall that didn't sell out.

The next week, we headed down to Dallas in the September heat to play the Mustangs of Southern Methodist University. As part of our preseason goal list, we had a lone mission in the Lone Star State—win a game on the road for the first time since 1985.

I was struck by how small the SMU's Ownby Stadium was. It looked like a glorified high school field, and we played as if we were still in high school. Our play on both sides of the ball resembled the deposits left on the field by the horse that was SMU's mascot. We went into the locker room down, 13-0, at the half. We were in danger of losing yet another road game if we didn't rear up and kick these Mustangs back in the second half.

We rallied and came out of intermission hotter than the evening's 94-degree air. Our offense put up 24 points behind the hard running of Brent Moss and a Bevell–Dawkins touchdown pass. Our defense allowed only three more points and got two key interceptions from Yusef Burgess and Scott Nelson.

Our road win proved there was a new sheriff in this Texas town. J.C. Dawkins put it best, "This is the '93 team, and we didn't have a road record yet." Giddy-up.

We kept the momentum going and made another check on our goal sheet by beating Iowa State and closing our non-conference season undefeated. We came into the game ranked 23rd in the Associated Press poll. Our offensive line dominated the game and spun the Iowa State defense, appropriately, like cyclones. Our defense continued to be stingy and tough. We easily won, 28-7, in front of the first home game sellout crowd in many years, with more than 78,000 fans in attendance.

We then marched through our first three Big Ten games with comfortable wins, on the road at Indiana and Purdue, and at home against Northwestern, to put our record at 6-0.

At Indiana's rain-soaked, half-empty stadium, Brent Moss kept his feet and ran for a career-best 198 yards for an offense that amassed 477 total yards against the Big Ten's top-ranked defense at the time. Our defense held Indiana to only 101 yards rushing and forced them to punt nine times. The win put us at 4-0 in the conference, the best start for a UW team since 1978.

While we didn't spend a lot of time focusing on it, revenge was in the back of everyone's minds as we hosted Northwestern for our homecoming game. After all, we'd had almost a year to think about how the Wildcats had put a nightmarish end to our bowl dreams the previous season.

Well, our demons were unleashed; we terrorized Northwestern, 53-14. Once again, our offensive line owned their opponents as we ran for seven touchdowns, Moss and Fletcher both picking up more than 100 yards. Bevell was nearly perfect, completing 17 of 18 passes for the day.

On defense, Mike Thompson remembered Lenny Williams, Northwestern's quarterback, talking a lot of smack the previous year. Mike said he didn't hear anything from him on this day...and he should know, because he sacked Williams five times himself.

In this blowout, many reserves got into the game, including linebacker Dan Schneck, who made a key tackle on a goal-line stand. Because of this, guys on the team started calling him Rudy, after the underdog movie character who made a tackle for Notre Dame at home.

I did not get in until the game's very last play. In a post-game interview, Northwestern coach Gary Barnett complained that Alvarez ran up the score: "I feel sorry for Wisconsin's second-string players because they didn't get to play very much." Seeing as how we were just running out the clock for most of the second half, I didn't miss much action.

Despite what I viewed as our team's dominance, there were still those who didn't seem to be paying much attention. Heading into our road game against Purdue, our opponents and the media provided plenty of inflammatory material for our locker-room bulletin board. Purdue receiver Jermaine Ross said, "I think we're a better team than they are, but they're getting more attention from the media right now." The week of the Purdue game, a sportswriter for an Indiana newspaper wrote, "Wisconsin a top 25 team? Don't be fooled. The Badger program is not as advanced as it may appear, and the Boilers will prove it with a rare national TV win."

Our offense jumped on and through Purdue, taking a 35-0 lead into the third quarter. Our defense lapsed and allowed them to score 28 points in the second half before our offense got one more TD to put the final score at 42-28, closer than it should've been. Bevell equaled his Nevada game output by throwing five touchdown passes, and Brent Moss ran for his fifth straight 100-yard game. For the first time in my four seasons, the Wisconsin offense was considered stronger than the defense.

Our record now stood at 6-0 for the first time in school history since 1912. Upon hearing this, Cory Raymer said, "Eighty-one years? Jesus Christ ...1912? OK ... my grandfather played on that team, I think." Actually, Cory me boy, it probably would've had to have been your grandfather's grandfather.

We already had more wins in a season than any UW team since 1984, had a lock on a winning season, and had already qualified for a bowl game. We were ranked 12th by the CNN coaches' poll and 15th by the AP. We were clearly showing ourselves to be a Badgers team the likes of which hadn't been seen around Madison for a while. Alvarez said, "Right now we're setting new standards. Every week we go out, we set new records. Hopefully, we'll continue to do that but they're not real hard to break."

As someone who'd been around since 1990 and a fan since I was a young boy, it was so much fun to watch our team, my teammates, have so much success. To see our skill players running away from and through people for a touchdown. To see our linemen pushing opponents all around the field. To see our defense sacking a quarterback or picking him off. To see the opponents hanging their heads after a game while WE celebrated the win.

It was fun to see the tables turned and to be on the winning side of things…to watch from the sunny side of life. It was a nice feeling to walk out onto the turf and truly believe you were on the better team in every game. It was all so special to witness this turnaround and be a part of it. We'd been working so hard to get to this point and now it was paying off. We deserved it, but we also felt fortunate. How could we not, after witnessing all the senior classes before us work so hard and not achieve the success they wanted? I think we had a cautious optimism. Like, hey, we're good but let's not get cocky and blow this, OK?

For the first time in my four years, we were a complete team: our offense was good, our defense was good, and our special teams were good. Alvarez emphasized this.

SPECIAL TEAMS

Coach Alvarez always talked about the three areas of any football game, the offense, the defense, and the special teams. He felt if you could win two of the three, you would win the game. He considered the special teams as important as the offense and defense. To prove his point, Alvarez had some starters on the special teams, which are normally made up of reserves and second-string players. He also scheduled significant practice time for special-teams work.

Coach Alvarez always spoke about the pendulum of momentum of any game, saying it will swing back and forth from team to team. Coach said this to illustrate that players shouldn't "flinch" when the pendulum swings to the other team, but also to show how you can get the pendulum to swing back your way. There are many times when a special-teams play can have a huge impact on the momentum and outcome of a game: a blocked punt, a botched snap, a field goal.

Special teams are where the biggest collisions and emotions of the game can happen as well. They are ideal for back-up linebackers, tight ends, and fullbacks, along with undersized, mobile linemen, bigger defensive backs, and tough, surehanded receivers. The keys to being a good special-teams player are mobility, toughness, and throwing your body around the field with reckless abandon.

I recall a special-teams play I was in on. I was on the right side of a kickoff return team. My job was to create an open pathway for one of the two kickoff returners behind me. Upon kickoff, I had to retreat about 10 yards and partner with another upback. Once the ball was caught, we were to head upfield and block or kick out our assigned men. My target was the kickoff team's outermost player, closest to the sideline, usually called "the killer." The killer, in this instance, was sprinting down the field in quite a hurry, trying to get to the ball carrier as soon as possible. Since I was taking a "bananalike" route to him, I stood a good chance to kick him out of the running lane, because he likely wouldn't see me coming in from the side. I was sprinting at him, heart and breath pounding as I envisioned knocking him into the stands. I briefly imagined my demolition of him on ESPN's highlight reel of the day's "greatest hits."

Just as I was about to launch him into the cheap seats, he turned his head and shoulders to engage me. Damn. So much for catching him off guard. We both lowered our shoulders—in football, the lower man wins—and exploded full-speed into each other. The contact caused us both to leave our feet and end up face first on the ground next to each other. Before I could register what had happened, I noticed our return man's legs just near my head, as did the killer.

Realizing I was still responsible for the killer, I attempted to push myself up with my left arm and push him off-balance with my right arm as he tried to get up. We both went down again and now I could see our returner had made it past me a few steps.

I attempted to get up to my feet to continue running down the field to block for him but was pushed facemask-first into the ground. I furiously clawed and tried to pull myself up before being slammed into the turf again. With all the colliding and clamoring for position going on above me, it was as if someone was just standing there waiting until I almost got to my feet and then knocked me back down. Sort of like how a cat will give its prey a little room to escape before pouncing back on it.

As legs and arms and feet crashed like a whirlpool around my body, I finally got to my feet as the whistle blew. I saw that our ball carrier had made it out to the mid-field line. A nice return. And like that, the play was over. Though it seemed time stood still during my attack on the killer, and then as if it took me an eternity to get to my feet, the whole play lasted less than 10 seconds.

I sprinted to the sideline while our offense took the field, and I got a few supportive smacks on the helmet from some teammates. My coach approached me and told me I had to keep my feet out there. He said I did no good lying on the ground. I nodded my head.

I was disappointed to be replaced on the next kickoff. I wished I had another chance to get the hang of it, to get accustomed to the pace of it. But I didn't. I also realized that every play is important and if someone on my team could keep his feet in that scenario, he was more deserving of the spot than I was.

I wanted to be on the field in any way possible, and since it didn't seem likely to happen at receiver any time soon I looked to the special teams. A fellow walk-on,

Dave Anderson, was able to find a spot on the traveling squad as the long-snapper on the team. His main task was to get the ball to the punter. Dave didn't play any downs outside of the punts, but he made the traveling squads, lettered, and most importantly, got to play in games.

I thought my next best shot at getting some playing time was to be a holder for the team's placekicker. The main attribute a holder must possess is good, quick hands, and poise. I was confident I had the former and with practice, I'd gain the latter.

I approached the special-teams coach, Paul Winters, and told him of my desire. He welcomed me to stay after practice and take reps with the third-string kicker, Matt Krueger. Matt was a tall, lanky redhead who was quiet and dedicated. Matt and I worked together as a tandem.

I found holding to be more difficult than I expected it to be. I guess being a holder falls into that category of things that look easy but in actuality are not: playing guitar, ice skating, and golf. The ball is snapped to you at various angles by a backup center (no pun intended), and because you're facing sideways in a crouched position, your range of motion is limited, so snagging the ball can be quite challenging.

Ideally, a backup quarterback is the holder, in case there's a bad or bobbled snap, or a fake-kick play that calls for a pass into the end zone. My throwing abilities were passable (pun intended) but not to the level of our backup quarterbacks who were inserted before me in any serious scrimmage. Even though I'd stayed after practice for half the season to enhance my skills, I soon realized it wasn't worth the extra time.

The punter and the field goal kicker seem to have the best jobs on the special teams. They don't practice as long and almost never get hit. But they are also the positions that get the most focus and the most pressure. Our punter and my good friend, Sam Veit, was cool as a cucumber in almost any stressful situation, and he encountered many of those his freshman year. Sam was a walk-on who ended up starting in his first year and quickly was put on scholarship for the next season. Sam kept his calm as he scooped up many of long-snapper Eric Unverzagt's hikes that skidded and bounced toward him off the turf.

In Unverzagt's defense, he was a linebacker by trade and only stepped into the long-snapper position because no one else could do it any better. Sam focused on getting the ball in his hands and off his foot without even acknowledging the fact that large, fast men were clawing and sprinting maniacally toward him and the ball. Sam's concentration and great hands made him our team's ideal punter.

Off the field, Sam was very dry, only cracking his stoic face to laugh at a joke he made that someone didn't get. I don't think I ever heard him raise his voice. Sam was a bit different from many players on the team, an outsider, in keeping with the kicker's role on most any team. He didn't drink, he studied hard, and he had a long-time serious girlfriend, Amy, who he went on to marry and have two girls with.

Our kickers were interesting characters. My first two seasons, the job was held by Rich Thompson, an Oklahoman who loved to joke around. He was well-liked by his teammates and was a fairly good kicker. Succeeding him were two kickers who shared the position depending on who was kicking better.

John Hall, a freewheeling wild-child from Florida, was very social. A scholarship kicker with a very strong leg, John was fairly big, 6' 2" and around 200 pounds. John worked out a lot and would roll up his sleeves like a lineman to show off his arms. John had a great leg, if not great aim, to start out his career. He was sort of like the golfer John Daly, a big hitter, but prone to inconsistency. I liked John a lot and thought he brought a good energy to the team. John went on to have a long NFL career (10 years with the New York Jets and Washington Redskins) after his time at Wisconsin. My mom and step-dad often sat next to his parents in the players' ticket section for home games, and they got along quite well. My mom got a kick out of how the Floridians considered 50-degree temps to be cold weather.

His first year, Coach always used John on long field-goal attempts and kickoffs, but on shorter field goals he would sometimes use walk-on kicker Rick Schnetzky. Rick was a walk-on from the Milwaukee area who looked like the fraternity guy he was. He was nearly unflappable, kicking extra points and some field goals.

WATERLOO, MINNESOTA

I think it's important to note that while our team had a tremendous amount of confidence in ourselves, we didn't take any opponent lightly and treated every game as if it were the season. Our focus was razor sharp and narrowed to our opponent of the week. This group of upperclassmen had seen too many years of "almosts" and "coulda beens" to take anything for granted. This team came to play every Saturday.

We headed into the Minnesota game with the same intensity, if not more, than we'd had in every game all year. Some might speculate that we disregarded them, but it's just not true. We'd beaten them handily, 34-6, the previous season and retained Paul Bunyan's Axe, but we knew that the Minnesota game was always up for grabs. We headed to the Metrodome in Minneapolis with that Axe, fully intent on bringing it back to Madison with us.

The Metrodome is one of the worst facilities in the Big Ten. It has the charming lighting of an office building, the stagnant air of a litter box, and a field with the consistency of one. The locker rooms felt like a sauna—in fact, the entire stadium did. The dome had its second largest attendance in history for this game, half of it because of the Badgers fans. The heat caused lethargy among our team. This was in stark contrast to the Gophers' energy, heightened because it was their biggest game of the year. All these things combined to thrust us into a bizarre world. Our normally potent, precise offense committed five turnovers, including an uncharacteristic four interceptions thrown by quarterback Darrell Bevell. We fell into a 21-0 hole but managed to get back to our old ways in the second half.

Our offense came out and put up 223 yards in the third quarter, while Brent Moss scored two touchdown runs to bring the score to 21-14. But the interception wand waved over Bevell's arm once again.

Despite our poor play, we still had a few shots to win it at the end. With 1:14 to play, we advanced the ball to the Minnesota 32-yard line. But we threw four incomplete passes, and Minnesota came away with a 28-21 upset. It was so frustrating to lose to a team we were better than but just as frustrating not playing up to our ability. We played in a daze and watched in that same daze as the Gophers grabbed the Axe and paraded it around their stadium as we had done the previous two years.

There were no longer any thoughts of an undefeated season. The team was shocked and upset. We'd hoped to go into the game against the 12th-ranked Michigan Wolverines with a 7-0 record, riding high on a mountain of momentum. Now, we were going to have to traverse back up one step at a time. Having slid from 15th to 21st in the AP poll, we now shared one loss with four other Big Ten teams trailing Ohio State on top of the conference.

What a difference a week can make in the college football world. Practice the next week was going to be rough, but the team's attitude was best captured by Panos. "We hit a stumbling block. Now we know how bad it hurts to lose, and we're not going to let it happen again."

SAY YES TO BEATING MICHIGAN

Coming off our upset loss to Minnesota in a game riddled with mistakes, the Michigan game loomed large as we sought to recapture the momentum we'd worked so hard to build. This would be the week we'd find out whether we were contenders or pretenders. Many prognosticators took our loss at Minnesota as an indication that we weren't as good as we thought we were. Some fans were even murmuring, "Here we go again" and were expecting us to begin an inevitable decline for the rest of the season. This cynicism was the natural outcome of the football program's many years of mediocrity.

Our team was not of this mindset. We knew we weren't like the teams of the past, and we were going to prove that. We wanted a chance to redeem ourselves, and what better way to do that than by beating the reigning Big Ten champions, the Michigan Wolverines? They were coming to play us in Camp Randall Stadium, where we had a five-game home winning streak. Coach Alvarez wanted us to establish Camp Randall as a place no opponent wanted to step foot in, and beating Michigan on our turf would send that message very clearly.

We had a tough, focused week of practice. Especially Darrell Bevell, who came under a lot of criticism for throwing five interceptions against the Gophers—a school record. No one was feeling sorry for himself, and everyone, from the bottom of the depth chart to the top, was doing his best to prepare to beat highly ranked Michigan. Even though our opponents boasted such future NFL players as Tyrone Wheatley, Amani Toomer, Derrick Alexander, and Ty Law, by Friday's practice we felt confident we had the game plan and the confidence to beat Michigan.

No doubt, this was the biggest game of any of our careers and the biggest of Barry Alvarez's tenure. During pregame warm-up drills, the stadium, usually only about a quarter full, was already more than half full. The TV networks were positioning their cameras for the game. I'm sure many media personnel and even some fans were expecting a Michigan win. Even the Michigan players seemed to think so as they circled the W at midfield and yelled taunts at us like, "We're Michigan! We're Michigan, baby!" I couldn't believe they would be so brazen and I looked around at my teammates to see their reaction. No one even turned their heads to acknowledge them. There was a quiet intensity, and it seemed like most of the players were mentally filing the insults away for later repayment.

Michigan's arrogance and our intensity were not lost on the coaches. In the locker room before we took the field, there was an eerie quiet. The kind of quiet you wouldn't even think was possible among 100 intense men.

Coach Alvarez addressed the team, each of us down on a knee in the center of the locker room. I'd never seen Coach Alvarez and the other coaches so concentrated and so anxious.

Alvarez stood in front of us and said, "This is it men. I'm heated up. They're out there strutting around like it's their fuckin' field!" Murmurs from the coaches and players started to swirl as Alvarez continued, "Last I checked, this was OUR house!"

Voices of agreement arose from the players, and Alvarez went on: "And what do you do to someone who comes into your house?" Grumbling began to build. Alvarez yelled, "You kick their ass!" Supportive yells flew through the air as a storm of tempers quickly brewed. Alvarez said, "They think they can roll out those…ugly fuckin' helmets and we'll just lie down."

Alvarez adopted a mocking tone, "Because they're Michigan. They got *tradition*. Well, so what? *Tradition* doesn't win football games. *Tradition* doesn't get down in a stance and play!" A chorus of "That's right, uh-huh, fuck yeah" arose.

Alvarez grew as impassioned as any of us had ever seen him, "*Tradition* doesn't win football games! Guys with *heart* win football games!" Alvarez's voice cracked with emotion on the word "heart."

The intensity in the room was now the groundswell of a storm. Players pounded shoulder pads. Fists clenched harder onto the facemasks they were holding and drove the helmets against the floor, creating a thunderous sound. Coach

McCarney wiped tears from his eyes as he stood behind Alvarez, listening and watching our reaction. There was no question on the part of anyone in that locker room that this game was like no other we'd ever been apart of. This was something special. Wisconsin hadn't beaten Michigan since 1981, when most of us players were learning to tie our shoes.

Today, we had a chance to solidify a new era of Wisconsin football, just as we'd wanted to do the first day we put on our jerseys. Tradition is just a construct of the past. Today, tradition was put in proper perspective.

Alvarez finished his speech: "Well, they got something comin'! This is OUR house; this is OUR game to win! Now, let's go out there and show them and the nation what Wisconsin smash-mouth football is all about!" Alvarez punched a fist in the air and the players all jumped up and smashed into a huge huddle. One of the captains yelled, "Win on three!" "One, Two, Three! Win!" the team responded.

Joe "The Big Greek" Panos, in a crowd of happy Badgers.

As we made our way up the tunnel toward the stadium, the players were screaming, smacking shoulder pads and bouncing up and down. The team was so torqued it wouldn't have surprised me if we'd just busted right through the stadium

177

walls to take the field. I felt sorry for Michigan. I really did. I was a scout-team player and I would have sworn to God I could beat up on the Michigan all-Americans that day.

As we snaked our way through the tunnel onto the field, we each hit the sign above the door, often mocked by outsiders, that read, "The road to the Rose Bowl begins here." Now was our time to make that sign prophetic instead of pathetic. As we marched in the corridors of the stadium, the fans' screams of support were almost deafening as they echoed in through the ear holes of our helmets. As is customary, we gathered just inside the end zone entrance tunnel. The red fire truck carrying the Wisconsin cheerleaders roared out of the tunnel in front of us, as the marching band played "On Wisconsin." That was our cue, and we took the field like buckshot out of a rifle. The sold-out crowd gave us a raucous greeting.

As I looked across the field at Michigan's players and our own players, I was struck at how beatable Michigan looked. They were guys just like us, but with different-colored uniforms. To be honest, in previous years, Michigan held a noticeable edge on our team. They looked, and for the most part were, bigger, faster, and stronger. But not this year. We looked just as formidable, if not more so, because of our determination.

We got the ball first and moved it on Michigan all the way to their seven-yard line, before getting stopped and having to settle for a field goal. Our defense held them scoreless through the first quarter.

In the second quarter, our offense put together another nice drive deep into Michigan territory but again had to settle for a field goal. The score stood at Wisconsin 6, Michigan 0.

Right before the half, Michigan drove to the Wisconsin seven-yard line but this time our defense held them out of the end zone, and they, too, settled for a field goal.

With only two minutes left in the half, our offense put together an impressive drive, with Bevell hitting DeRamus and Dawkins on four straight passes, putting us deep into Michigan territory. Then Terrell Fletcher made a great zig-zagging run through Michigan's defense and found the end zone with less than a minute left. The score at halftime: Wisconsin 13, Michigan 3.

Our locker room at halftime was fired up but not overly so. We broke off into our position meetings in separate areas of the locker room. We discussed all the plays that were going well and what plays we thought would work in the second half. We knew there was still a second half to be played and we knew we had to play a full four quarters to beat Michigan. We also knew we could do it. Alvarez reminded us that we needed to keep the pressure on them. "You're the better team, now go out there and win this game because it's yours!"

The second half was more physical than the first as we fought to hold our lead and Michigan fought to take it from us. Yusef Burgess caused his fifth fumble of the season by smacking Michigan running back Ricky Powers and Kenny Gales recovered, stopping a long drive. On a subsequent drive, Michigan converted a fourth-and-nine pass and then scored with two minutes left in the third quarter, bringing the score to Wisconsin 13 and Michigan 10.

Our offense couldn't get back into Michigan territory, and so now it was the defense's turn to win it for us. Early in the fourth quarter, Michigan was driving when UW linebacker Chris Hein pressured Michigan QB Todd Collins to throw the ball to avoid being sacked. The ball landed in the outstretched hands of Jeff Messenger, who pulled in his fifth interception of the season.

With one last attempt to score before time ran out, Michigan's offense made their way into Wisconsin territory, but our defense stopped them on three straight plays. Michigan went for it on the fourth down. Collins completed a pass to Walter Smith who was gang-tackled so ferociously that he couldn't make it the one yard he needed to get the first down. UW's offense got the ball back and ran out the rest of the clock. The game was over and Wisconsin won, 13-10, defeating Michigan for the first time in more than 10 years. Our win was considered an upset by all the odds-makers and virtually everyone in the entire nation—except for us.

As the final whistle blew, our team and our fans were ecstatic. We players were jumping around the sidelines, hopping on each other's shoulders, and waving towels at the crowd. Before we even made it across the field, there were already fans hanging on the goal posts.

I was one of the first players to make my way off the field, through the tunnel located under the student section. Normally, after a game I could run through the tunnel with my arms spread wide, high-fiving the fans hanging over the railing. But after this game, I had to turn my shoulders just to get through the mass of humanity crowding the field and the tunnel.

The players in the locker room were celebrating with dances, hugs, and screams of joy. After about 10 minutes or so, a strange energy seeped through the air. Some of the later-arriving players entered the locker room looking scared and shaken up. It was a strange juxtaposition indeed.

Some were crying but not the tears of joy one would expect. I remember Joe Panos, in particular, looked distraught. The jubilation was bridled and now the noise in the room waned to inquisitive whispers.

Word spread in the locker room that the railings in the student section had collapsed under the weight of the fans rushing to get onto the field. The stadium announcer was heard asking for the field to be cleared so more medics could attend to the injured. Players said there were ambulances all over the field. Many people had been trampled in the fracas, and they were seriously hurt.

The room was already silent when someone reported that two students were dead. Shock filled the locker room. It was like a bad game of operator, the stories slightly changing after each person relayed it to the next. I felt guilty for getting so excited and for possibly stirring the crowd up too much.

I now feared for my sister, Katie, who I knew had tickets in the student section. We heard that it was mostly females who'd been injured. Teammate John Rhymes said he saw a girl we both knew being put on a stretcher and getting put into an ambulance. I was devastated. I didn't know what to do but try to run back outside to the field and check things out. I was still half-dressed in my uniform as I ran to the roped-off area outside the tunnel to check on Katie. I argued that I was on the team and wanted to help. The security personnel said that the best thing to do was to stay out of the area and let the paramedics do their job. I asked whether it was true that people had died, and they said they'd not been told that.

I went back to the morose locker room and quickly got dressed. Several players still in uniform were being consoled by other players. The coaches were not around to address the team post-game as usual. The atmosphere resonated bewilderment and chaos.

My parents met me outside the locker room as they usually did. None of us had heard from Katie. They said that the announcer was saying that there were people who weren't breathing but they hadn't heard of any deaths. My mom decided to try to call Katie's dorm room from a pay phone outside the locker room and thankfully my sister answered. Turns out, Katie had left the game early because she'd felt sick.

Katie was a freshman on the UW women's basketball team and was often exhausted by the hectic schedule and the early morning practices. Incidentally, Katie and I both earned a varsity letter at the University of Wisconsin in the same year, a rare brother-and-sister accomplishment that has only been equaled a few times in the history of UW athletics.

Since the spotlight had been on the game because of the high-powered matchup, the disaster that occurred afterwards got even more publicity. You couldn't find a station that didn't have some sort of report on the game and footage of players pulling students, pinned against the railings by the surging crowd behind them, onto the field. One repeated image was of Joe Panos lifting a limp female student out of the crowd, over his shoulders, and laying her down in a safe area so the paramedics could easily get to her. Other players could be seen yelling to the clueless fans toward the back to stop rushing the field and to step back.

After all was said and done, Joe Panos and several other players were singled out in the press as heroes for jumping in and helping these students, possibly saving lives.

One player, a fellow walk-on receiver, Mike Brin, gave a girl mouth-to-mouth resuscitation. The next week he was featured on ABC's news as its hero of the week. Upon hearing this, some of us players hassled Brin for copping a feel. Nothing like getting national acclaim and still getting crap from your teammates to keep you humble.

Thankfully, the reports of students dying turned out to be false, but seven girls did have extended stays in the hospital to treat their injuries. I knew one of the girls who was hospitalized. I wrote her a letter thanking her for her support and telling her how much the team cared about her well-being. Some fans who had been in the student section reported the surging was so strong that they traveled down 20 some rows without their feet touching the ground. Many of the students toward the back had no idea that students in the front were being pinned against the barriers. Some people blamed security for not just opening the gates to the field and allowing the rush of fans onto the field as it became congested.

The Sunday following the game, many of the players went into the stadium to check out the damage. The student section area looked like a war zone. Whole chunks of concrete were torn out of the seats. Parts of the steel railings, with pieces of concrete still attached, were lying on the ground. Orange, netted-plastic temporary fencing was substituted where the railings used to be. There was some question whether we'd be able to have the game in Camp Randall the following Saturday against the third-ranked team in the nation, Ohio State.

Our big win over Michigan led to near-disaster and left Camp Randall a mess.

Needless to say, the coaching staff was very concerned about the players' state of mind following the emotional roller coaster the team had gone through over the weekend. It was almost unprecedented that a team could have one of the biggest wins in school history then have such a dramatic reversal of events immediately following.

As a player, I should have been feeling elation, pride, and optimism about the victory and the upcoming game against Ohio State. I had those feelings but also a deeper sense of how unimportant football was if people could actually lose their lives over a game. As momentous as the game was for us, it certainly paled in comparison with students' lives.

At the Sunday meeting, Coach Alvarez assured us the game would be played at home and that the student section would be fixed in time for the game. He congratulated us on the win and said that everything would be back to normal this week. The coaches didn't want us to be unfocused for the big Ohio State game coming up and did their best to convey that we didn't want to lose our massive edge and momentum gained in the Michigan win.

At Monday's practice, Coach Alvarez introduced a group of counselors and trauma specialists who would be available all week if any of us wanted to talk about what some of the guys had witnessed. It was a smart move. All of the players were in their late teens, early twenties, and many had never seen unconscious people, much less carried them to safety. Certainly not on a football field, after a big game.

Before Tuesday's practice, Coach Alvarez gathered the team together again. He read a letter from one of the girls in the hospital. She said to tell the team she was fine, that all the other girls were fine, and she was thankful for our concern. She ended the letter imploring us to keep up the amazing season and to beat Ohio State on Saturday. Alvy rallied us around this by saying, "See guys, the only thing you can do now is take care of your business on the football field. The doctors are taking care of everything on their end, now you take care of everything on your end. Let's have a great week of practice, a great week of focus, and let's beat Ohio State on Saturday, dammit!" The team responded positively to this and we put on our helmets and relasered our focus.

OH S YOUGOTTABEKIDDINGME

As if it wasn't tough enough to have Ohio State University coming into town ranked third in the country and loaded with future NFL stars like Dan "Big Daddy" Wilkinson, Joey Galloway, Terry Glenn, and Eddie George, we had the residual emotions of the Michigan win and frightening aftermath. There was also the emotional component of this being the last home game for the seniors.

This group of seniors was made up of fifth-year players Scott Nelson, Reggie Holt, Todd Orlando, Jason Levine, Nick Rafko, Joe Panos, Todd Anthony, Tyler Adam, Lee Kreuger, Jeff Wirth, and fourth-year players Carlos Fowler, Mark Montgomery, Phil Chavez, Henry Searcy, Yusef Burgess, Melvin Tucker, and Lamark Shakerford. And me.

The seniors, as is customary, were introduced in a special ceremony before the kickoff. We congregated at the entrance of the tunnel while the rest of the team sprinted onto the field. The band members and pom pon girls lined up to form a lane for us to run through. There were several ABC game cameras around the field. I wondered whether the national audience was seeing this part or whether a commercial was playing. The jam-packed student section was lined with the much-publicized temporary breakaway fences and numerous security personnel. I knew many friends and family were in the crowd, and that made me happy. I imagined them cheering a bit louder when my name was called.

We lined up and were introduced in alphabetical order, announcing our height and weight, hometown, and then our name. I did my best to drink in the moment, as did the rest of the seniors I suppose. I noticed a friend in the band standing nearby who waved at me. We'd known this day was coming, but I'd never really put much thought into what it would be like or how I would feel. There's not much foresight in a life taken one practice, one day at a time.

As my mind was wandering, my body followed. I fell out of line and Scott Nelson, ever the leader, snapped me back to the moment, "Chris?" I turned around and he gestured for me to get back in line, a few spots in front of him. I felt honored to stand in line with my fellow seniors. I did my best to appreciate how fortunate I was to get to run out in front of a crowd like this. The crowd was already raucous, and the game hadn't even started. A field worker put his hand on my rib cage and told me I was next. I looked around the horseshoe-shaped stadium one more time and thought of how quickly it all seemed to have gone by. My playing days, which at one time moved like molasses, were now coming to a close in the snap of a ball.

I heard the PA announcement echo through the tall stadium, "From Waunakee, Wisconsin, a 5-foot 10-inch, 180-pound receiver...Chrrrrriiissss Kennedyyyyy!" The field worker released his hand like a gate opening, and I sprinted past a blur of faces, pom pons, and instruments out onto the open field. The crowd was much louder than I thought they'd be when my name was announced, which made me feel pretty damn good. Maybe there were lots more friends and my hometown folk in the sold-out stadium than I'd thought.

I ran until I reached my parents who were standing on the 50-yard line waiting with hugs for me. They were all bundled up in ski coats, and my mom wore a pin on her puffy jacket with my football picture on it. We were all beaming and joined the other parents along the sidelines. My father has a picture taken of me sprinting onto the field this day still hanging in his office. The parents all shouted last words of encouragement before being escorted off the field.

The game started and was a typically physical Big Ten game. This was essentially for the conference title, and no one from either side was ready to concede an inch. The first half was a back-and-forth slobber-knocker slugfest. The score at halftime was tied at 7.

Because the game began later than usual due to ABC's schedule, the second half and the night came with a light snowfall. The scene in the stadium with the crisp night air covered in snow flurries resembled one of those little Christmas globes after you've turned it upside down.

I recall a few specifics about the game. Our offense moved the ball pretty well but only found the end zone twice. We were stopped in the red zone (the 20-yard line to the end zone) on two separate occasions without getting any points.

J.C. Dawkins (1) and Lee DeRamus (2) manage to celebrate a touchdown over the head of a Buckeye.

Our defense played tough, only allowing one touchdown into the fourth quarter. Safety Scott Nelson broke a couple of ribs on a punt return, so Jeff Messenger moved to free safety to replace him, and Donny Brady came in at cornerback to replace Messenger.

Brady did an admirable job filling in, intercepting a pass thrown by Buckeyes quarterback Bobby Hoying. Unfortunately, Brady also gave up a few long passes and a touchdown to Joey Galloway. Ohio State tied the game at 14 in the fourth quarter.

We got the ball back and made our final push to win this game and the conference crown for the first time in 31 years. Our offensive line and running back Brent Moss controlled the ball and moved into Ohio State territory at the 22-yard line with seven seconds to play.

We set up for a 39-yard field goal. Our season, the seniors' final home game, our Rose Bowl hopes came down to one snap, hold, and kick—The immensity of the moment in the collective minds of the entire stadium full of people. Not knowing what else to do and feeling almost powerless about our fate, almost our entire sidelines grabbed hands and knelt down together. A prayer chain was formed. We were willing the ball to go through the uprights with all the powers of God, or mental telepathy, or whatever you want to believe. OSU called a time-out to "ice" our kicker, Rick Schnetzky. Rick seemed calm and simply practiced his kicking motion off to the side while the rest of the team huddled up. Very soon, Rick would be a hero or a goat.

The whistle blew and the teams lined up for the snap. The whole crowd inhaled and in eerie quiet, Steve Stark snapped the ball perfectly into the hands of the holder, Bevell. Darrell caught the ball and planted it cleanly on the ground. Rick made his approach and kicked the ball hard...right into the outstretched hands of OSU's Marlon Kerner dashing in from his right. The ball made an audible thud off his hands and careened out of bounds. The screams of the Ohio State players broke the stunned silence in the stadium, and the game was over. A tie. OSU celebrated like they'd just won while our sideline acted like we lost and sullenly walked off the field. I suppose the fact that the third-ranked team in the nation was wildly celebrating a tie against us, and our utter disappointment, showed how much respect we had and how far our team had brought the UW football program.

The tie, the non-win, was hard to swallow. How could such an important game, for the Big Ten championship, end in a tie? I'd envisioned a win and us seniors dancing on the field during the fifth quarter under the lights with confident smiles as we left the stadium after a game for the last time. Instead, we walked off in a trance feeling numb, thinking about what might've been and should've been. Despite all the extra security personnel and new regulations, there was no need for the fans to rush the field this week.

The locker room was quiet. The coaches and players did their best to put on a stoic face, but it was clear everyone was deeply disappointed. The thud of the ball bouncing off the OSU player's hands kept echoing in our minds. It wasn't supposed to go like this. Weren't we the Cinderella story? Cinderella didn't show up at the ball to find the door locked.

The silver lining of this dark cloud of frustration hanging over us was that we were still in the hunt for the Big Ten title and the first Rose Bowl berth for UW since 1963. We needed to win our remaining two games against Michigan State and Illinois, and hope that Michigan would beat Ohio State in their annual rivalry game.

CATCH THE PASADENA

My father and I had a conversation the night after the OSU game. I was mired in frustration, too much to realize that things weren't so bad. My dad pointed out that with an OSU loss against Michigan (which certainly wasn't out of the question given that they had home-field advantage) and victories in our final two games, we would get the Rose Bowl bid. I was heartened with that realization, as I had no doubt we could win our final two games of the year.

The coaches at the Sunday meeting after the OSU game pointed this out as well. Coach Alvarez addressed the team, "Guys, there were a lot of good things yesterday. There were some mistakes that'll kill you when you watch these films. But you competed until the very end. That guy doesn't sneak through and we put that ball through the uprights and we win the game. The important thing is, we can still accomplish every goal we set. This tie doesn't affect that one bit. Sure, now we need a little help. But we need to take care of our business and that's to have a great week of practice, and go down there and beat Illinois this week, and then Michigan State after that. That's all we need concern ourselves with."

Coach Alvy gave us a couple of days off since we had a week off on our schedule before we headed to Champaign-Urbana to play our next opponent, the University of Illinois Fighting Illini. The break couldn't have come at a better time. Many guys needed the time to recover physically and mentally from the back-to-back Michigan and Ohio State games.

When we came back to practice, the team refocused and prepared very well for the Illinois game. We were back to being as sharp as we'd been all season. Illinois had started the season looking as if they'd be a Big Ten title contender, but their inconsistent play showed many weaknesses. We studied them and went down there with a game plan to expose those weaknesses and showcase our strengths.

The Illini boasted one of the best defenses in the country with three all-Big Ten linebackers, including all-American Simeon Rice. Watching the game films all week, we thought they were overrated and our offense soon proved it. Our linemen pounded the Illini defense and their star linebackers all day. They not only blocked the Illinois defensemen, they put them on their backs. When this happens, we called it a "pancake." That Saturday afternoon, our offense made more pancakes than an IHOP cook on a Sunday morning. Both running backs, Moss and Fletcher, ran for more than 120 yards as our offense put 35 points on the scoreboard.

On the other side of the ball, Illinois had a prolific quarterback, Johnny Johnson, leading their offense. But on this day, they were only able to manage 10 points the entire game against our tough, feisty defense. We whopped Illinois, 35-10, and took care of our business. Our team showed its character by bouncing back after two tough games and re-established ourselves as a dominant team in the conference. We also won our fourth road game of the year and won for the first time at Memorial Stadium in 23 years.

I can't imagine there was a player or Wisconsin fan who didn't then turn their full attention to the OSU–Michigan game right after ours. Capitalizing on their home-field advantage, the Wolverines inexplicably pounded Ohio State, 28-0, in one of the most lopsided victories in the long storied tradition of the two schools. Some unknown force was guiding us toward Pasadena. Our team and our fans got what we had wished for that day—an OSU loss, a UW win, and control of our own destiny.

Alvarez and his staff were especially happy with the Illinois win. The Illinois and Wisconsin coaching staffs had a lot of animosity toward each other. Earlier in the season, Coach Callahan was scouting a game and was caught in the Illinois coaches' box after a game, looking at a depth chart the Illinois coach had mistakenly left behind. Callahan was suspended for one game for the infraction, which many considered too severe a punishment.

We now assured ourselves of a top-four finish in the Big Ten and a January 1 bowl bid. We had two weeks before we were to play Michigan State for the opportunity to win the Big Ten championship and make that New Year's Day bowl a granddaddy one.

TOKYO ROSE

Just after the season started, our academic advisor, Coach Fishbain, stopped me in the hall. When Coach Fishbain stops you in the hall, it usually means you're in trouble for skipping a class or flunking an exam. This had never been the case for me, so I was intrigued. He informed me that since our Michigan State game was going to be played in Tokyo, Japan, I should sign up for a six-week Japanese culture course that was put in the curriculum for the trip. The completion of this class was a requirement for anyone who would be making the trip. Purportedly, it was also a requirement to be in good academic standing to be allowed to travel.

Basically, the class was established so that ignorance wouldn't be an excuse if we happened to accidentally insult the Japanese people or run roughshod over their customs. We were, technically, a place of higher education and we football players would be representatives of the University of Wisconsin.

The class met every Tuesday night after practice for six weeks. Besides the football players on the traveling squad, there were cheerleaders and band members who were making the Japan trip.

The class curriculum consisted mostly of watching Godzilla movies and eating raw fish. There was no homework in the class, and we didn't receive any credit for it. We didn't learn any Japanese other than the bare basics like hello (*konichi wa*), goodbye (*sayonara*), and watch out for the blitzing strong side linebacker (AHHH!).

The team administrators set up times to get our passport pictures taken, and a few weeks later I received my first passport free of charge. I was happy to learn it could be used not only for travel in Tokyo but anywhere in the world for the next 10 years. I imagined all the places I'd go with that passport in my hand once I was released from my university obligations.

Perhaps this is a good time to explain why we were playing a "home" game in Tokyo. It's not like the Japanese are huge Badgers fans, although we may have converted a few. Every year an exhibition football game known as the Tokyo Bowl is played in Japan. It was the Big Ten Conference's turn in 1993, and the game was scheduled a few years prior. Since the prospects of the Wisconsin Badgers football team making a bowl game seemed highly unlikely at the time, UW had agreed to give up a home game to play in Tokyo.

Of course, now that we were in the midst of one of the most miraculous turnarounds of any program in the Big Ten, the move no longer looked so wise. It would've been a huge benefit to play the biggest game of our careers in Camp Randall Stadium, where we'd won 10 of our last 11 games, to qualify for the Rose Bowl.

But the die had been cast, and there was nothing we could do about it now. This had been such a crazy, unexpected year that our team was basically unfazed by anything, even the fact that we'd be flying halfway around the world to play our final home game.

Coach Alvarez is a great spin doctor. He made it sound as if things couldn't have worked out better. He announced to the team several times throughout our two weeks of preparation for the Tokyo Bowl, "Guys, I can't think of a better situation than we have now." He reasoned that we got a bonus trip out of our season, that we'd have essentially two bowl games this year. He somehow had us convinced the jet lag would affect Michigan State more than us.

Some players joked that Coach Alvarez could have pumped up the passengers of the *Titanic*. He would say, "I can't think of a better situation than this boat sinking right now." The passengers would look befuddled and Alvarez would continue,

"Listen, those rooms are cramped, this gets you out in the fresh air, you go for a little swim, and you take a nice gondola ride. To top it off, some of you will get picked up by a better ship. You'll make history. It's perfect!" We all knew, though, that if given the chance to bring the game back to Camp Randall, Coach Alvarez would have gladly bowed and said sayonara to the Tokyo plans.

We were given a couple of days off from practice after the Illinois win and started with a few lighter practices on Wednesday. Coach Alvarez wanted to get us used to the time-zone change and so on Saturday, a week before the game, we started to adjust our schedules to Japanese time. We began starting practice later each day until one night practice started at midnight. Despite the abnormality of the practice start time, pretty much everything else—the intensity, the length, the focus—was the same as it normally was.

Michigan State was a good team with a winning record in the Big Ten and overall, but we were confident we could beat them if we played our game.

The Monday before the game, the travel squad was posted in the locker room. My name was not on it. One other senior and I had been left off of it, and we were upset. I went to speak to Coach Norvell about it. I told him I thought I deserved to be on the travel list. I was supposed to be on that list. He took my questioning as a challenge to his authority and got angry, saying, "You were never supposed to be on that list." If he hadn't walked away immediately after he said that, I could've shown him my passport photo and my transcript showing I'd completed a six week Japanese culture course. I was supposed to be on that list.

Basically, only the top couple of players at each position were going on the trip, save for a few exceptions. I, and apparently, Coach Fishbain, thought that the upperclassmen would fill those extra slots, but that wasn't the case. Very disappointing. The argument could be made that since I was unlikely to play I didn't merit one of the coveted spots. Though I'd counter that they saw fit to travel tangential people (athletic department personnel, band members, cheerleaders, etc.) who, believe it or not, had less chance to play than I did.

It seemed ridiculous to me that the coaches were not allowed to take the entire team. Wasn't this for the players? Why were so many left behind? Who cares if they didn't play a lot? They were on the team. Why were athletic department personnel going with their families? They should have given up their slots for the players, in my biased opinion. Or have I lost sight of who the games are really for in the end? The policies surrounding college football are confounding and often seem contrary to the players' interests.

Despite my getting snubbed, I was too excited for the team's opportunity and wished nothing but the best. The other senior and I got a phone call from a reporter who asked me to comment on how I felt about the slight. I was tempted to be honest and tell him how unfair it was we were left behind. But I told him I didn't really want to say anything about it. I didn't want anything negative in the papers about the team. It was too big of a deal for us to be playing for the opportunity to get a Rose Bowl bid, to have any one person voice his personal concerns in a public way like that. It seemed selfish and I like to think, if nothing else, my four years of volunteer service to the team proves my unselfishness.

I spoke to my father, and he agreed we should say nothing. The reporter certainly still could have done the story without our comments but he didn't have much when we wouldn't talk.

The team left for Tokyo a few days before the game, so I had some unwanted time off. I attended class, and one of my professors—from whom I'd gotten a permission slip to miss class the week before—was more than a little surprised to see me. He asked what happened, and I lied and told him I was injured. He genuinely felt bad for me that I'd miss out on such an experience and couldn't believe they still couldn't take me. I just agreed as it was easier than trying to explain the screwed-up priorities at work. Not that I could have explained them anyway.

A few players who were left behind got together to watch the MSU game at a house party in Madison. As hard as it was to not be with the rest of our team that night, it was still exciting to realize we were on the verge of possibly going to the Rose Bowl.

Just from watching the game on television, I could tell the scene in Japan was surreal. Exactly half of the stadium had red flags to wave, the Badgers fans, and the other half had green flags, the Michigan State fans. These red-flag waving people, by virtue of their seat number, would be the lucky "Wisconsin fans" in attendance to witness us securing our first Rose Bowl berth in 31 years, while the true fans who'd sat through the last nine losing seasons watched from their couches. Too bizarre. The Japanese fans had no idea when to cheer. The television shots often caught their bewildered expressions, the inappropriate timing of strange cheers, and their overall indifference to the game's magnitude.

Wisconsin came out of the gate slowly. We'd been too long without a game; due to the strange scheduling, we'd played only one game in the past month. Despite Alvarez's calming mantra of "This is just another game on the schedule," it was impossible to escape how big the game was for our team, the university, and our fans. Combine too much time off with the emotion of the biggest game of our lives, and it made for a sluggish brew. Michigan State was ahead, 7-3, in the second quarter.

However, Scott Nelson picked off a pass, our offense took over, and the real Wisconsin team finally appeared. Our potent offense scored the next six times we had the ball! Moss and Fletcher both ran for more than 100 yards each. This team was on a victory march, and no one was going to stop it.

Down, 34-17, in the fourth quarter, Michigan State made an attempt to rally by successfully recovering an onside kick. However, two plays later UW cornerback Kenny Gales intercepted a pass and we took possession. We beat Michigan State,

41-20, and became Big Ten champions. The Wisconsin Badgers were heading west to Pasadena via the Far East.

Our teammates told us it was weird to be partying in Tokyo instead of Madison after the game. Many of the players went out in the "American district" of Tokyo. They were by far the largest people in Tokyo and were viewed in awe by most of the citizens they came across. Joe Rudolph got his foot run over by a cab because he was looking the wrong direction while crossing the street.

Apparently, everywhere the players went they were comped, which was a good thing as drinks were north of $20 each, which basically equaled a player's entire weekend budget. Other players stayed in their rooms, still abuzz with the thought that they'd be playing in the Rose Bowl game.

Back in Madison, a group of us headed down to State Street, joining about 20,000 of our best Badgers friends in celebrating the win. It was mayhem. Students climbed up trees, lamp posts, and bus stops. The streets and the sidewalks were shoulder-to-shoulder full of celebrating fans.

At one point, call it "group consciousness" perhaps, the majority of the crowd made the one-mile trip from State Street to Camp Randall Stadium, which had been opened up, much to my surprise.

Fans were on the goalposts, lying on the field, and tackling one another. One guy was sitting cross-legged on the field and crying. It was a 20,000-person group hug. I bumped into a few people I knew. They were understandably confused as to why I was there and not in Tokyo. I hid my embarrassment as best I could and repeated the "injured" story.

Nonetheless, I was happy and I was over not going to Tokyo. There were bigger things on which to focus. The next morning, I spoke with my father who congratulated me. He observed that when something really big happens, you know it's really big because when you wake up the next morning, it still feels really big, if not bigger. The temporary highs aren't so temporary when there's a monumental achievement involved. A lot of accomplishments lose their excitement pretty quickly, but this was something essentially enduring. I had a warm glowing feeling of knowing I helped make history.

I'm a chronic dreamer and being a member of a Wisconsin Badgers Rose Bowl team held the promise of exceeding my wildest dreams. I was experiencing a fantasy in real life. I eagerly awaited the journey to come.

CHAPTER ELEVEN:
ROSES AND THORNS

Some of the bowl rumors, promises, and speculation turned out to be untrue. We'd heard that everyone would go to the bowl game, and we assumed that everyone would suit up and be on the field. This was not true. For some reason, the NCAA dictated that only 95 players could suit up for the game. Why they picked that number is unknown to me. We had 106 players on our team. This meant 11 teammates would have to watch the game from the stands.

Why not suit up the entire team? It's certainly not a space issue. Look at a college sideline sometime. There are at least 50 non-players on those sidelines, some working the game (trainers, equipment managers, security personnel) and some not (boosters, coaches' friends and family, and athletic department personnel). Yet, the NCAA feels the need to institute a rule that deprives student-athletes from having a complete Rose Bowl experience. Eleven guys who'd gone through all the practices, meetings, film sessions, voluntary workouts, weightlifting sessions, and all the rest, were told, "Thanks for your dedication, sacrifice, and service to the team, here's a ticket to the game." It was another example of the way NCAA player policies demonstrate a lack of respect and thought toward the student-athletes. Again, who was this bowl experience supposed to be for?

I was suddenly filled with dread that I could be one of these 11 players. I'd been left off the 60-player travel squad to Japan, and now I didn't know where I stood. I voiced this concern to some friends on the team and they told me I was being paranoid. I was a senior; I was going, end of story.

I was still nervous about it though, so I decided to try to make one last attempt to ingratiate myself to the staff. After one of our first practices after we won the MSU game in Tokyo, I approached Coach Norvell. I thought I'd illustrate my loyalty to the program and remind him of my unselfish contributions, so I told him about the reporter who had contacted me about being left off the Tokyo travel squad. I told him I'd said nothing. Norvell didn't really know what I was talking about but said OK.

About 15 minutes later, Coach Norvell came into the locker room and signaled for me to come with him. We went to an area outside the locker room. He was visibly upset and pointed at me threateningly. "Listen," he said. "We don't need people calling the press around here, trying to take us down." I was confused and responded, "What? I'm not doing that." He ignored my comment. I wondered who these "people" he was referring to were. All I could think of was my friends and family. Give me a break. Why would they do something behind my back and jeopardize my career? They wouldn't, but he didn't know them and didn't care to know them. Coach Norvell continued, "We're all in this together, what goes on in here stays in here. The outside world has no clue." I was still confused and just said, "Yeah, I realize that. That's why I didn't say anything." He countered, conducting some sort of heated argument that didn't exist: "We don't need people making us look bad. We clear?" I just shook my head confusedly and said, "Yeah. Listen, my family, nor I, had anything to do with this. I'm telling you." He walked away. I was baffled at being scolded for exposing something about the team to the outside world by refusing to comment to anyone from the outside world.

My moment in the spotlight, being introduced to the crowd at the OSU game.

Why would I want to call attention to the fact I'd been left off of a traveling squad? All I would have gained was the public humiliation of pointing out my low status with the team. Besides, no story was ever printed. As a journalism major, I knew how to get a story out of this if I wanted to. Hell, I could've written it myself and had it printed in one of the student newspapers. Why would I have done this in the midst of the most successful season in our school's history? Why would I do anything to jeopardize this team I'd sacrificed for and dedicated myself to my entire college career? The miscommunication between Norvell and me was maddening, frustrating, and nerve-racking, as it had been for our entire four years. I was more nervous than ever now, especially if the decision would be influenced by Norvell.

The next day, the 95-player travel squad was posted in the locker room before practice—and my name was not on the list. I was the only senior not on there, but all my friends were. Freshman reserves were on the list; guys who had less chance than I did of playing in the game. My nightmare had come true. I was shocked, hurt, and humiliated. It was unbelievable.

Buried under the avalanche of my despair was the hope that there was a mistake or that this could be rectified with some much-needed clarity of the reporter situation.

Before practice, as other players were laughing and playing catch with casual ease, my stomach was in knots and I was in a state of shock. I walked toward Coach Norvell for clarification. He pulled me aside and said, "Listen, you're going to go out on that second plane. I don't expect any problems from you or you'll not go at all." He walked away and said over his shoulder, "That's it." I couldn't even begin to respond.

The whistle blew to start practice and I was in my own world while I got in line and stretched. I watched the coaches laugh and joke with each other and the players. I wondered whether the coaches all knew I'd been left off the travel squad or whether they even cared. It didn't appear so. Suddenly, with one piece of paper posted on our locker room wall, I felt like a stranger, an outsider from my own team.

I was split by rage, humiliation, and my heavily developed sense of duty. I didn't know what to do. Part of me wanted to throw off my shoulder pads and tell everyone to stick them where the sun doesn't shine, and walk off the field. Would that be the way to defend my honor? Did I even care what these guys thought of me anymore? By staying and practicing, was I doing the right thing or being a whipping boy?

Needless to say, my enthusiasm for practicing and helping the team was drained empty. I caught some balls in warm-up drills and thought, "What's the point?" I no longer felt the need to impress anyone. I purposely sat out a few drills and almost defied anyone to say something. I ignored idle chit-chat. Several players asked me what was wrong and I just shook my head. It was the worst practice of my life.

My roommate and best friend on the team, Phil Chavez, told the other players who had no idea what was going on, so I didn't have to. Guys started coming up to me and telling me they thought it was bullshit. They told me to talk to Alvarez. Some advised me to keep my head up, finish out the season, and get the fuck out of there. Most had no idea how to handle it, much the same way I felt.

Phil told me one of his fellow linebackers and friends, Dan Schneck, felt so bad about my predicament, he said he'd offer up his spot on the travel squad for me. Phil told him I wouldn't want him to do that and he was right, of course. Taking the experience from another player would have made me feel worse and didn't change the fact that the coaches' decision to not put me on the squad was the wrong one.

I was moved at the beauty of Dan's gesture. I was moved at how this young guy was so willing to do the right thing, even at his own expense.

I pondered going to the captains of the team, letting them know the story, and perhaps using their influence to change the matter. But I really didn't want to disrupt things. It felt selfish, and the team needed to be focused on other things than my own predicament. I felt this was a personal issue between me and Norvell.

I spoke to Coach Alvarez after a senior meeting about Rose Bowl stuff the next day. I remained in the room as the others filed out. I told him I wasn't on the travel squad and he nodded. I asked him why, and he explained that he told his coaches to make a list of the players they thought deserved to go. Alvarez continued, "I have to stand behind that." Then he added, "I wish you were going too, but…." He shrugged and I nodded. We both knew things weren't going to change, I guess, and there was nothing left to say.

The 11 players who weren't suiting up were going to the Rose Bowl as well, but a few days after the travel squad went. Joining me in that group was one of our injured starting linebackers, Chad Yocum.

Chad had begun the season playing very well. He was one of our best pass rushers and contributed greatly to the team. Unfortunately, he had a serious back injury and couldn't play any more games. He should've been allowed on the field, but instead would be given a seat next to the very fans who were cheering for him weeks earlier.

Our group would miss out on a few of the experiences the first few days and would even be staying at a hotel separate from the team. We'd be loosely supervised. We were going to be given a ticket to the game.

Everyone was talking about the Rose Bowl, and everywhere you looked was some sort of sign about the big game. I contemplated moving to some remote island for the next couple of weeks to keep my sanity.

I broke the bad news to my girlfriend, Stephanie, who immediately gave me a hug and cried. She was incredibly supportive. She went with me as I drove to my father's house to break the news to him.

This was going to be rough. He'd been invested in my four-year journey, and I knew this news was going to hurt him. I just hoped it wouldn't ruin the experience for him. He'd been a fan for so long, and he deserved to enjoy the Rose Bowl experience.

My dad knew right away something was wrong, so I just came out and told him I wasn't suiting up for the Rose Bowl game. I tried to put a positive spin on it: "Well, it sucks but I still am going out for the game."

My father didn't know what to say. He was shocked. He managed to give this advice, "Hey, keep practicing hard and keep your head up." This seemed really important to him, so I pledged that I would finish out with full effort.

I then went and told my mother. She had posted outside of her house a sign with my name and number, congratulating me. It broke my heart to see that, and I was infuriated with Norvell and college football in general. I told her that I loved the sign, but I wouldn't be on the travel squad. My mom was supportive of me and angry at the football program for treating me so poorly.

Alone in my room, I did some private soul-searching. I was so sorry, not just for myself but for what I was putting my family through. Their reward for four years of unconditional support shouldn't have been dealing with this. I blamed myself, not just Norvell, for the situation. Maybe if I'd worked harder in practice, maybe if I hadn't let the younger guys take some of my reps on the scout team, I wouldn't be in this position. But plenty of other upperclassmen in my predicament did the same thing, and they were going to be suiting up. So I realized it did boil down to my relationship with Coach Norvell—or the lack thereof. We were both to blame for that. I set a meeting with him.

Coach Norvell and I met in his office. I asked him whether he thought it was fair that underclassmen with less chance of playing than I did were going on the trip. I was the only senior not on the travel squad. He stated that seniority didn't matter to him and that he thought I'd done the bare minimum required of me the past four years. He acknowledged that our lack of communication and relationship may have been his fault as well. He said he would not let that happen in the future, but regardless I was not going to be on that first flight.

Coach Norvell and I should have clicked. He was a young coach, and I was a young guy. We were both football players from the Madison area who loved the Badgers and wanted the best for them. I still don't have much of an explanation why we didn't get along; I guess sometimes people's personalities just don't mesh. Unfortunately for me, I was the one who had to suffer the consequences of this bad relationship.

I didn't know how Coach Alvarez felt about the situation and doubt he even thought about it beyond our brief conversation. He was obviously busy with all that was happening. This was a crazy time for everyone involved.

I decided I'd better go in and talk to Alvarez myself so that we knew where each other stood. I made an appointment to meet with him the next day. I was received warmly by the long-time football office receptionist, known to everyone as "Ski."

WHERE DO I STAND?

Sitting in the chair directly across from Coach Alvarez, I noticed a few big candy jars on his desk. They seemed out of place to me for such a disciplined and strict leader. So did his wardrobe; instead of a Wisconsin sweat suit, he was dressed in a sweater vest and tie.

Coach Alvarez spoke first. He said he didn't care if I wanted to go to the press, that I was free to do that. I stopped him. "Coach, I don't want to do that. I've never gone to the press. My family has never done that, and it's not going to happen now." I was sincere, and he seemed fine with that explanation.

Coach Alvarez explained that he wished he could bring everybody on the trip. He thought it was silly to not let everyone suit up, but those were the rules and he had to follow them. I believed him. If he didn't care about his reserve players or think they were important to the team, he wouldn't have taken time out of the busiest, most important week of his coaching career to explain himself and listen to me.

Coach Alvarez said he delegated travel squads to his assistant coaches and stood by their word. He assured me I'd still get to do all the stuff the travel squad was going to get to do. He said I'd still get a Rose Bowl ring and would have a great experience.

I realized Coach Alvarez wasn't my therapist, and I would keep my tortured feelings about the whole situation to myself. I told him I understood what he was saying, and that I would abide and continue to practice as I always had.

I was still flummoxed by the idea that he couldn't possibly get me on that field. There had to be a way. I told him I felt I deserved to be and wanted to be on the field even if I wasn't suited up. Coach Alvarez seemed empathetic and said that could possibly be arranged. I thanked him and we shook hands.

I left our meeting feeling that it was a success. I realized that what I most wanted was to have Coach Alvarez acknowledge me and my contributions to the team for the past four years. I obviously hadn't been feeling very appreciated after being left off the game roster. But I really got the sense from Coach Alvarez's tone, and the fact that he took the time to meet with me at all, that he really did appreciate me and my contributions to the team.

My sense of Alvarez's respect for me was confirmed a few days later. My father attended an event where Alvarez was present, and the coach made himself available for a little chat. My father asked for clarification of the situation. Alvarez repeated that he was upset that he couldn't dress everybody for the game. Alvarez lamented that one-time starter Chad Yocum couldn't suit up for the game because he'd been injured during the season. He added that he was impressed I'd come in face to face with him to set things straight. I was happy to hear Alvarez thought well of me. I guess I hadn't totally gotten over my need of approval from father figures.

One more meeting was arranged, I honestly don't recall how, with someone in the athletic department. I really didn't want to talk about the situation any more. I just wanted to get the whole thing over with and put this mess behind me. But I went in anyway. I'm not sure what the athletic department worker wanted out of the meeting, and I was absent an agenda myself.

We met in an office on the other end of the stadium from Alvarez's office. I'd seen this man around the athletic department facilities before and on TV a few times speaking about athletic department business but never met him. He was friendly and congratulated me.

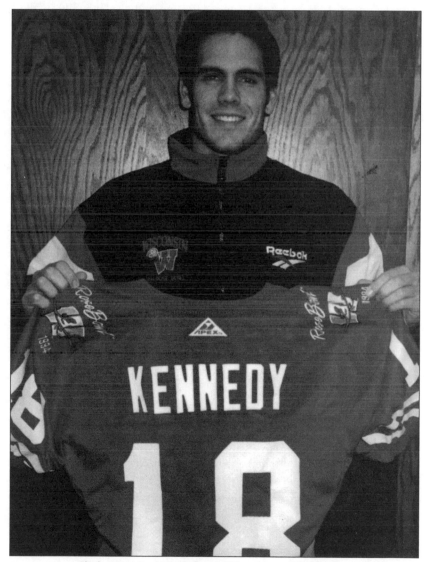

I had my Rose Bowl jersey—but would I get to wear it in Pasadena?

He started in on an unsolicited monologue about his job. He oversaw the football operations. He said if there was any wrongdoing in the program, he'd be the one to investigate it. But he didn't think there was any wrongdoing in my case. Since he hadn't heard my side of it, I wondered how he felt he could make a decision like that but kept it to myself. He said, "Heck, the way everyone viewed Wisconsin football now, Alvarez could have me fired." He was probably right. Alvarez could have run for mayor.

He explained his theory that athletes like me, and like he had been, think they are better than they actually are. He said athletes had to be this way to be competitive and to be successful. He said maybe I was right about deserving a spot on the team but the coach's word will always win out over the player's. He was right on this too.

He thought it was unfortunate that my career had to end this way, but he said he was sure I would look back on my experience as a Badger and feel very proud of everything I'd done. He hoped that for me. He thanked me for coming in and then asked me if I had any questions. I hadn't gotten a word in, which was fine because I had nothing to say.

I did mention the only thing that I was still upset about was that it was insinuated that my family was trying to drum up negative publicity for the team by supposedly calling that reporter. I explained that was just not the case; it was unfair and it was really the only thing that was bugging me. My father is a proud alumnus of the university and had been a season-ticket holder long before Alvarez or anyone else in the athletic department had been there. My mother simply supported anything I did and would never jeopardize anything for me. I found it ludicrous that the athletic department was considering my family to be culprits at all. They didn't deserve to be associated with this mess.

If nothing else, my four years of good grades, service to the team, and my impeccable behavior should count for a benefit of the doubt when it came to my word. The fact that the football team and athletic department saw fit to have me speak on their behalf at various charity events and youth organizations throughout the years shows they believed me to be someone of good character. Their sudden reversal on this didn't make me question myself, but them.

He said he understood and again congratulated me on my accomplishments, saying he only heard good things about me. The meeting ended, and he wished me luck.

I thought I liked him, until I found out a few days later that he'd had a follow-up conversation with an acquaintance of mine after our meeting, and he said he didn't believe me. He said he knew that my family had to be involved, since I was virtually unknown, in leaking the Tokyo information to the press. For a story that was never printed, by the way. I was disappointed to hear this but not surprised.

I was just sad for him that he couldn't even be straight-up with a football player like me who held zero power in the system.

The mere suspicion that I had pulled the curtain back and told the outside world what was happening inside the secret world of college football was enough to have me banished. I'd been hit many times throughout the years on the playing field but I'd never expected to be so blindsided off of it.

THE PLEASURES OF FOOTBALL

Amid the ugliness of things, let me assure the reader that I have not forgotten the beauty of the sport.

Running away from the pack, in the open field at your fastest speed, with heavy, excited breath as the end zone grows closer and closer, and you know no one is going to catch you. And crossing the goal line in an explosion of triumph and release.

Throwing a perfect spiral. Watching it twist tightly through the air, right on target.

Catching a perfect spiral. Catching a pass without having to break your stride.

Thinking that a ball thrown to you is out of your reach, you run as fast as you can anyway, stretch out your arms and dive with your whole body laid out, and the ball sticks softly, right into your enclosed fingertips.

Seeming like you're trapped by advancing players, but cutting back to find a small opening, diving through it into the end zone with a ball in your outstretched arms.

Making a tackle in perfect form, feeling the player you're tackling become weightless on your shoulder.

Getting hit so hard you see stars…and the subsequent recovery a few moments later.

The adrenaline rushing like Niagara Falls through your body in the midst of a game.

Breaking through the line and blocking a punt, having it ricochet off your stinging hands and insides of your wrists, and the ensuing struggle for the ball. You're the harbinger of chaos.

Walking toward the stadium in full gear past supportive fans. Hearing the crescendo of sounds—the marching band warming up, the lively chatter of a crowd, whistles cutting through the crisp air.

Working hard to pull off your sweat-soaked shirt after a practice or game, and dropping it to the floor in a clump.

Admiring the scratches you earned on your helmet.

Your significant other discovering your nicks and bruises after a game.

Wearing a dirty jersey. Noticing blood on your uniform yet feeling no pain.

Helping a teammate to his feet after a play. Being helped to your feet by a teammate after a play.

Seeing a teammate throw his body in sacrifice to stop someone from tackling you. Doing the same for a teammate.

Respectfully shaking hands with an opponent after a hard-fought game.

Playing in a descending shower of lights from towers on high.

A long, slow hug from a loved one after a loss.

Removing your helmet and feeling the steam erupt off your sweaty head.

Greeting family and friends outside the locker room after a win.

Walking off the football field healthy, regardless of winning or losing, knowing you got to play one of the greatest sports ever invented.

ROSE BOWL PERKS

Reporting for meetings and practices after earning the Rose Bowl berth was paradoxical for the team. Known for its "down-to-earth," roll-up-the-sleeves work ethic, the team was now hovering a few inches off the ground. Everyone seemed a bit buzzed, almost tipsy, drinking in this newfound, unprecedented success. So much talk about us was floating around the city, the state, and the country.

In my four years, I'd watched the press corps outside of practice expand from a handful of reporters my freshman year to an army of 30 or so by the Rose Bowl practice weeks.

Students and professors applauded some of the players when they entered the classroom. I understand the term instant celebrity a bit better. It seemed every other stranger you'd pass on the street would shake your hand or say congratulations.

For the most part, though, our isolated existence as players pretty much continued as usual: Attending classes, practices, meetings, doing homework, and hanging out with our roommates.

Since none of us had experienced qualifying for a bowl before, rumors and speculation abounded. It was said we'd be receiving all kinds of Rose Bowl gifts: A ring, a watch, sweat suits, T-shirts, baseball caps, and so forth. This was true. Seems like every day, there was a new article of clothing with a Rose Bowl insignia in our lockers.

There were footballs laid out on tables that we were to sign for various charities. Now it was a commodity to have our signatures on anything. Realizing this and being a broke college student, I improvised my Christmas shopping. I had my teammates sign shirts and baseball caps for me so that I could give them out as presents.

It was both strange and necessary to get back to our usual "focus hard, practice hard" mentality that got us here. For the next few weeks, we'd practice three days a week, with film and workouts mixed in. Since we typically had a week during the season to prepare for an opponent, the three-plus weeks for UCLA seemed like overkill. As a scout-teamer, I would soon know the UCLA offensive plays better than my own.

Coach Alvarez and the staff were very tuned in to where the players were mentally. Perhaps to guard against too much complacency, the coaches held some very physical practices with live scrimmages. Coach Alvarez enjoyed the fact that bowl teams got extra practices that non-bowl teams wouldn't get. It allows time for the younger players to get some more practice and experience, and it's a nice head start on building for the next year's team.

Coach Alvarez said the highlights of his playing and coaching career were the bowl games. He told us that he wanted us to enjoy the experience of going to a bowl. He promised we'd do all the fun things associated with the bowl experience, but he also warned us that the point of going to a bowl game is to win it. He expected extra focus and extra-hard preparation for the game.

The practices leading up to the Rose Bowl were going well. The team was exuding confidence. Everyone was having the same thoughts: "Hey, that receiver catching the ball right there, that linebacker making the tackle next to me, that guard blocking here, is on the Big Ten championship team. We're pretty good!" Yes, we still had to beat the Bruins to cap off the season properly, but regardless, we'd achieved more than we'd set out to do before the year began.

There are many perks in going to a bowl game, especially the Rose Bowl. The most talked about is the Rose Bowl ring. The Rose Bowl ring is actually a Big Ten championship ring, so it is awarded whether or not the team wins the game. We received our rings a couple of months after the game, if I recall correctly.

Our ring was designed with our particular season in mind. The face has a red W surrounded by many small diamond chips. One side of the ring has the player's name, number, and a Badgers helmet on it. The other side has the score of the Rose Bowl game and the Japanese symbol for victory. The ring is made of solid 24-karat gold.

Usually, when people find out I was on the Rose Bowl team one of the first things they ask about is the ring. I can honestly say that I don't know where my ring is. I think it's at my mom's house somewhere but it could be at my dad's house as well. It's not that I don't appreciate it, I just don't wear jewelry and since I've lived my whole life in rented apartments, I don't feel it's safe to lug it around with me from place to place. It's not that I take it for granted; I just think people assign too much importance to it.

ROSE BOWL WEEK

Along with all the material gifts emblazoned with Rose Bowl insignia, many adventures were included in the trip. The typical day in Pasadena consisted of a practice in the morning and an excursion in the afternoon—Universal Studios one day, Disneyland the next. It was funny seeing these big guys squeezed into the rides and getting their pictures taken with the park's costumed characters. Several players documented the theme parks on their camcorders.

One night's dinner was the Lawry's eat-off. Wisconsin and UCLA were both guests of the restaurant, which held eating contests between the teams. Our coaches actually wanted us to win this as well. They said anytime there's a competition, you guys win it. We won.

Then there were the unexpected perks. The week of the game, Shane Kreke, Carl Heidemann, and I went to get something to drink at a gas station across the street from the hotel. Kreke was notorious for getting into trouble on campus—nothing major, he just liked to have a good time. The coaches viewed him as a big embodiment of unfulfilled potential and constantly derided him. It seemed they wanted to drive him out, get his scholarship back, and be done with him. Kreke was a fun-loving party guy and didn't seem to let it affect him much. I suppose as someone who wanted to attain a scholarship, I should've also detested Kreke. But, along with many of my teammates, I liked him because he was a lot of fun.

The gas station was in the middle of the block, so instead of using the crosswalk, we cut diagonally across the street to get there. A police car happened to be driving by when we did this. The car U-turned and drove slowly right behind us as we walked through the parking lot. One of the cops told us through the car microphone, "Stop and put your hands up." We looked at each other in puzzlement and did as instructed.

The two cops, one older with a moustache, the other young and muscular, got out of their car and walked over to us. They asked for our identification and we gave it to them. We'd heard about Rodney King and LA cops on the news, but this didn't make sense as we were all young, white guys.

One of the cops, the moustached one, asked us whether we knew why we were being stopped. I wanted to answer mistaken identity but reconsidered, as I sensed these guys took themselves very seriously. It then occurred to us the only thing possible was that we were technically jaywalking. I thought there was no way I could say that without chuckling, and Kreke and Carl seemed to feel the same because we all looked at each other to see who would answer. Kreke took the bullet and said, "Uh, jaywalking?" "That's right, JAYWALKING," the cop responded hastily. We hid our smirks.

The moustached cop looked at our licenses and asked, "So what's someone from Wisconsin, Illinois, and Indiana doing in California?" We told the cops we were members of the Wisconsin Badgers football team in town for the Rose Bowl game. Heidemann and I were regular-sized guys who he might not have believed, but fortunately Kreke was 6' 6" tall and weighed around 300 pounds. Kreke added, "Yeah, it's just on campus we're used to pedestrians walking all over the road." The younger cop, a.k.a. "the good cop," said, "Ah, let's go easy on them." The moustached cop, a.k.a. "the bad cop," said, "Well, listen, against my better judgment, I'm gonna let you guys go."

We responded with the most sincere thank-yous we could muster. Before they headed back to their car, the bad cop added, "Now, you use those crosswalks from now on, otherwise we'll be sending you back to Wisconsin, Illinois, and Indiana in body bags."

The cops drove away, and we looked at each other and started laughing. We couldn't believe we almost got a ticket for jaywalking. Kreke threw up his hands saying, "I'm out here two nights? I knew I shouldn't have left the hotel."

A pep rally was held at the Century Park Plaza Hotel with thousands of Wisconsin fans in attendance. This was the headquarters of the UW fans in town. It seemed like every balcony of the high-rise hotel had a Badgers flag hanging off of it.

The Plaza Hotel is also the site of the Big Ten Dinner of Champions, a Vegas-style entertainment show put on for the team and its boosters. Our show was hosted by Alan Thicke, who did a stand-up routine, which became a "Growing Pain" by the end of the night. Ba-dum-bum.

Gladys Knight and the Pips performed a few songs. They even invited up a few players to dance with them at one point. I recall freshman Tony Simmons getting up on stage and cutting the rug so impressively, I thought Gladys was going to make him a Pip.

Madison native, Badgers fan, and *Saturday Night Live* star Chris Farley also made an appearance. I was sitting at a table near a short set of about five stairs when Farley made his entrance from the back of the large room. As Chris made his way past the dinner tables toward the stage, he paused at the top of the stairs near me and did a pratfall, dropping the entire length of the stairs. It was like a belly flop onto the hard ground. Since Farley landed only a few feet from me, I could tell that he landed right on his stomach and didn't reach out to break his fall in the slightest. I imagined how that must have hurt. I admired the way he sacrificed his body for the sake of the joke.

Chris had made several appearances during the season after games and practices. He often did a "Matt Foley" motivational speaker routine. Matt thought we had "the world by the tail now! And, oh boy, we'll keep marchin' and marchin' all the way down the road to successville!" He was totally committed, screaming as loud as he could, his body gyrating all over the place, spit flying from his mouth. He had everyone in the room laughing, coaches included. Many people were impressed to have Jesse Jackson come speak to the team earlier in the season, but I was more impressed by Farley's visit.

Former Playboy playmate Randi Rhodes, hostess of USA Network's late-night show, *Up All Night*, also appeared on stage. She did a little bit of comedy and then did some famous Playboy poses, but fully clothed. She then asked for a volunteer player to come up and see whether he could perform the poses. Immediately, everyone chanted for Nick Rafko to go up. He did.

Nick was wearing a suit with loosened tie and a few days of scruff on his face. Nick maneuvered his 6' 4", 260-pound frame into various pouty and seductive poses, the crowd loving every one of them. It was scary how good he was. His years of researching the magazine had paid off. I was glad the boosters and others outside the team could witness how funny Rafko was.

The headliner for the evening was Joe Pesci. He was a short guy and a huge disappointment. He came on last and had no jokes. He admitted on stage he didn't know what he was doing there. He wasn't funny at all and was only on stage for about three minutes. He said Coach Alvarez had asked him whether he wanted to be on the Wisconsin sideline during the game. Joe didn't know what to say, and Alvarez asked, "Did they [UCLA] ask you?" The crowd laughed at this. Joe shrugged and said, "I guess I'll be on your sideline." He didn't end up doing it.

There is also an invite every year for the Big Ten champion to visit the Playboy Mansion, courtesy of University of Illinois alumnus Hugh Hefner. This is made after the game, as there are distractions…and then there are distractions. A small number of players went; I was on my way to Vegas and skipped the visit. Those who attended said it was nice but that they only met a couple of Playmates, who were dressed in sweatpants.

Of course, one of the big perks is spending more than a week in balmy, beautiful southern California in late December and early January while Wisconsin shivers.

HOT TICKET

The mood around Madison and the state was unprecedented. Gleeful. Obsessed. Rabid. Rose Bowl mania. This trip to Pasadena was 31 years in the making. You couldn't pass a shop window or street corner without seeing some sort of Wisconsin logo with a rose on it. Every TV station had a football story running every night. You heard something about the game anytime you scanned the radio stations. You know it's a big story when the news, weather, and sports all feature the team and the game.

There seemed to be a mandate that everyone in the state of Wisconsin have some article of clothing advertising the trip to the Rose Bowl.

If you hadn't booked a travel package to Pasadena the next day or two after the Tokyo game, you were out of luck—or were going to be out of a lot of money. Travel companies were selling tour packages with airfare, accommodations, and game tickets included. The problem was a lot of these companies didn't have actual tickets to the game. Many Badgers fans found this out the hard way. They showed up in Pasadena thinking they had tickets but found the vouchers they had paid good money for were worth nothing.

My mother and step-dad booked their tickets before I could inform them that, as a senior player, I would receive eight complimentary tickets to the game. By the time the news got out that some of the ticket vouchers sold along with travel packages were not going to be honored, my spare tickets were already distributed. I was livid, and my parents were nervous. Thankfully, they were among the lucky ones whose tickets were legit, but they obviously went through some unnecessarily anxious days.

My eight allotted tickets went fast: Two went to my father, one to an uncle, three to my girlfriend and her family, and the other two to friends of the family. The face value on the ticket was only $48 each at the time, but because of the demand from Wisconsin fans, the average ticket was going for more than $200 and some fans ended up paying more than $1,000 apiece for good seats. UCLA students were selling their tickets to Badgers fans for enough to pay their rent for a month or two.

The day of the game, most of those selling tickets were scalpers, not fans. These guys were opportunistic and were making huge profits off the loyalty of Wisconsin fans. On the flip side, there were reports of Wisconsin fans selling extra tickets at face value to fellow Wisconsin fans. Even a few UCLA folk sold their extra tickets to Wisconsin fans at face value. Good sportsmanship warms my heart.

The sad truth is that some fans never found a way into the stadium and had to watch the game on television. Knowing the spirit of Badgers fans, I'm sure they made the best of it.

A tent was set up outside the Rose Bowl for these unlucky UW souls to watch the game. Not like being in the stadium of course, but at least they could celebrate together.

Also, it was reported that liquor stores near virtually every hotel Badgers fans occupied ran out of beer. Nice to know our fans were leaving their mark on Los Angeles.

I contemplated selling my game ticket. After what I had been through, I didn't care much about the NCAA rules against it. I had a good seat available and could've garnered around $1,000 for it. That would've paid the rent for the apartment I shared off Langdon Street for four months. I figured I'd get a pass onto the field anyway and even if I didn't, I wasn't completely sure I wanted to be in the stands for our biggest game ever.

I started asking around at a New Year's Eve party at a hotel full of festive Badgers fans. I had a few drinks and was feeling a little reckless. I flashed my ticket around. Those I approached were suspicious as to how I had such a good seat. I said I had good connections with the team.

After comparing the ticket with another party-goer's and seeing it was real, one guy offered me $500 cash on the spot for it. Another guy overheard this and told me to wait right there as he wanted to bring his friend over. I was happy to start a bidding war, a New Year's Eve ticket auction right there in the hotel bar. A group was forming around me.

My girlfriend Stephanie saw what I was doing and pulled me out of the room. Very interested potential buyers asked where I was going, and I told them I'd be right back.

Stephanie and I were both strong-willed types, and had our share of arguments. Heck, we met once in high school competing against each other in a mock trial tournament. Her team trounced mine and even as we dated later in college, she still trounced me in most arguments. I respected her opinion very much. She carried an almost-perfect grade point average as an engineering major and went on to graduate from Harvard Business School years later.

Stephanie sat me down on the back steps of the kitchen just outside the hotel and asked me whether I realized what I was doing. I was surprised how upset she was. I said I knew what I was doing and I didn't care anymore. If, for some reason, I wasn't able to get on the field for the game, I just couldn't bear to watch from the stands. This is the team I'd been on for four years and now I was just another fan? It would be too difficult to look at the names on the backs of the jerseys while my own was absent.

Stephanie said, "I think you'll regret it for the rest of your life if you give up your ticket to the game." I told her they were offering me a lot of money and she said, "You're going to give up the experience for $500?" "I could probably get more," I responded. She gave me one of those looks, and I didn't know what to say or do. There was no way around this hurt.

Sitting in that back alley under the orange-yellow light, I felt as disposable as the cigarette butts lying on the ground around me. Steph gave me a hug and my throat felt like it had a thousand needles stuck in it. New Year's Day had come in the midst of our talk. While everyone else was drunk and loud, we walked beside each other and I leaned over and kissed her. She sacrificed her New Year's celebration to save me. I now knew I wasn't going to give up my ticket…and I knew I was lucky to have someone to pull me out of the dumpsters.

CHAPTER TWELVE:
THE GRANDDADDY

The Rose Bowl game is nicknamed the "granddaddy of them all." It is the longest running bowl game, first played in 1902. The score in that game: Michigan 49, Stanford 0. Stanford not only got beaten badly but gave up in the third quarter. It would have been nice if their fellow Pac-10 school UCLA had followed suit, but it didn't happen.

Almost as famous as the game is the Rose Bowl parade. The parade is televised every year, and as many as a million spectators watch it in person. Parade-goers camp out on sidewalks in mini-tents and sleeping bags the night before the parade to save their spots.

The parade is just part of the ceremonies that also include a Rose Bowl court and the coronation of a Rose Bowl queen. The theme for the Rose Bowl that year was "Fantastic Adventure," a pretty apt description of the four-year journey the team and I had been on.

On this game day, January 1, 1994, the area surrounding the small valley the Rose Bowl resides in was covered with Wisconsin fans. Large inflatable Bucky Badgers fronted roped-off beer gardens, the smoke of grilling meat swirled around RVs adorned with red Badgers flags, and clusters of fans gathered by the stadium entrances. Fans played catch, danced, and reveled in the fact that they were a part of UW history. Large chartered busses with tinted windows delivered the teams. The fans parted, waved, and cheered at the behemoth vehicles.

I approached the secured entrance to our locker room. An equipment manager spotted me and looked puzzled as to why I wasn't inside already. I shook hands with him and asked him to get Coach John Chadima, Alvarez's right-hand man. Chadima came out a short time later and I asked him for the field pass promised to me. He didn't know anything about it but told me to hold on a moment and he left. He returned with a plastic laminated card attached to a string, and I stepped through the barrier. Now, I had a useless ticket in my pocket.

The Rose Bowl locker room was surprisingly barren and dull. It's a bit of a misnomer to call it a locker room; there were no actual lockers, simply hooks and footstools to store your gear. It reminded me of an elementary school gym locker room.

We had the home locker room, even though it was UCLA's locker room all season. The "home team" designation for the Rose Bowl alternated between the Big Ten and the Pac-10, and this happened to be our conference's year. At a meeting earlier in the week, UCLA's coach, Terry Donahue, had asked Coach Alvarez if it would be okay if UCLA just stayed in the home locker room since their gear was already there. He said both locker rooms were the same size anyway, so it wouldn't really make a difference. Coach Alvarez said we were the home team and that we wanted the home locker room. Perhaps he was setting a tone for the feistiness our team would show on game day. Coach Alvarez wanted us to feel comfortable, to feel that this was our home field, and so we had the home locker room.

I made my way onto the field. It's truly a stunning sight to walk out of the tunnel onto the natural turf manicured like a putting green. I felt like I should've been walking on it barefoot. The end zones and sidelines were painted in vibrant colors. A mountain range peeked over the top edges of the stands. The crowd was overwhelmingly red and white—estimates were that anywhere from 60,000 to 80,000 Badgers fans attended, occupying all but two sections of the stadium. It was a breathtaking sight.

UCLA players said it was awe-inspiring and disorienting for them to see so many Wisconsin fans in their stadium. An inflatable air balloon in the shape of a cow floated overhead. UCLA assistant coach Ric Neuheisel commented upon seeing the airborne bovine, "I thought we might be in trouble when I saw that hanging above the red-and-white-colored crowd."

Coach Alvarez wanted the team to be as focused as possible. In his pregame speech, Coach emphasized that this was a home game for us: We had the home locker room, we had more fans, and so we had the advantage, not UCLA. He said we couldn't have asked for a better scenario and that the game was ours to win, "We didn't come out to LA to stop doing what we've been doing all year." We were going to go out and play smash-mouth football and win this game like we had all year long. He called the Rose Bowl "Camp Randall West."

William Shatner was the Grand Marshal of the Rose Bowl parade that year and was parked on a truck right behind our sideline when the game started. Fitting to have Captain Kirk there as our team was trying to go where no Wisconsin team had gone before…the win column of a Rose Bowl.

I greeted a lot of my teammates on the sideline. My sour mood instantly changed as I felt a member of the team again. I couldn't have wanted us to win the game more. "Why aren't you suited up?" Brent Moss asked. "Long story, man," I responded. He just shook his head in a "that's messed up" way. "Aw…well, good to have you here, man," Moss said as he gave me a hug. A few guys helped pull me up to stand on the bench, and I settled in next to my cohorts as I'd done all season.

Looking around on this beautiful, sunny day, I was happy to see how this game provided such a service and a unique opportunity for so many connected to the university. To give Wisconsin fans the chance to cheer on their team in sunny 70-degree weather in January. To give the band a chance to march in the famous parade. To give the cheerleaders, the trainers, the equipment guys the chance to get out of our humble town and work in the big leagues for a day.

There was a lot of concern that UCLA star wide receiver J.J. Stokes would have a field day against our smaller, slower defensive backs. Even he thought so, as he claimed in interviews leading up to the game. It's usually not a good idea to say things like that in the media. It doesn't go unnoticed.

While we couldn't get in the end zone on our first drive of the game, my former roommate and punter Sam Veit put UCLA on their own 2-yard line. A few plays later, UW free safety Scott Nelson gave Stokes a taste of his shoulder pads, leveling him on a pass play. Stokes had to be removed from the game for a while

MIKE DEVRIES/CAPITAL TIMES

Celebrating a score in front of the "home crowd" in Pasadena.

to recover. A player from our sideline wondered, as he was being helped off the field, how he was going to run all over our defense as he said he would if he was going to be sitting on the bench. Stokes returned to the game later in the quarter.

UCLA kicked a field goal to take the lead. Our team responded to the challenge as we had all year. Our offense pounded the ball at UCLA's defense, marching down the field behind Brent Moss's hard-charging runs. Moss scored a touchdown right before the end of the quarter, to bring the score to Wisconsin 7, UCLA 3.

In the second quarter, our defense revealed its penchant for taking the ball away from offenses, causing two turnovers. Cornerback Jeff Messenger intercepted a UCLA pass at the Bruins' 44-yard line. Later, Stokes fumbled a catch, perhaps still rattled by the hits our defense was putting on him, and the ball was recovered by UW defensive tackle Lamark Shackerford at the UCLA 32.

Our offense mustered another drive that culminated in Brent Moss scoring on a one-yard touchdown run. Rick Schnetzky kicked his second extra point of the game to put Wisconsin up, 14-3.

Not to be outdone, our other kicker, John Hall, who was handling the kick-off duties, booted the ball into the UCLA end zone for a touchback.

Our defense again stopped UCLA, and we got the ball back. Right before the end of the half, we marched into field-goal range. Schnetzky's 38-yard kick sailed wide right, and the score at the half remained Wisconsin 14, UCLA 3.

The mood in the locker room was confident but not celebratory. There was still half of a game to play. But things were looking good. Our offense was moving the ball, and though our defense allowed some yardage, it had only given up three points to UCLA's prolific offense.

John Hall started the second half off by booting the kickoff into the end zone, unreturnable. On UCLA's first drive of the second half, they marched to the Wisconsin 8-yard line. But Bruins quarterback Wayne Cook was stripped of the ball by defensive tackle Carlos Fowler and the other defensive tackle, Mike Thompson, recovered it. Our tenacious, opportunistic defense came through again.

It was our offense's turn, and the second part of our one-two punch at running back, Terrell Fletcher, ran for 50 yards on several carries to put us deep in UCLA territory.

Several plays later, with about nine minutes left in the third quarter, a fight broke out on the field after a Brent Moss fumble. During the scramble for the ball, a UCLA player took a cheap shot at our quarterback. Several of our linemen saw it and responded by shoving him away, and things escalated from there. Some players from UCLA's sideline jumped in to join the fray on the field. Our sidelines were poised to do the same, but our coaches held everyone on the UW side back.

After the smoke cleared, two UCLA players and two key Wisconsin players, starters Mark Montgomery and Lee DeRamus, were kicked off the field. Apparently,

DeRamus and a former high school teammate from UCLA had gotten particularly heated and fought in plain view of the referees.

These suspensions were a much bigger blow to our team; we lost two starters and UCLA one starter and one reserve player. I don't think I'm being too biased here when I say we got the bad end of the deal from the refs. UCLA started the fight by taking a shot at our quarterback away from the play, many players from their sidelines jumped in while ours didn't, and UCLA got possession of the ball.

UCLA moved into Wisconsin territory and looked like they would take advantage of their newfound momentum with a score; however, our defense responded like they had all year. Reserve defensive lineman Rob Lurtsema, stepping in for Carlos Fowler (who had broken his wrist), sacked Cook and forced a fumble. Reserve cornerback Henry Searcy recovered. Another key turnover had been forced by our defense, and by two reserve players at that.

MIKE DEVRIES/CAPITAL TIMES

I think Darrell Bevell was channeling Crazylegs Hirsch during his 21-yard touchdown run.

Reserve wide receiver Michael London, who replaced the ejected DeRamus, and reserve fullback Jeff Wirth, who replaced Montgomery, came in and barely missed a beat. That's just the way our UW team had been all year. One guy goes down, another steps in.

Despite their efforts, our offense didn't move the ball very well and we were forced to punt.

As UCLA's offense was moving down the field, UW safety Scott Nelson intercepted a pass. However, the refs called an interference penalty and UCLA kept the ball. The third quarter ended with Wisconsin still leading, 14-3.

As the game entered the fourth quarter, both teams had players raising their arms with four fingers in the air, trying to claim the quarter would be theirs. As they already had the ball in Wisconsin territory, UCLA struck first, scoring on a 12-yard run to bring the score to UW 14, UCLA 10.

We got the ball back and needed to eat some clock and get a score, but we did neither. Our offense went three and out. We punted, and UCLA got the ball on their own 22-yard line.

Our defense, sensing that our offense needed a boost, did what they had always done best. As UCLA ran the ball around the right side, the ball carrier was hit hard and fumbled the ball. Mike Thompson recovered his second fumble of the game.

Our offense got the ball on UCLA's 34. Moss gained some yardage on a few runs. From UCLA's 21-yard line, quarterback Darrell Bevell dropped back to pass, didn't find any receivers open, and decided to run it.

In one of the most memorable images of the game, Bevell bobbed and weaved toward the end zone, legs spinning like legendary UW football player Crazylegs Hirsch. His teammates, throwing their bodies in front of UCLA defenders, cleared a path for him; just as Bevell neared the end zone, he got one more key block from wide receiver J.C. Dawkins and crossed into the end zone untouched to cap a 21-yard touchdown run.

The Rose Bowl stadium crowd erupted in ecstasy and some surprise. Bevell was not considered a running quarterback, and no one would have predicted that he'd run into the end zone to give UW an 11-point lead in the fourth quarter of the Rose Bowl game.

The score was now Wisconsin 21, UCLA 10 with about 10 minutes left in the game.

The UCLA offense needed to score to have a chance at winning the game. They moved the ball for a first down. After a completed pass, our defense forced yet another fumble, which was recovered by UW safety Scott Nelson.

So our defense had given our offense the ball back on our own 36-yard line. We now desperately needed to grind yardage and time off the clock. But UCLA's defense bristled, and UW could only manage one first down. Veit and the coverage unit did a great job, pinning UCLA on their own 10-yard line with six minutes left in the game.

Our defense was tired and battered. Two key defensive starters were out of the game due to injuries: Along with Carlos Fowler's broken wrist, senior Reggie Holt sprained his ankle in the third quarter. Junior reserve defensive back Jamal Brown filled in nicely for Reggie, recording several tackles, and Lurtsema, a freshman, did the same for Fowler.

UCLA's offense absolutely had to score on this drive if they were going to have a shot at winning the game. They mustered their offensive strengths and moved the ball down the field, with the help of some nice catches and a couple of Wisconsin penalties. At the end of their drive, the Bruins completed a five-yard touchdown pass to bring the score to 21-16. The small UCLA crowd went bananas.

A successful two-point conversion would bring them to within a field goal of UW. Our defense summoned their courage and stuffed the UCLA offense, preventing them from converting on the two-point play. The large Wisconsin contingent in the stands roared.

Pandemonium: Darrell Bevell joins the shouting as the final gun sounds.

MIKE DEVRIES/CAPITAL TIMES

215

The score was now Wisconsin 21, UCLA 16, with just under four minutes to play.

Even with two key offensive starters ejected, Wisconsin had to try to score or at least run out the rest of the clock. We got the ball on our own 18 after the kickoff.

Our offense was back on track. Running back Brent Moss gained 21 yards on the next three plays, moving the first-down chains and the clock. UCLA used the first of their three timeouts.

After a Wisconsin false-start penalty, Moss ran for a 10-yard gain and UCLA used up another timeout. A few plays later, on a critical third-and-one, Moss was stopped for no gain and UCLA called its final timeout of the game.

MIKE DEVRIES/CAPITAL TIMES

The prize.

Coach Alvarez chose to punt the ball rather than attempt a fourth-and-one play. One yard on offense and the game would be over. But a UCLA stop would give them the ball in Wisconsin territory with plenty of time to score a touchdown to win the game. Coach Alvarez believed our defense and our special teams could pin UCLA in their own territory and keep them there.

We punted the ball, and UCLA returned it to their own 38-yard line. With 1:43 remaining in the game and no timeouts, UCLA began their final series of the game. They had some success throwing the ball on previous drives and now went back to the air. Cook completed 4 out of 5 passes on the drive and added a 10-yard run. This left UCLA on Wisconsin's 18-yard line with 15 seconds remaining in the game, no timeouts, and a first down.

On the next play, Cook dropped back to pass, presumably looking for wide receiver J.J. Stokes, but he, along with other UCLA receivers, was well covered by our pass defense. As our defensive line closed in on Cook, he panicked and ran right into the arms of defensive tackle Mike Thompson, who dropped him to the turf. As the seconds ticked away, UCLA couldn't line up fast enough to get another play off. Time expired.

The stadium exploded in pure pandemonium as the final gun sounded. The scoreboard read Wisconsin 21, UCLA 16.

On the Wisconsin sideline, all of us standing on the bench leapt into the air. We danced and hugged and hopped on each other. It was just pure elation, a soaring, surreal feeling. The crowd was so loud; the stadium shook so much it seemed like an earthquake had started.

Players ran around the field, some making "snow angels" on the rose at midfield. Most made their way toward the students' seats at the stadium and took off their helmets in tribute, as is the custom after a win at Camp Randall Stadium.

In the midst of the mayhem, love bloomed like the rose on the 50-yard line. UW safety Scott Nelson dropped to a knee and proposed to his girlfriend, Becky, whom a security guard had brought down to the field. (Some people thought Nelly just snapped during all the chaos, but it turns out he planned it that way. Had we lost, he was going to propose in Vegas.)

A few of the upperclassmen hadn't had the chance to play a big role. Their excitement was mixed with hurt and disappointment that they didn't get to contribute to such a big game. I remember seeing one of them walking off the field, lost in thought, unhitching his shoulder pad straps as the crowd lining the tunnel all reached to high-five him. Looking back, you want to tell him to just enjoy the moment, but trying to get a highly competitive young athlete to accept a moral victory is like convincing an artist of the merits of a 9-to-5 paycheck.

On the other side of the field, UCLA could do nothing but hang their heads. They were defeated on their home field by a team they were favored to beat, a team that had brought three times the number of fans they had in their own stadium.

J.J. Stokes, who caught 14 passes but never scored a touchdown, commented about the UW team after the game, "They're real physical, I can tell you that much. To tell the truth, I'm relieved [the game's over]." Another UCLA player said, "This is the best of the Big Ten, they're better than Ohio State, they're better than Michigan. We knew they'd come in here and play smash-mouth football and that's what they did."

UCLA coach Terry Donahue credited the upset to Wisconsin's fierce determination: "Players yearn to be respected. Wisconsin's a very good team. You have to give them credit, they created those turnovers." The Wisconsin defense caused UCLA to turn the ball over six times.

Mike Thompson said, "This team kind of embodies Wisconsin. We're not flashy. We work hard. We get the job done. That's what Wisconsin's all about."

This Rose Bowl win was truly a Wisconsin victory. From Racine alone, Rose Bowl MVP Brent Moss ran for 158 yards; J.C. Dawkins had several key plays in the game; and punter Sam Veit pinned UCLA in their own territory several times. Brookfield's Joe Panos captained an offensive line that also included Fond du Lac's Cory Raymer and Kimberly's Mike Verstegen. Portage's Mike Thompson had one fumble recovery and multiple sacks, and Marinette's Jeff Messenger had one interception and another key pass deflection. Sun Prairie's Scott Nelson recovered a fumble. Plymouth's Chris Hein had a key pass deflection. Chad Cascadden of Chippewa Falls had several key tackles; Salem's Vince Zullo had several crucial blocks (especially on Bevell's touchdown run); and Mequon's Rick Schnetzky kicked three extra points to seal the touchdowns. And I can't forget to mention Schofield's Jeff Wirth, who replaced starter Mark Montgomery after his ejection from the game while continuing his stellar special-teams play.

After the game, Coach Alvarez said that despite coaching on many championship teams, including a national championship at Notre Dame, "It's by far the hugest game in my career. This gives our program a lot of credibility."

The celebrations back home rivaled anything happening in Pasadena. State Street in Madison was invaded by thousands of fans cavorting in the single-degree temperatures, as nearly every sports bar overflowed with revelers. This scene was replayed in virtually every town in the state. Cory Raymer wanted to join them in his hometown. "I wish I could get on a snowplow and go at Mach 10 back to Fond du Lac," he said.

The game and its aftereffects reverberated throughout the nation. Bob Verdi, a *Chicago Tribune* sports columnist, wrote, "The Badgers may have won because they had a better game plan. That's for the X's and O's freaks to dissect on film. Live and in color though, there was no doubt. Wisconsin had more emotion. Wisconsin had plenty of occasions to cave in, like too many of their Big Ten predecessors, but the Badgers wouldn't lose. You wonder about Wisconsin's arteries, given the beer and bratwurst diet, but don't worry about their heart. Just when you fear all the fun has been drained from sports for the sake of profit, along comes a story like this."

Well, history was made. Wisconsin won the Rose Bowl for the first time in school history. It was even more impressive because of the tumultuous season that led us there. The Minnesota loss followed by the Michigan win, immediately followed by the student section collapse. The heartbreaking tie with Ohio State.

Then having to travel halfway around the globe to beat Michigan State and secure our Rose Bowl berth. Finally, getting to the Rose Bowl only to end up losing five starters in the third quarter and still clinging to victory.

There were so many chances for our team to pack it in, so many excuses to lose, to not finish the season with a win. But true desire and passion doesn't fade. We burned bright for the whole nation to see.

Wisconsin state pride was restored and brought to a level many hadn't seen in their lifetimes. I, along with the other 20 seniors, got to walk out a winner after so many years of hardship…even if it was with a limp.

HANGING THE ROSE

What do you do after you win a Rose Bowl? Well, our options were to hang around the Los Angeles area a few days, relax, accept the invite to the Playboy mansion, and then fly back to Madison on the fourth of January on a chartered team plane.

You could also choose to fly back to Madison on your own whenever you decided to. We were given the money to fly one way from LA to Madison. A lot of players took that money and applied it toward a cheaper one-way flight out of Las Vegas to Madison. Since school didn't start until January 20, we had plenty of time to carouse in the nice weather. This was our time to really let our hair down and party—no more practices, no more games.

I opted to do the Vegas route. Defensive lineman Steve Kouba's family friend had a Vegas strip condo that Steve, Alex Illich, Terry Glavin, and I were going to stay in. Kouba was like a 50-year-old man in a pudgy 21-year-old's body. You could already see him sitting in an office, taking over his dad's insurance sales business. Steve had a sharp, dry wit and a '50s haircut. He and Bevell must have gone to the same barber.

Alex decided to rent a small convertible in LA that we would use to drive to Vegas. Alex was 6' 6", 300 pounds; Glavin weighed about 225 and Kouba about 240; with all of them packed in a compact car, there wasn't much space left. Somehow I managed to ride shotgun, probably by playing the seniority card, or just quick thinking and quick feet. Since we were in a convertible, Alex wanted to drive with the top down the entire time. Unfortunately, we left just before sundown and spent the majority of the trip driving through the cold desert night.

With the heat blasting in the front, Alex and I were quite comfortable, and I must say it was a lovely feeling. Glavin and Kouba huddled together in the back seat like a couple of immigrants coming into Ellis Island in steerage class. We drove into the bastion of sin just before midnight.

Our condo would have made Austin Powers blush: mirrored walls, white leather furniture, and tan shag carpeting. We settled into our '70s love nest and met up with another group of players around 1:30 a.m. for a night on the town. We returned at 7 a.m. the next morning. I know that what happens in Vegas stays in Vegas, so suffice it to say we had a good time. Especially when Wisconsin fans were in the casinos or when we ran into random gamblers who'd bet on us to win. We had plenty of comped buffets, extra chips at the tables, and VIP treatment at nightclubs.

Illich's birthday was coming up, so we took him out pretty hard. He had run out of money gambling but kept going to the ATMs so conveniently located in the casinos. Glavin suggested to me that we stop him from doing that. The fact that Alex outweighed us both didn't stop us from shuffling our feet and doing our best offensive lineman drills to keep him from the ATM.

Stifled by our efforts, he snorted and stuffed his hands in his empty pockets. He went to the bathroom, and we lost track of him. We searched the casino and couldn't find him.

Glavin called the night manager of the condo building to find out whether Alex was there. The manager asked for a description and Terry said that Alex "looked like a mountain…wearing a large gold chain."

We arrived back to the condo a little while later to see him laid out in front of the door, still wearing his nice, long leather jacket. It took all three of us to get him in the condo and set him on the pullout couch.

I tell that story not to embarrass Alex but because it was one of the last times I hung out with a group of players like that. Once the second semester started, I had a degree to finish and they were going to be burrowed back in Camp Randall.

The return to Madison correlated with my disconnect with the team. I was relieved to no longer have to deal with winter conditioning and spring ball. I looked forward to gaining control over the scheduling of my life. I was happy to have some afternoons free again. But I did start to miss some of the guys. They were back into the football grind and as hard as you may try to keep things like they always were, changes came.

The other seniors and I got to hang out with the whole team once again at the annual awards banquet in a huge hall at the Marriott. This year was obviously much more celebratory than those of years past.

As a senior, I got to sit at the head table with the rest of my class and be served first—which is nice, considering there are about 80 tables of people in attendance. Fans came up and thanked me, including some from my hometown, telling me how proud they were.

When I returned from Vegas, my hometown paper interviewed me about the Rose Bowl experience. Another guy from my high school was in the band, and they did a story on him and his experiences the week before. I don't feel that I effectively communicated much of the experience, but it's notoriously hard to come across the way you'd like to in an interview. I also left out any mention of not being able to suit up. I couldn't handle tarnishing anybody else's Rose Bowl experience, and no one else outside of my family needed to hear about my situation.

A few months after the Rose Bowl game, the seniors received a letter from Six Flags Great America amusement park outside of Chicago. The public relations director for the park was a UW grad who was inviting the seniors and their family and friends to spend a free day at the park. She asked whether we could just make an appearance for a couple of hours as part of their interactive sports exhibit. In return, we'd be free to spend the rest of the day for free in the park with our family and friends. I love rollercoasters, and I have a big extended family which includes 16 aunts and uncles and 40 cousins.

I called and asked how many tickets I could get. The woman was very excited and just asked me how many I needed. I said that she should give me a limit because I could have 50–60 of my family members alone invading her park if she didn't pick a number. She said she could do about 20 tickets, and I used every one of them. Only a few players, including me, Phil Chavez, and Reggie Holt, took her up on this generous offer.

Once at the park, the sports exhibit happened to be mainly under construction that day and so we only ended up putting in about 20 minutes signing autographs and saying thanks to the crowd, which was made up mostly of Reggie's and my family. Our obligation was fulfilled, and we were free to roam the park the rest of the day. I felt a little guilty I didn't have to do more to earn the tickets, but I guess my four years on the team were sufficient.

CHAPTER THIRTEEN:
NO PLACE IN
THE STANDS

The follow-up season to the Rose Bowl proved to be a disappointment. Key players were lost to injury, academic problems, and suspensions. The team still did relatively well, finishing 7-5 and qualifying for the Hall of Fame bowl, but their hopes of a Rose Bowl repeat victory were dashed early in the season. While the team may have been more talented, you can't argue with the significance of team chemistry.

I attended a game and tried my best to enjoy it as a fan. I had good player seats courtesy of a buddy on the team, but it just didn't feel right to be in the stands watching the team. I felt isolated from the team now, and thought of how I'd already missed a whole spring practice, a summer conditioning, and a fall camp.

New players wore the numbers of friends I'd known so well. It's the same feeling I had when I drove by the house I'd grown up in, years after we'd sold it, and saw strange cars and strange people beside it. The new inhabitants had torn down the fence in the front yard and taken down my basketball hoop. I loved the house still in some way, but couldn't look at it without feeling sad. I could see only what it wasn't anymore, and I quickly departed. In the same way, watching the team play was so uncomfortable for me, I almost left at halftime, but I stayed until the end out of respect to the players.

Despite having attended games for most of my life and wearing a red-and-white uniform myself for four long years, I actually felt quite removed from my beloved Badgers. It was so different being a fan once you've been a player. The fan enjoys the products of the work, but the player makes the product. Once you know how it's made, you can't help but view it differently.

My friends were baffled when I turned down tickets to upcoming games, and I don't know that I could adequately explain why. Other players, I came to find out, felt much the same as I did and many of them didn't attend games anymore either.

In the college football world and in life in general, I guess, things move forward. Today's news wraps tomorrow's garbage. You clean out your locker and a new player moves in. The transition is as immediate and clean as sliding out your name plate and sliding in a new one.

The fans cheer for the new players the way they once cheered for you. You thought you were special, that it was really about you, and it sort of was, but mainly you were playing a role and so were they. When your playing days are over, you realize it wasn't as important as you once imagined it to be. After all, those same fans fight for position in the hot dog line at halftime.

The 1993 seniors and Rose Bowl champions celebrating at the year-end football banquet.

FORMER GLORY

In the midst of our playing days, we college football players think we'll be kings forever. But in reality, we're one-term presidents.

College athletes have been successful enough to play at an elite level for most of their young lives. When you enjoy a lot of success in youth, you tend not to be very introspective. Introspection is usually instigated by some sort of failure.

At the end of your college career, all that hard work you did served its purpose, but it's not going to get you any farther than it already has. Those coaches you worked so hard to impress aren't going to be in your life much anymore.

A former player has to establish a new identity in the world, and there probably won't be a stadium full of people who care much about it. This is when the guys who developed other interests in school and outside of football could be relatively secure setting a new life in motion. Those who hadn't…well, they were in a pretty lonely place, and maybe still are. To find his new identity, the former player has to break his football connection for awhile. To face the facts outside the stadium, unmasked, in a world that is much more indifferent than he'd once imagined it to be.

I had all this football experience and knowledge that I didn't know what to do with. But a phone call changed that.

BACK TO THE BEGINNING

That fall, Coach Rice asked me to help coach the varsity football team at Waunakee. I was hired, for minimal pay, to be the wide receivers' and outside line-backers' coach. This was a job I took for the love of my school team, and to find the purity of the game again back where I first discovered it. I jumped at the opportunity to pour all that I'd learned into the young minds of my hometown.

There was something affirming about being back around high school foot-ball away from the blinding lights and mess of big-time college sports. I found it a welcome release. I spoke up and tried to impart as much football wisdom as I could to the young players. I worked hard to help them achieve their goals.

I felt great that both of my starting receivers, who had not started before, made second-team all-conference. I felt even better about the other receivers, the backups who enjoyed their experience on the team despite not getting to play much. I made it a point to play everyone I could, because I knew what it felt like to work so hard and not have any playing time to show for it. In fact, I remember pointing to the guy lowest on our depth chart during one of our wins and telling him he was going in next. His eyes got bigger than the moon. I nodded yes, then nudged him out onto the field. Coaching football saved me from abandoning the game I'd stud-ied and enjoyed so much in my life. My playing career was over, and while I liked coaching I didn't feel I wanted to do it the rest of my life.

Ironically, in the place where I ended my football career, my next career began.

MY LONGEST YARD

In my last semester at UW, I was notified that Burt Reynolds was shooting a football instructional video, *Basic Football*, at Camp Randall Stadium. I went down to check it out. The UW cheerleaders and I, along with a few others, were put in the background to help with the shoot. We were considered "extras" and were told to not ask Burt for autographs or even speak with him. Nonetheless, it was cool to see the whole production and chat with the cheerleaders on a beauti-ful sunny day.

The production was setting up a shot to show a passing play, but it looked terrible. They were using the extras and everyone was out of position and the alignments were way off. I casually mentioned to a crew worker standing next to me that it didn't make any sense. I explained a better way to set up the play. The crew member asked me to demonstrate, and I did.

The crew member made an announcement to the whole crew to change the formation and walked back over to me and shook my hand. "Hi," he said, "I'm the director." He asked me how I knew so much and I told him I had played here.

A little while later, I was back chatting with the cheerleaders when the director walked up to me and said, "Burt wants to meet you." The director brought me over, and Burt asked him, "This is the player?" He gave me a rough hug and said, "You played here?" I said, "Yes, sir." Burt continued, "I saw your Rose Bowl game. That was great. Moss. Bevell." I was impressed he knew his stuff. Burt talked about playing for Florida State as a running back. He said he was good but injured his knee as a sophomore and couldn't get back to form after that. We chatted a bit more, and then he was needed for a shot.

A little while later, the director approached me again, "We want to add a scene with you and Burt. That okay?" Yes! So they set up the shot, showed me my tape marks on the ground where I was to stand, and gave me my line, "Hey Burt, can you teach me a little something about women?" To which Burt replies, "Not anymore, kid."

As the lighting was being adjusted on me, the assistant cameraman says, "Can we get the kid to move to his left?" Burt jumps in and shouts, "Kid? His name's Chris and he played in the Rose Bowl!" The man apologized to me, and I didn't mind in the least but accepted his apology. And technically, I hadn't actually *played* in the Rose Bowl, but who's going to correct Burt Reynolds?

It took me several takes to stammer out my one line. I couldn't believe how much harder it was than it looked. It was intimidating to have Burt Reynolds standing a few feet away staring at me, and behind him a whole crew with a multitude of equipment, just waiting on me. After a couple of takes, Burt walked up to me and roughly hugged me again and said quietly, "Just relax and have fun with it." I took Burt's acting lesson to heart, and he helped me be playful by responding differently to my line each time. One take, his response was "Not anymore, kid," the next, it was "Later," and the last one was "No…cuz you're too young and you're too good-looking, now get off my set!" With that he threw a football at me and I caught it. The crew all cracked up laughing and applauded. I felt like I'd won the Academy Award.

I went back to the cheerleaders and gloated in my newfound fame. How had I gone from an extra who wasn't supposed to even look at Burt to acting opposite of him? Because I played UW football, and I can't keep my mouth shut.

Burt's manager, Rob, gave me Burt's business card at the end of the day and told me Burt really enjoyed meeting me. I walked up to Burt to say goodbye and he again pulled me in for a hug. We took a few pictures together and he asked me what I was doing after I graduated. I told him I was moving to Chicago to be an actor. He encouraged me, said Chicago was a good place, said to leave my info with Rob and if anything came up in Chicago, they'd give me a call.

About six months later, when I was settled in Chicago, I called Burt and a secretary answered. I asked for Burt, and she said he wasn't home. I just said, "Tell him Chris from Madison called." I doubt he ever got the message and I never heard back. Nevertheless, I consider it one of the highlights of my football career.

THE NAME GAME

While I was in college, I don't think an introduction went by that wasn't some version of, "This is Chris…he's on the football team." Immediately labeled. When I dated a sorority girl, her whole house knew she was dating a football player. Not a cute guy or nice guy or friendly guy, but a football player. I had nothing against being known as a football player, but it would have been a lot nicer to be judged for who I was. I realize almost everyone can be labeled in some way, but usually they're not immediately judged. For example, someone doesn't say, "This is Ron, he's a frat guy." Sure, Ron may divulge that information later, but it's his choice.

While I was proud to be on the team and be considered special among the 40,000-plus students on campus, I hated being summed up by one term as most people do: Jock. Nerd. Druggie. Even though my label was meant as a compliment, I was both flattered and offended when someone would remark, "You don't seem like a football player." In fact, most of the guys on the team were nice, relatively humble, hard-working guys who wouldn't "seem like football players." The bad image came from the few rotten apples that spoil the bunch, I guess. Or more to the point, the image of there being rotten apples.

Long after my playing days, there are many who still associate me with those four years of my life: "This is Chris. Chris was on the Rose Bowl team—weren't you, Chris?" I dutifully answer yes. Most of the time, it's fine. It's a conversation starter, and I can usually steer away from it. Sometimes it's said to inappropriate people at inappropriate times. Does a Wal-Mart cashier need to know I played for Wisconsin? Ah, you win some, you lose some, I guess.

As time has passed, I'm better at discerning where, when, and to whom I mention I played football. I have taken more control over my identity. I'm Chris Kennedy, UW grad, football player, actor, and now, author.

BREAKING BREAD

In 2006, Coach Alvarez and I had a nice chat at a Los Angeles National W Club dinner. Alvarez had just retired as head coach and was now the UW athletic director. I was seated next to him and was surprised at how much time we spent chatting, catching up. I think we spoke more at that dinner than we had during my entire four-year career. Coach was warm and relaxed, so different from the way I was used to seeing him when I was a player 16 years earlier and we were working to re-establish the football program.

Coach Alvarez told me he liked my letter recounting our Rose Bowl team reunion the year before. He'd posted it in the locker room for the players to read—in fact, they had to read it and sign their names afterwards to prove it. It made me feel reconnected with my former team for the first time since I played.

It all came back to me; the camaraderie that was so special and as I came to find later in life, so unique. All those people who said when I got older I'd really appreciate the experiences, good and bad, that I'd disregarded as a feisty youth, were now being proven right.

During our chat, I asked Coach Alvarez about what had happened to Brent Moss. Maybe it was a bit inappropriate to bring up at a back-slapping cocktail event, but Alvarez took the time to talk about a difficult subject.

From my removed perspective, it seemed to me that Brent Moss got a raw deal the season after the Rose Bowl. Instead of going pro after his Rose Bowl MVP performance, Brent decided to come back and play one more year at UW. The coaches were undoubtedly happy about this and I assumed nudged him in that direction. I would have advised Brent to take the money and run to the daylight of the NFL. What more stock would he need with pro scouts than being the Rose Bowl MVP? But he didn't ask me.

Well, Brent passed on the NFL and draft and decided to come back that fall. After a few games, Brent was caught with illegal drugs when the Madison police stopped his car, and he was suspended from the team for the rest of the season.

That next spring, Brent was not drafted and he signed a free-agent contract. He played only sparingly for the St. Louis Rams one year, bounced around a couple of different teams and never really got any significant playing time in the NFL. He signed with Amsterdam of the World League of American Football, but that didn't work out either.

He ended up back in Racine, his hometown. He got an assistant coaching job with a semi-pro football team but that didn't last either. He's been arrested several times throughout the years on various drug possession charges.

It's hard to see a teammate I got along with have such struggles, and especially hard to see him derided by the media and fans. I felt the football program he helped bring to national prominence and the fans who once adored him turned their backs on him when he needed it most. It didn't seem to me that the university, the boosters, or the coaches did enough to help Brent.

So I asked Coach Alvarez whether he knew what was up with Brent Moss. Coach wrinkled his forehead and said, "He's probably in jail."

Coach explained that after the Rose Bowl, many guys came back to practice that winter and spring not knowing how to handle the new fame. Brent may have fallen into that trap. Coach said that he got a call in the summer from the Madison police informing him that some "activity" was occurring in front of Brent's apartment.

Alvarez called Moss' father, who said he'd talk to Brent. Alvarez said he told Moss that if he was doing anything that he needed to stop; otherwise Brent might as well go supplemental (a small NFL draft that takes place after the primary one in April) because Alvarez wasn't going to put up with it that season.

During the season, Moss came in and asked Alvarez for permission to miss practice so he could meet with a professor. Alvarez was suspicious and said no. Brent was upset. Two weeks later, Brent was picked up for the infamous bust and Alvarez released him from the team.

Alvarez said that years later, when Brent's pro career was finished and he wanted to re-enroll in school, he stuck his neck out to get him back in despite Brent's poor academic standing when he'd left UW. "I paid for his school when he came back," Alvarez said. School didn't work out for Brent either.

Nevertheless, I'm sad that most fans remember Brent Moss as "the guy who screwed up his career with drugs." Brent was one of the best running backs Wisconsin ever had, and he was loyal to his school and to his friends. He was the type of guy who would have your back if you got in trouble, and the type of guy you wanted to have your back. I wish things were better for Brent, because he's better than the poor circumstances he's in.

I was pleased Alvarez and the school hadn't turned their backs on Brent as I had thought. I was impressed that Alvarez kept tabs on many of his former players. He asked me about my acting career, wished me luck, and said he looked forward to seeing more of me on the big screen. I know that his former players mean a lot to Coach Alvarez. He's helped many players land jobs, written countless letters in their favor, and counseled them on career decisions long after their playing days.

At dinner, he even coached me on how to get more sauce onto my pasta. Good to know the coach still cares.

LESSONS

As a football player at UW, I learned how to win. Not just in terms of points on a scoreboard, but how to win battles, whatever those battles may be. Adversity, challenges, roadblocks can all be overcome. Sometimes it's by brute force, tenacity, and persistence. Sometimes it requires strategy, focus, and calm execution. Usually it's a combination of all of the above.

I learned that the magic of winning isn't based on miracles; it's based on believing in yourself and your teammates. Knowing that you'll give a full effort and taking comfort in the fact your teammate will do the same. When you have that, you can do anything.

The hardest lesson I learned is that life isn't always fair but that you've got to keep going on anyhow.

The most valuable lesson I learned is that what matters is not what others think of you, but what you think of yourself. My experience on the UW football team allowed me to discover my own character.

When I was a player I was stricken with near-sightedness, as young men often are. Most college football players can't see much further than the ends of their bloodied noses. For a college football player who is under so much pressure and is burdened with so many obligations, that's probably the only way to survive. My experience was nothing like I thought it would be, but it was worthwhile. I entered the program as a young player and left it a man. I was given an arena in which to chase my dreams and for that, I'm grateful.

Nobody gains success without help. Lots of it. I had a great support group of people—friends, family, coaches, athletic department personnel, teammates, roommates, fans—who were integral to me making it through all the good times and especially, the bad times.

The coaches and players alike were under a lot of pressure, and we were all doing the best we could to fulfill our duties. I wish it could've gone more smoothly for me; I wish I would have played more and enjoyed it more at the time. As it goes with most things, matters are never as clear as they appear in hindsight.

But the great thing is, while our time on the field was brief, there is no statute of limitations on celebrating the things we achieved together. Like my dad had told me after we won the Rose Bowl berth, you know it's a great accomplishment when you wake up the next day and it's just as exciting, if not more so.

Thousands of days later, I'm excited that time hasn't diminished our accomplishments but actually burnished them. History remembers and celebrates our 1994 Rose Bowl team as champions, and now, so do I.

While I appreciate my Rose Bowl ring, being associated with the 1994 Badgers, and playing for my favorite college football team, the true reward was being able to experience it. In the words of Ralph Waldo Emerson, "The reward of a thing well done, is to have done it."

INDEX

MORE GREAT SPORT TITLES FROM TRAILS BOOKS

After They Were Packers, *Jerry Poling*

Always a Badger: The Pat Richter Story, *Vince Sweeney*

Baseball in Beertown: America's Pastime in Milwaukee, *Todd Mishler*

Badger Sports Trivia Teasers, *Jerry Minnich*

Before They Were the Packers: Green Bay's Town Team Days,
    Denis J. Gullickson and Carl Hanson

Blood, Sweat and Cheers: Great Football Rivalries of the Big Ten, *Todd Mishler*

Boston Red Sox Trivia Teasers, *Richard Pennington*

Chicago Bears Trivia Teasers, *Steve Johnson*

Chicago Cubs Trivia Teasers, *Steve Johnson*

Cold Wars: 40+ Years of Packer-Viking Rivalry, *Todd Mishler*

Denver Broncos Trivia Teasers, *Richard Pennington*

Detroit Red Wings Trivia Teasers, *Richard Pennington*

Green Bay Packers Titletown Trivia Teasers, *Don Davenport*

Mudbaths and Bloodbaths: The Inside Story of the Bears-Packers Rivalry,
    Gary D 'Amato and Cliff Christl

New York Yankees Trivia Teasers, *Richard Pennington*

Packers By the Numbers: Jersey Numbers and the Players Who Wore Them,
    John Maxymuk

Vagabond Halfback: The Life and Times of Johnny Blood McNally,
    Denis J. Gullickson

For a free catalog, phone, write, or visit us online.

Trails Books

A Division of Big Earth Publishing

923 Williamson Street, Madison, WI 53703

800.258.5830 · www.trailsbooks.com